FAITH

HOLLYWOOD
AND VINE

JODY HOUSER | FRANCIS PORTELA | MARGUERITE SAUVAGE

CONTENTS

Collection Cover Art: Jelena Kevic-Djurdjevic

Editor: Tom Brennan
Editor-in-Chief: Warren Simons

VALIANT.

Faith™: Hollywood and Vine. Published by Valiant Entertainment
LLC. Office of Publication: 350 Seventh Avenue, New York, NY
10001. Compilation copyright © 2016 Valiant Entertainment LLC.
All rights reserved. Contains materials originally published in
single magazine form as Faith #1-4. Copyright © 2016 Valiant
Entertainment LLC. All rights reserved. All characters, their
distinctive likeness and related indicia featured in this publication
are trademarks of Valiant Entertainment LLC. The stories,
characters, and incidents featured in this publication are entirely
fictional. Valiant Entertainment does not read or accept unsolicited
submissions of ideas, stories, or artwork. Printed in the U.S.A.
Second Printing. ISBN: 9781682151211.

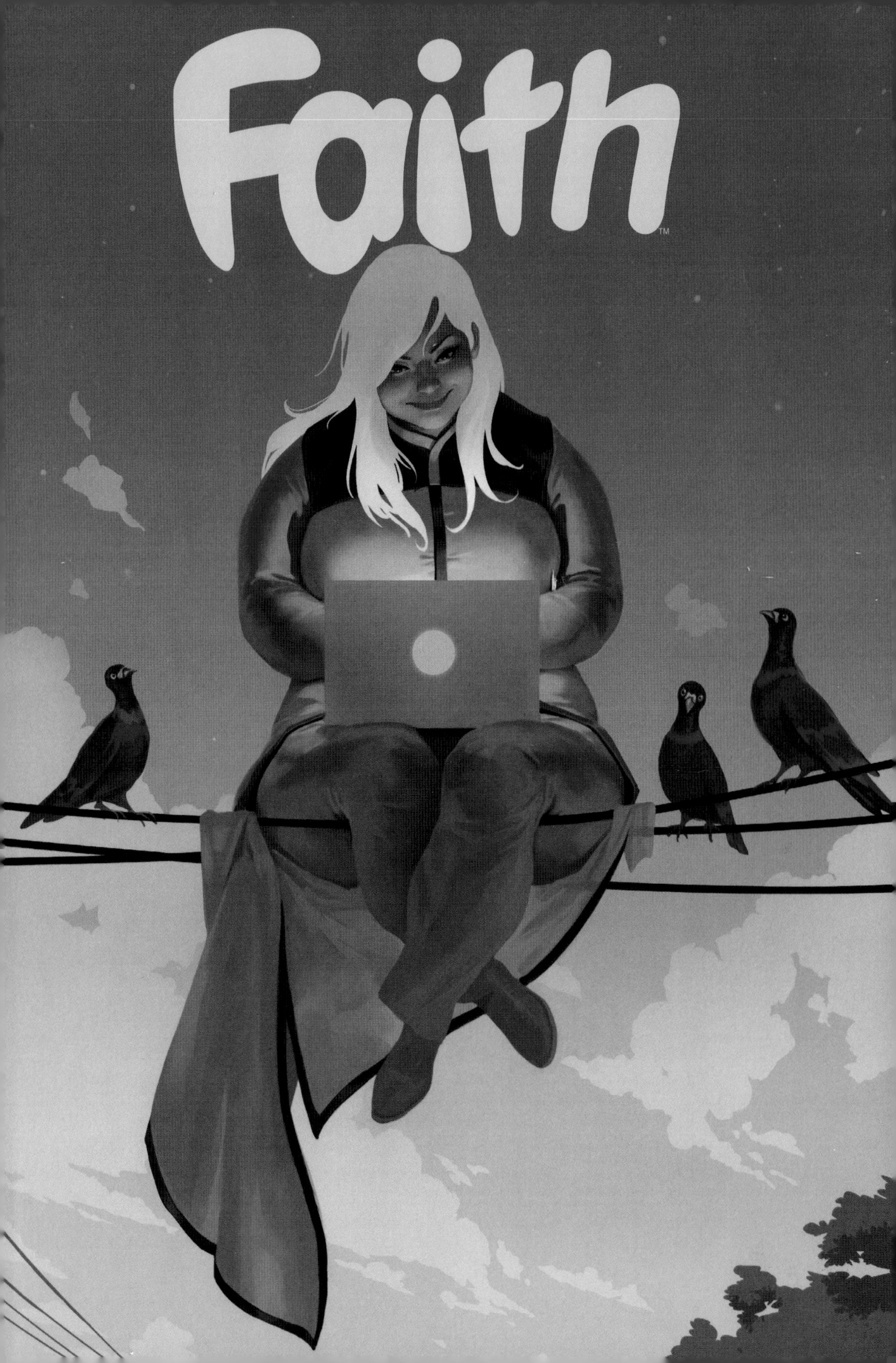
Faith™

When a car accident left her orphaned, Faith Herbert was raised by her loving grandmother and found comfort in comic books, science fiction movies, and other fantastic tales of superheroes. In her teens she would discover her fantasies were reality when it was revealed she was a psiot – a human being born with incredible abilities. Imbued with a telekinetic ability to fly and a companion field that allows her to physically move objects, Faith joined a group of fellow psiots called the Renegades to stand against the forces of evil. She's since left her Renegade family behind to take on the world's challenges on her own. She may have a lot to learn about the superhero game, but if there's one thing she's always had, it's...

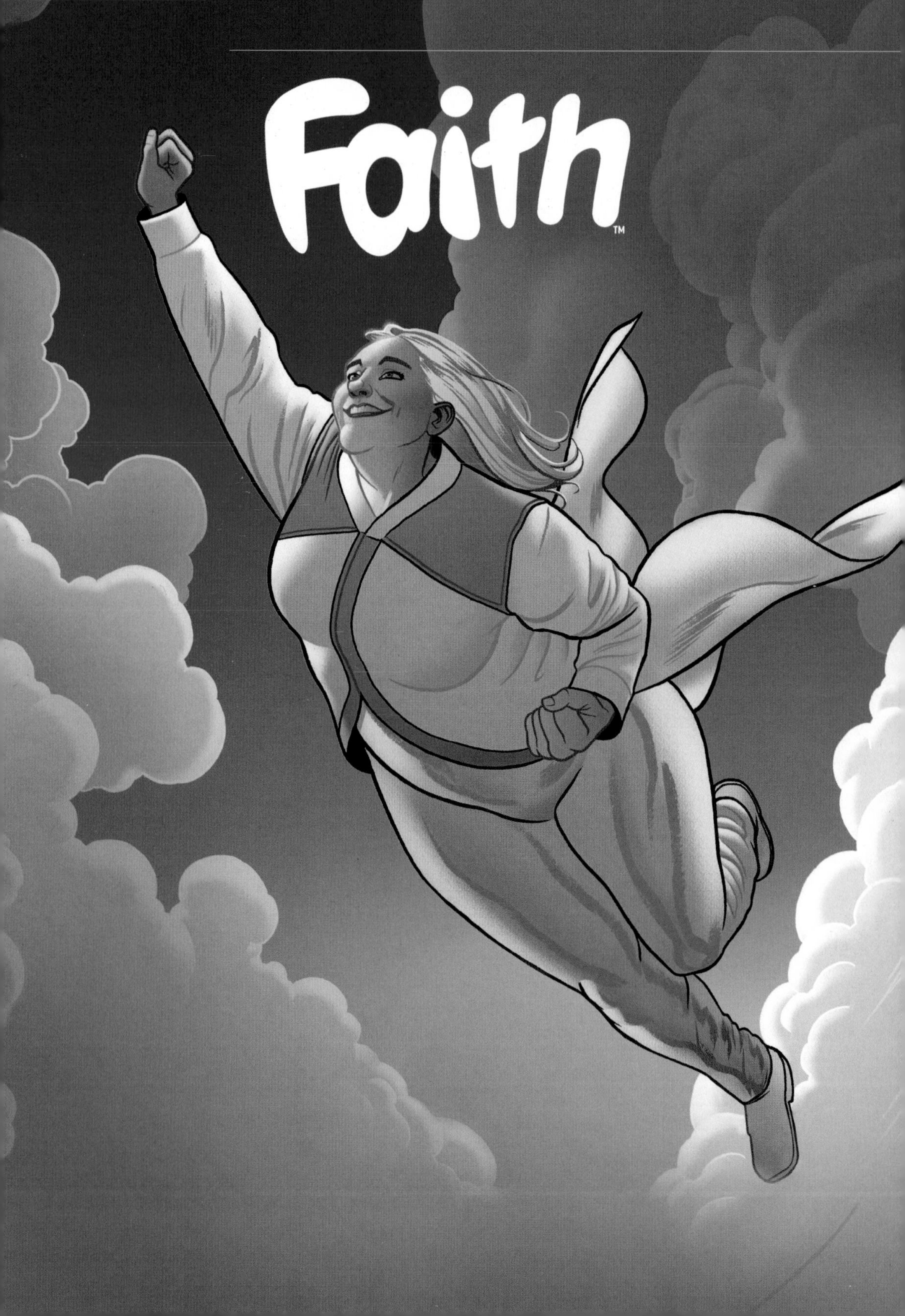
Faith™

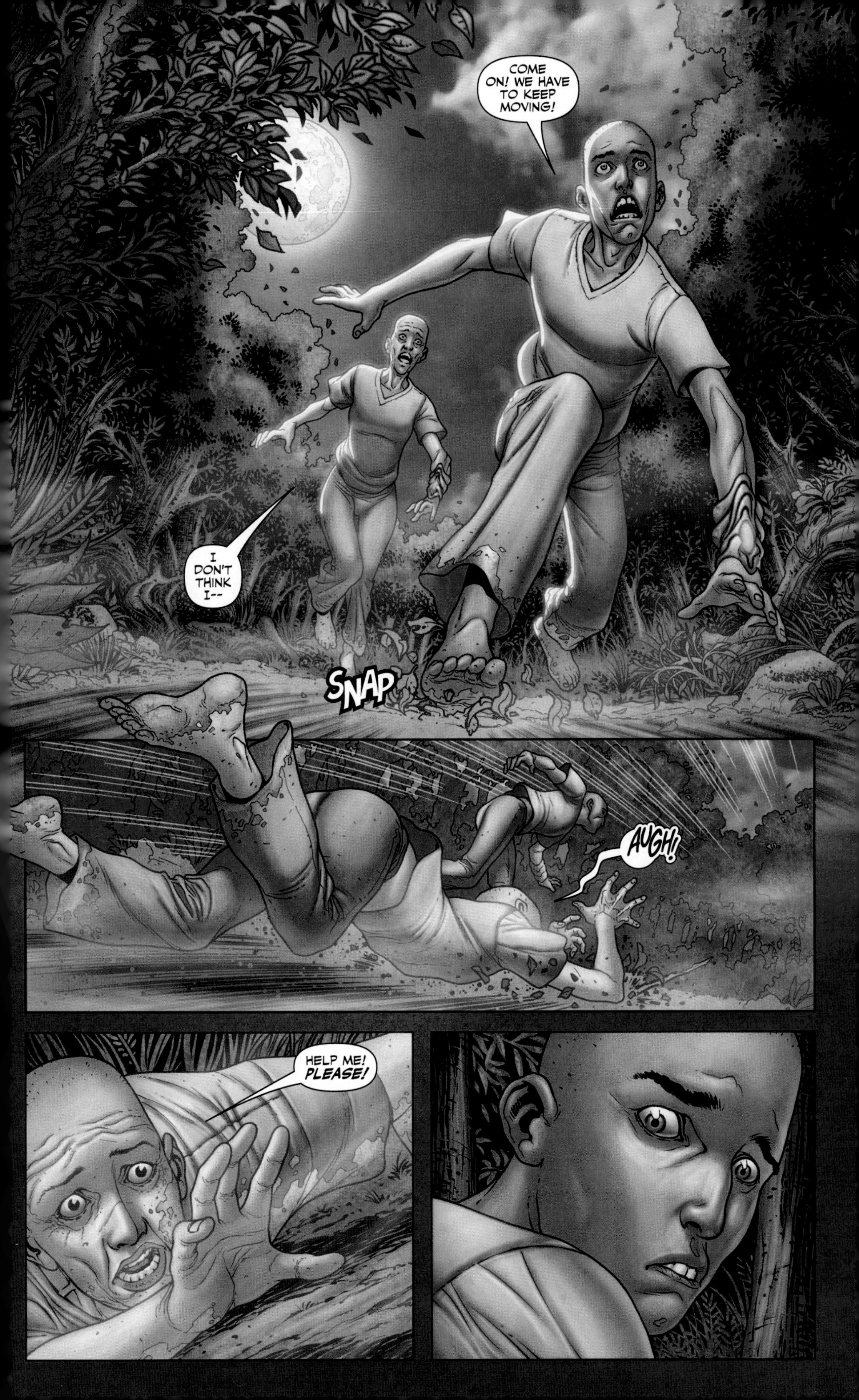

COME ON! WE HAVE TO KEEP MOVING!
I DON'T THINK I--
SNAP
AUGH!
HELP ME! *PLEASE!*

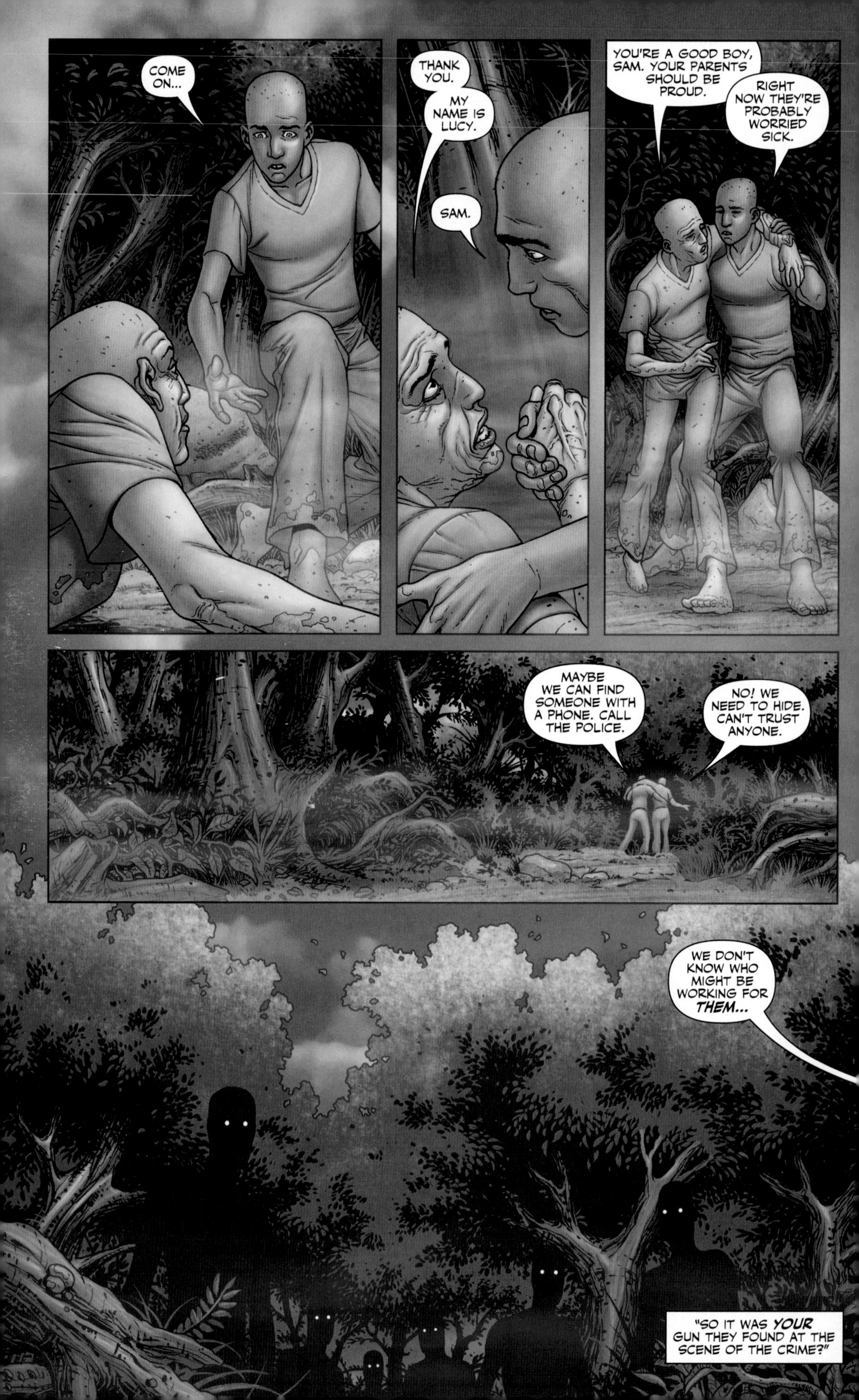
COME ON...
THANK YOU.
MY NAME IS LUCY.
SAM.
YOU'RE A GOOD BOY, SAM. YOUR PARENTS SHOULD BE PROUD.
RIGHT NOW THEY'RE PROBABLY WORRIED SICK.
MAYBE WE CAN FIND SOMEONE WITH A PHONE. CALL THE POLICE.
NO! WE NEED TO HIDE. CAN'T TRUST ANYONE.
WE DON'T KNOW WHO MIGHT BE WORKING FOR THEM...
"SO IT WAS YOUR GUN THEY FOUND AT THE SCENE OF THE CRIME?"

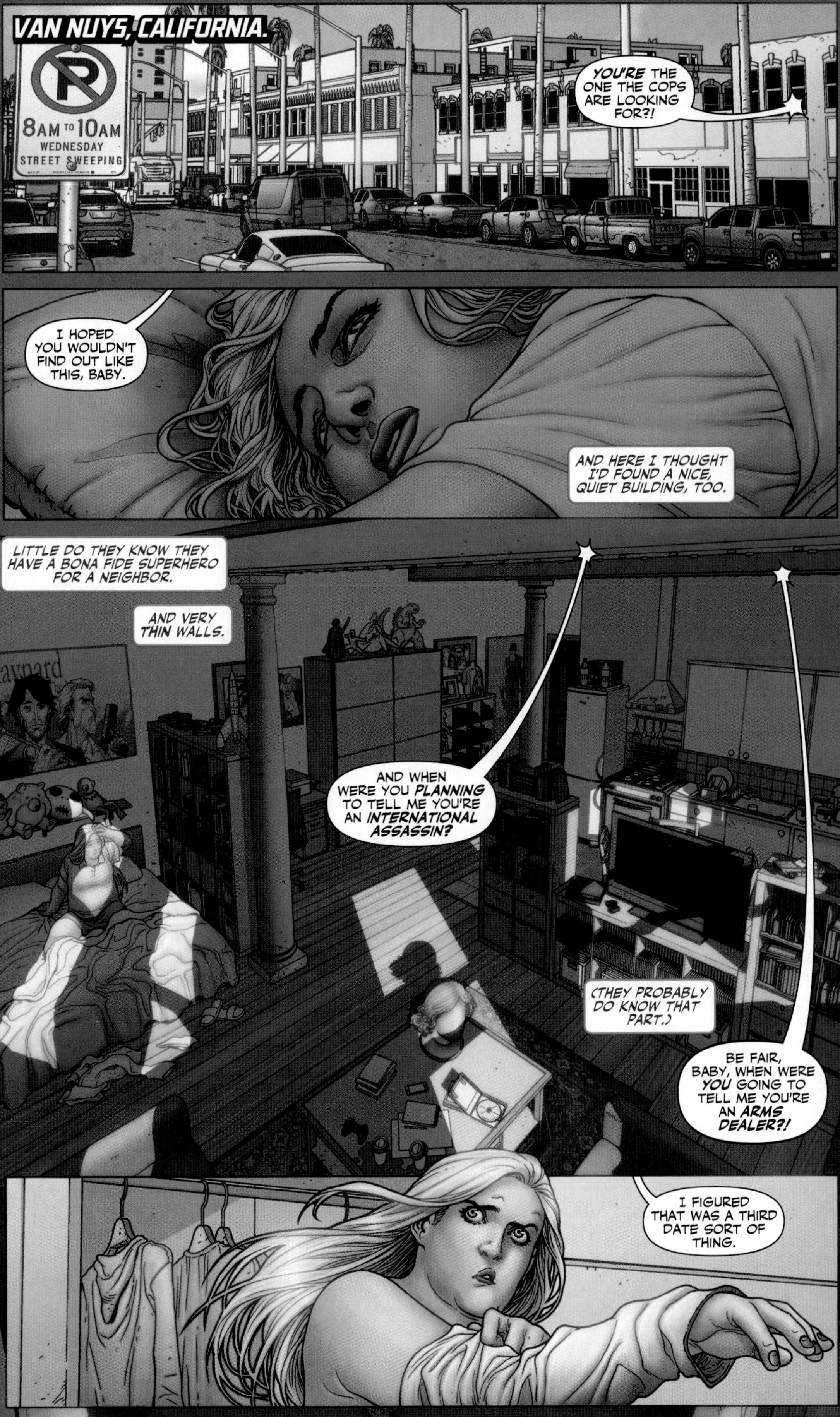
VAN NUYS, CALIFORNIA.
8AM TO 10AM
WEDNESDAY
STREET SWEEPING
YOU'RE THE ONE THE COPS ARE LOOKING FOR?!
I HOPED YOU WOULDN'T FIND OUT LIKE THIS, BABY.
AND HERE I THOUGHT I'D FOUND A NICE, QUIET BUILDING, TOO.
LITTLE DO THEY KNOW THEY HAVE A BONA FIDE SUPERHERO FOR A NEIGHBOR.
AND VERY THIN WALLS.
Maynard
AND WHEN WERE YOU PLANNING TO TELL ME YOU'RE AN INTERNATIONAL ASSASSIN?
(THEY PROBABLY DO KNOW THAT PART.)
BE FAIR, BABY, WHEN WERE YOU GOING TO TELL ME YOU'RE AN ARMS DEALER?!
I FIGURED THAT WAS A THIRD DATE SORT OF THING.

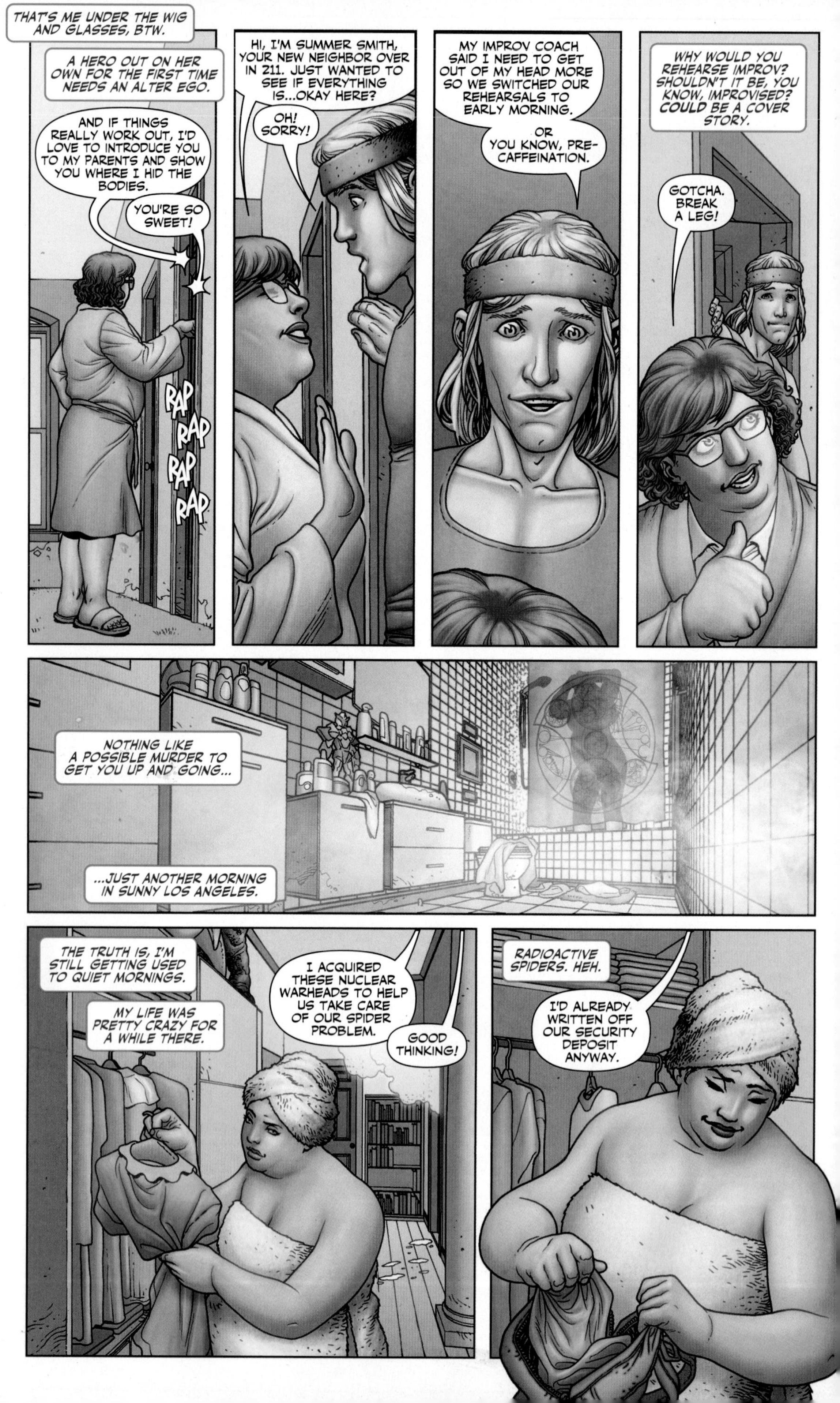
THAT'S ME UNDER THE WIG AND GLASSES, BTW.
A HERO OUT ON HER OWN FOR THE FIRST TIME NEEDS AN ALTER EGO.
AND IF THINGS REALLY WORK OUT, I'D LOVE TO INTRODUCE YOU TO MY PARENTS AND SHOW YOU WHERE I HID THE BODIES.
YOU'RE SO SWEET!
RAP RAP RAP RAP
HI, I'M SUMMER SMITH, YOUR NEW NEIGHBOR OVER IN 211. JUST WANTED TO SEE IF EVERYTHING IS...OKAY HERE?
OH! SORRY!
MY IMPROV COACH SAID I NEED TO GET OUT OF MY HEAD MORE SO WE SWITCHED OUR REHEARSALS TO EARLY MORNING.
OR YOU KNOW, PRE-CAFFEINATION.
WHY WOULD YOU REHEARSE IMPROV? SHOULDN'T IT BE, YOU KNOW, IMPROVISED? COULD BE A COVER STORY.
GOTCHA. BREAK A LEG!
NOTHING LIKE A POSSIBLE MURDER TO GET YOU UP AND GOING...
...JUST ANOTHER MORNING IN SUNNY LOS ANGELES.
THE TRUTH IS, I'M STILL GETTING USED TO QUIET MORNINGS.
MY LIFE WAS PRETTY CRAZY FOR A WHILE THERE.
I ACQUIRED THESE NUCLEAR WARHEADS TO HELP US TAKE CARE OF OUR SPIDER PROBLEM.
GOOD THINKING!
RADIOACTIVE SPIDERS. HEH.
I'D ALREADY WRITTEN OFF OUR SECURITY DEPOSIT ANYWAY.

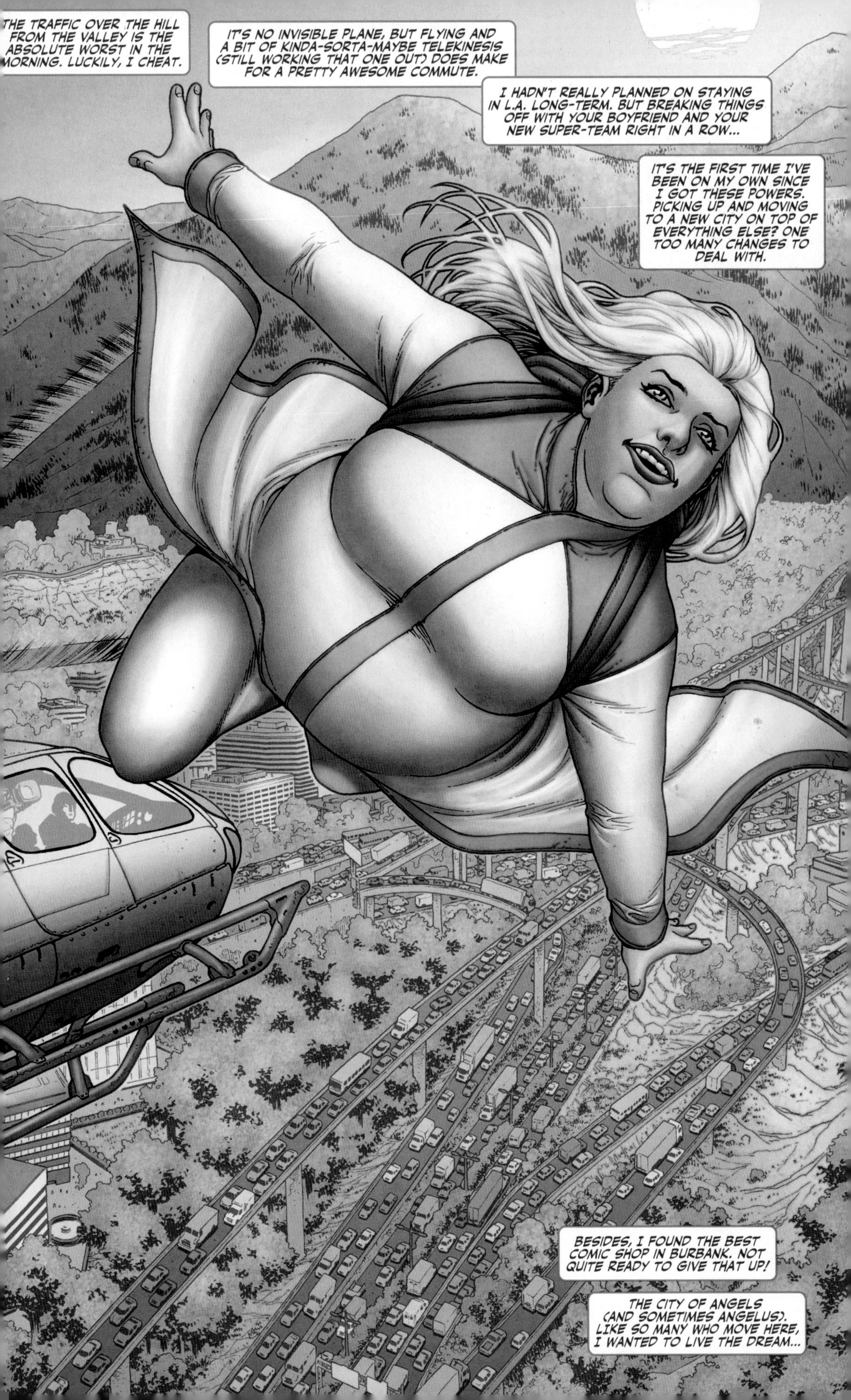
THE TRAFFIC OVER THE HILL FROM THE VALLEY IS THE ABSOLUTE WORST IN THE MORNING. LUCKILY, I CHEAT.
IT'S NO INVISIBLE PLANE, BUT FLYING AND A BIT OF KINDA-SORTA-MAYBE TELEKINESIS (STILL WORKING THAT ONE OUT) DOES MAKE FOR A PRETTY AWESOME COMMUTE.
I HADN'T REALLY PLANNED ON STAYING IN L.A. LONG-TERM. BUT BREAKING THINGS OFF WITH YOUR BOYFRIEND AND YOUR NEW SUPER-TEAM RIGHT IN A ROW...
IT'S THE FIRST TIME I'VE BEEN ON MY OWN SINCE I GOT THESE POWERS. PICKING UP AND MOVING TO A NEW CITY ON TOP OF EVERYTHING ELSE? ONE TOO MANY CHANGES TO DEAL WITH.
BESIDES, I FOUND THE BEST COMIC SHOP IN BURBANK. NOT QUITE READY TO GIVE THAT UP!
THE CITY OF ANGELS (AND SOMETIMES ANGELUS). LIKE SO MANY WHO MOVE HERE, I WANTED TO LIVE THE DREAM...

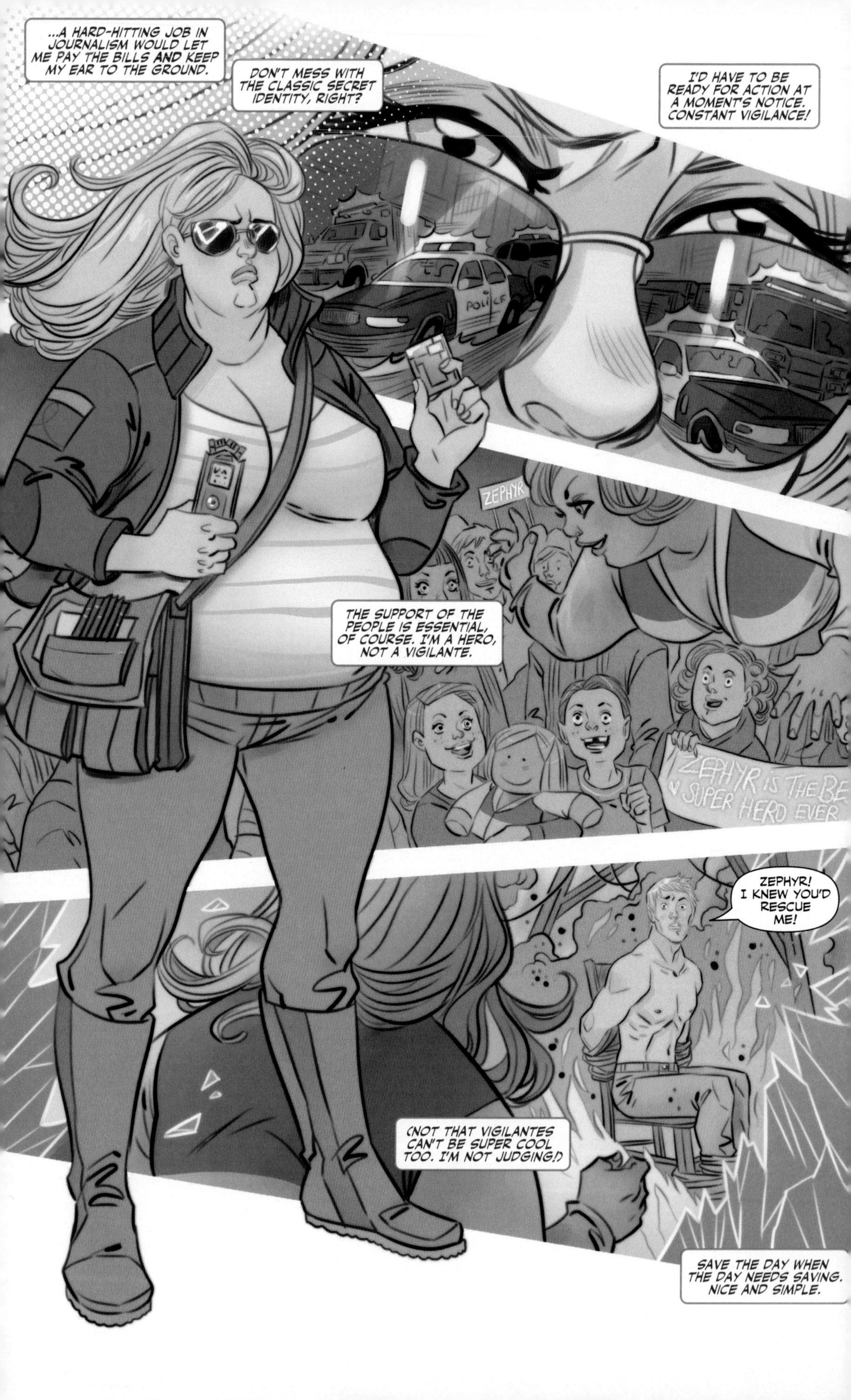
...A HARD-HITTING JOB IN JOURNALISM WOULD LET ME PAY THE BILLS AND KEEP MY EAR TO THE GROUND.
DON'T MESS WITH THE CLASSIC SECRET IDENTITY, RIGHT?
I'D HAVE TO BE READY FOR ACTION AT A MOMENT'S NOTICE. CONSTANT VIGILANCE!
POLICE
ZEPHYR
THE SUPPORT OF THE PEOPLE IS ESSENTIAL, OF COURSE. I'M A HERO, NOT A VIGILANTE.
ZEPHYR IS THE BE SUPER HERO EVER
ZEPHYR! I KNEW YOU'D RESCUE ME!
(NOT THAT VIGILANTES CAN'T BE SUPER COOL TOO. I'M NOT JUDGING!)
SAVE THE DAY WHEN THE DAY NEEDS SAVING. NICE AND SIMPLE.

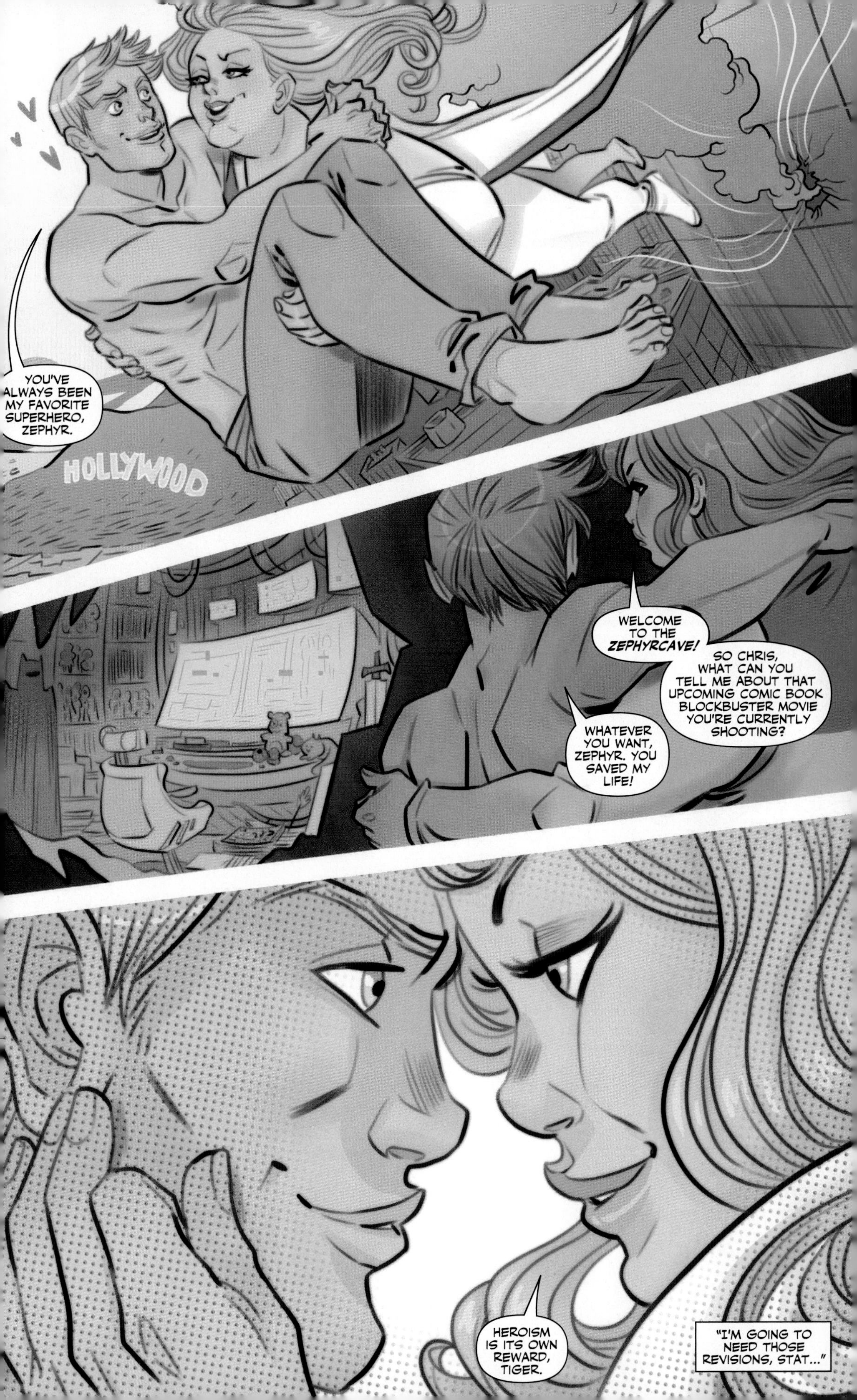
YOU'VE ALWAYS BEEN MY FAVORITE SUPERHERO, ZEPHYR.
HOLLYWOOD
WELCOME TO THE ZEPHYRCAVE!
SO CHRIS, WHAT CAN YOU TELL ME ABOUT THAT UPCOMING COMIC BOOK BLOCKBUSTER MOVIE YOU'RE CURRENTLY SHOOTING?
WHATEVER YOU WANT, ZEPHYR. YOU SAVED MY LIFE!
HEROISM IS ITS OWN REWARD, TIGER.
"I'M GOING TO NEED THOSE REVISIONS, STAT..."

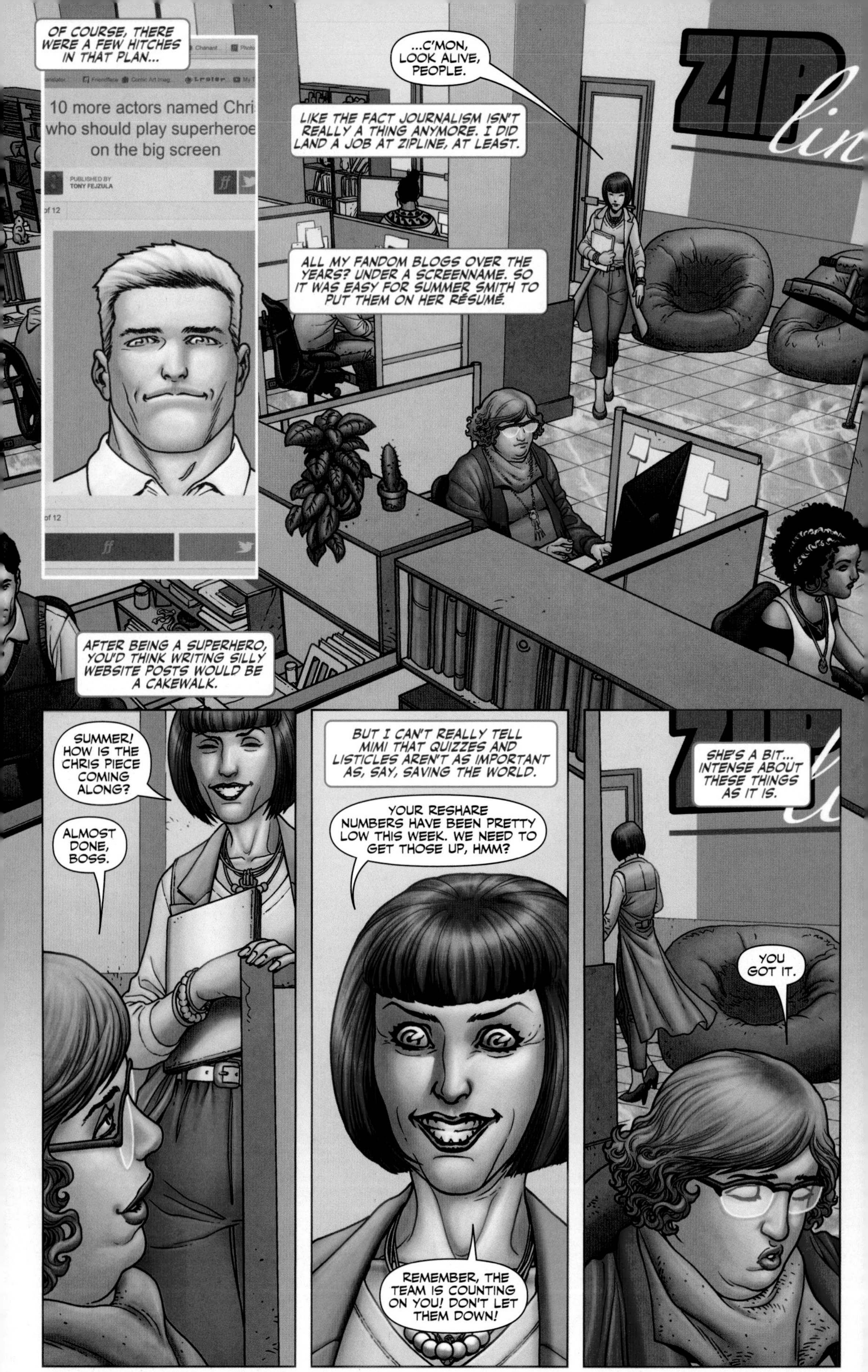

OF COURSE, THERE WERE A FEW HITCHES IN THAT PLAN...
10 more actors named Chri
who should play superheroe
on the big screen
PUBLISHED BY
TONY FEJZULA
of 12
of 12
...C'MON, LOOK ALIVE, PEOPLE.
ZIP
LIKE THE FACT JOURNALISM ISN'T REALLY A THING ANYMORE. I DID LAND A JOB AT ZIPLINE, AT LEAST.
ALL MY FANDOM BLOGS OVER THE YEARS? UNDER A SCREENNAME. SO IT WAS EASY FOR SUMMER SMITH TO PUT THEM ON HER RÉSUMÉ.
AFTER BEING A SUPERHERO, YOU'D THINK WRITING SILLY WEBSITE POSTS WOULD BE A CAKEWALK.
SUMMER! HOW IS THE CHRIS PIECE COMING ALONG?
ALMOST DONE, BOSS.
BUT I CAN'T REALLY TELL MIMI THAT QUIZZES AND LISTICLES AREN'T AS IMPORTANT AS, SAY, SAVING THE WORLD.
YOUR RESHARE NUMBERS HAVE BEEN PRETTY LOW THIS WEEK. WE NEED TO GET THOSE UP, HMM?
REMEMBER, THE TEAM IS COUNTING ON YOU! DON'T LET THEM DOWN!
SHE'S A BIT... INTENSE ABOUT THESE THINGS AS IT IS.
YOU GOT IT.

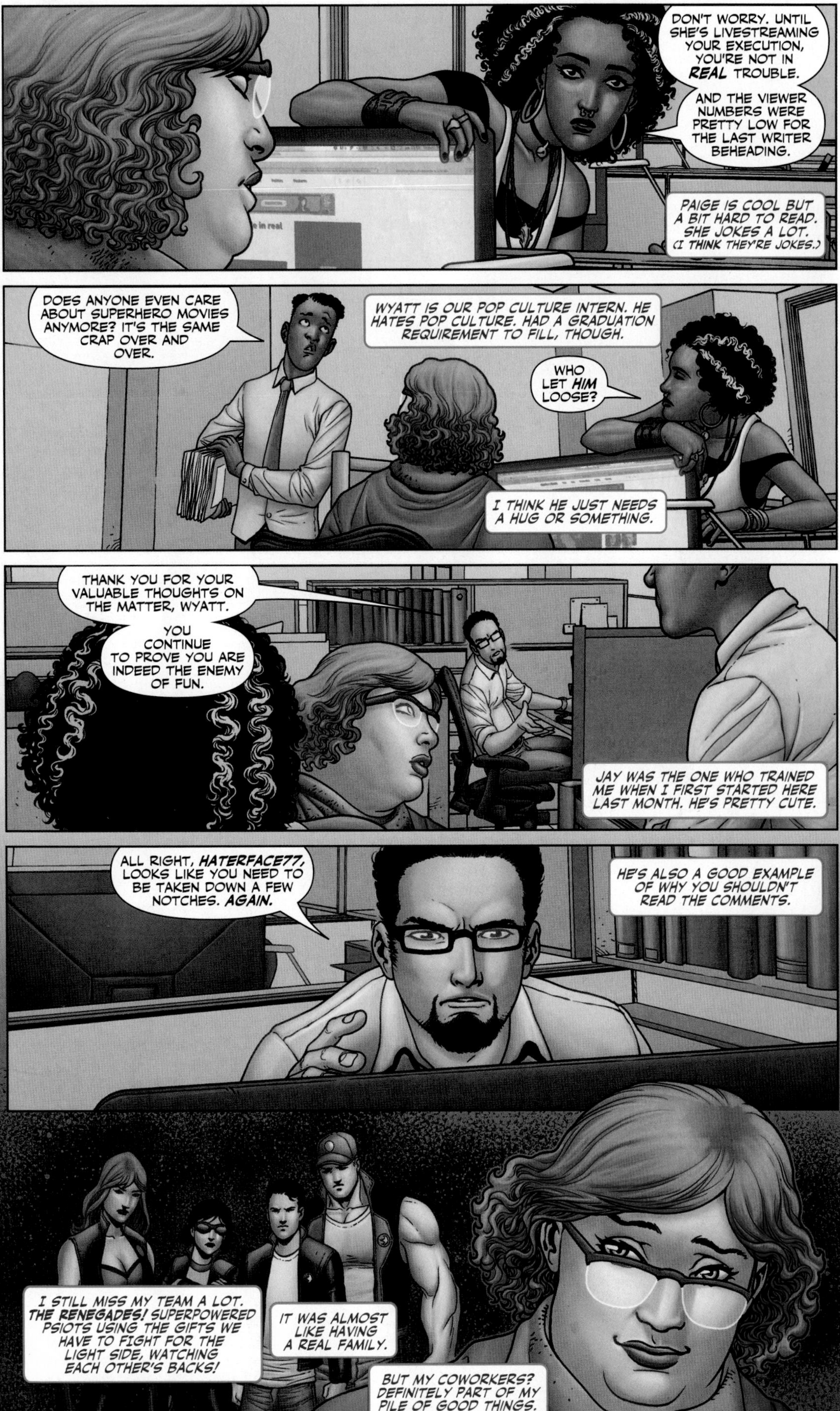
DON'T WORRY. UNTIL SHE'S LIVESTREAMING YOUR EXECUTION, YOU'RE NOT IN REAL TROUBLE.
AND THE VIEWER NUMBERS WERE PRETTY LOW FOR THE LAST WRITER BEHEADING.
PAIGE IS COOL BUT A BIT HARD TO READ. SHE JOKES A LOT. (I THINK THEY'RE JOKES.)
DOES ANYONE EVEN CARE ABOUT SUPERHERO MOVIES ANYMORE? IT'S THE SAME CRAP OVER AND OVER.
WYATT IS OUR POP CULTURE INTERN. HE HATES POP CULTURE. HAD A GRADUATION REQUIREMENT TO FILL, THOUGH.
WHO LET HIM LOOSE?
I THINK HE JUST NEEDS A HUG OR SOMETHING.
THANK YOU FOR YOUR VALUABLE THOUGHTS ON THE MATTER, WYATT.
YOU CONTINUE TO PROVE YOU ARE INDEED THE ENEMY OF FUN.
JAY WAS THE ONE WHO TRAINED ME WHEN I FIRST STARTED HERE LAST MONTH. HE'S PRETTY CUTE.
ALL RIGHT, HATERFACE77, LOOKS LIKE YOU NEED TO BE TAKEN DOWN A FEW NOTCHES. AGAIN.
HE'S ALSO A GOOD EXAMPLE OF WHY YOU SHOULDN'T READ THE COMMENTS.
I STILL MISS MY TEAM A LOT. THE RENEGADES! SUPERPOWERED PSIOTS USING THE GIFTS WE HAVE TO FIGHT FOR THE LIGHT SIDE, WATCHING EACH OTHER'S BACKS!
IT WAS ALMOST LIKE HAVING A REAL FAMILY.
BUT MY COWORKERS? DEFINITELY PART OF MY PILE OF GOOD THINGS.

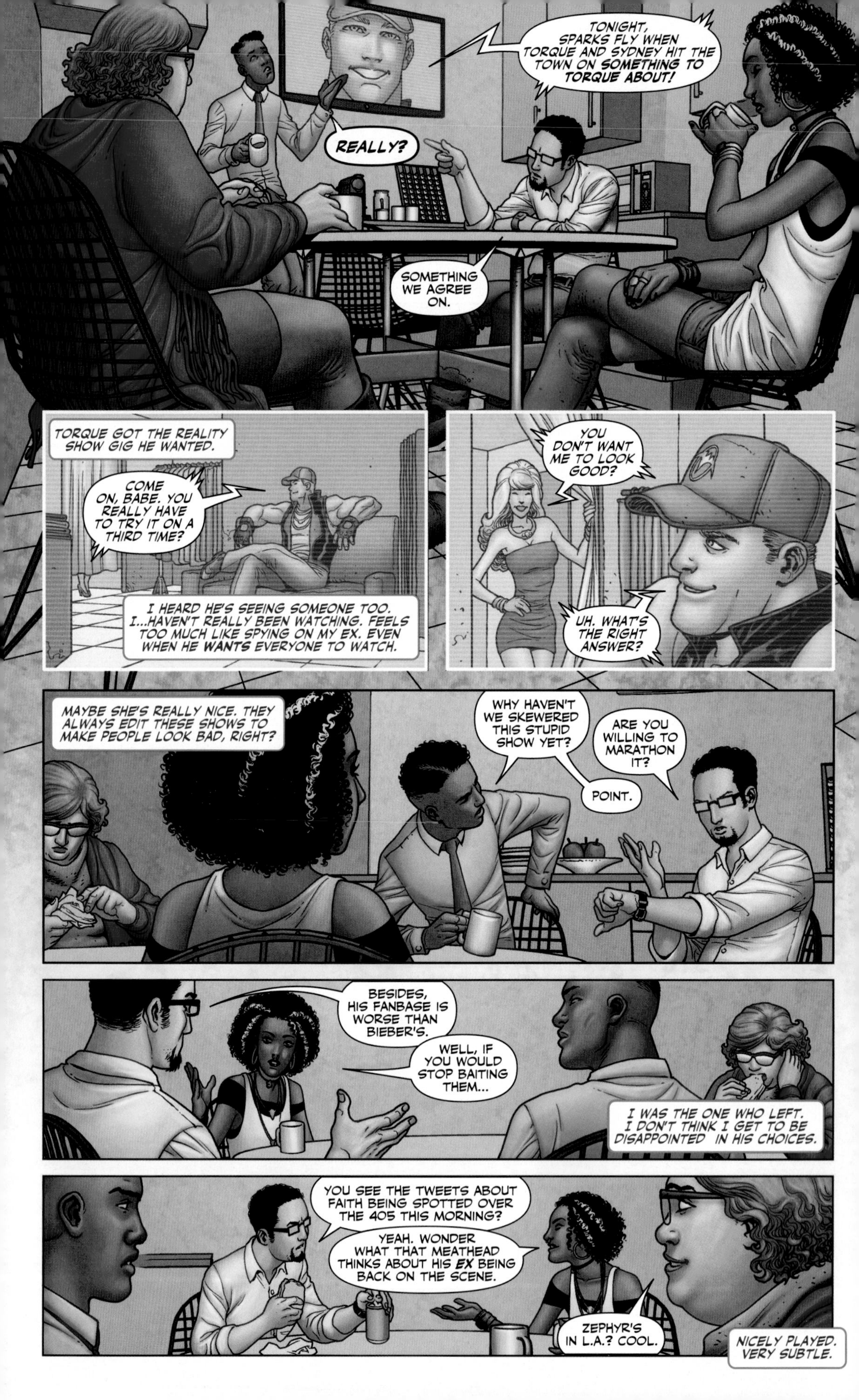
TONIGHT, SPARKS FLY WHEN TORQUE AND SYDNEY HIT THE TOWN ON SOMETHING TO TORQUE ABOUT!
REALLY?
SOMETHING WE AGREE ON.
TORQUE GOT THE REALITY SHOW GIG HE WANTED.
COME ON, BABE. YOU REALLY HAVE TO TRY IT ON A THIRD TIME?
I HEARD HE'S SEEING SOMEONE TOO. I...HAVEN'T REALLY BEEN WATCHING. FEELS TOO MUCH LIKE SPYING ON MY EX. EVEN WHEN HE WANTS EVERYONE TO WATCH.
YOU DON'T WANT ME TO LOOK GOOD?
UH. WHAT'S THE RIGHT ANSWER?
MAYBE SHE'S REALLY NICE. THEY ALWAYS EDIT THESE SHOWS TO MAKE PEOPLE LOOK BAD, RIGHT?
WHY HAVEN'T WE SKEWERED THIS STUPID SHOW YET?
ARE YOU WILLING TO MARATHON IT?
POINT.
BESIDES, HIS FANBASE IS WORSE THAN BIEBER'S.
WELL, IF YOU WOULD STOP BAITING THEM...
I WAS THE ONE WHO LEFT. I DON'T THINK I GET TO BE DISAPPOINTED IN HIS CHOICES.
YOU SEE THE TWEETS ABOUT FAITH BEING SPOTTED OVER THE 405 THIS MORNING?
YEAH. WONDER WHAT THAT MEATHEAD THINKS ABOUT HIS EX BEING BACK ON THE SCENE.
ZEPHYR'S IN L.A.? COOL.
NICELY PLAYED. VERY SUBTLE.

STANCHEK BLAH BLAH BLAH B...

ANYWAY, I COULD HAVE GONE THE REALITY SHOW ROUTE. BUT THAT WAS NEVER WHAT I WANTED.

...AH BLAH BLAH BLAH BLAH AND *UNITY*

anything cool happening??? :D :D :D

FAITH, BLAH BLAH BLAH BLAH...

I WANT TO FLY LIKE NO ONE'S WATCHING. I WANT TO HELP PEOPLE.

BLAH BLAH BLAH BLAH *HARADA.*

all quiet.

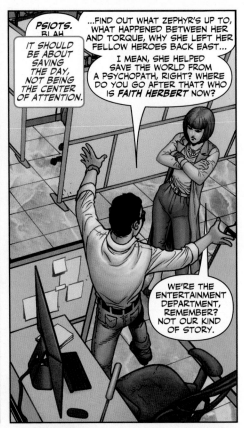

PSIOTS. BLAH. IT SHOULD BE ABOUT SAVING THE DAY, NOT BEING THE CENTER OF ATTENTION.

...FIND OUT WHAT ZEPHYR'S UP TO, WHAT HAPPENED BETWEEN HER AND TORQUE, WHY SHE LEFT HER FELLOW HEROES BACK EAST...

I MEAN, SHE HELPED SAVE THE WORLD FROM A PSYCHOPATH, RIGHT? WHERE DO YOU GO AFTER THAT? WHO IS *FAITH HERBERT* NOW?

WE'RE THE ENTERTAINMENT DEPARTMENT, REMEMBER? NOT OUR KIND OF STORY.

SEE, THEY UNDERSTAND.

I'M TRYING TO DO MORE THAN JUST SMILE FOR THE CAMERAS AND BE SOME CELEBRITY STORY.

HAVE A GOOD WEEKEND!

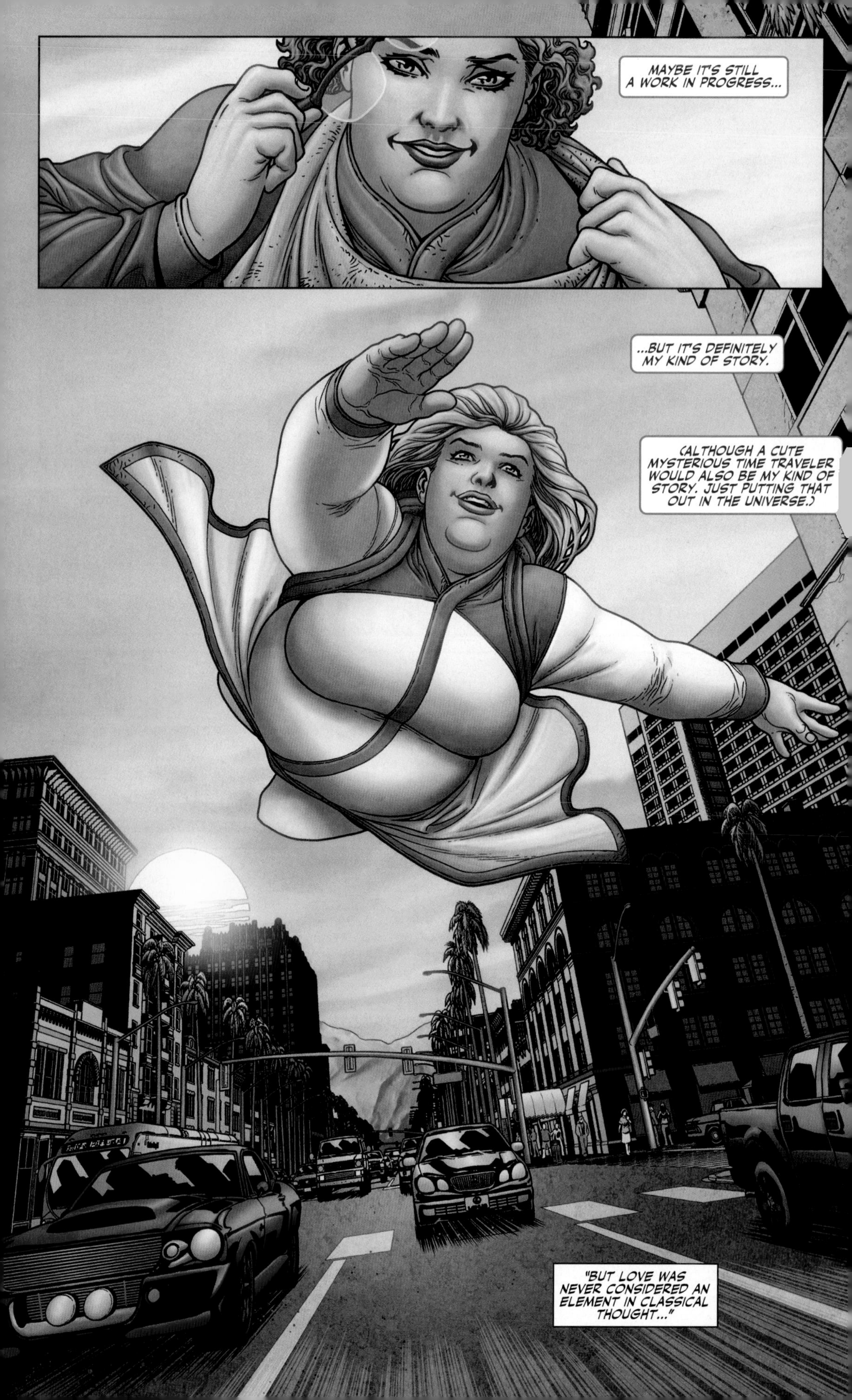
MAYBE IT'S STILL A WORK IN PROGRESS...
...BUT IT'S DEFINITELY MY KIND OF STORY.
(ALTHOUGH A CUTE MYSTERIOUS TIME TRAVELER WOULD ALSO BE MY KIND OF STORY. JUST PUTTING THAT OUT IN THE UNIVERSE.)
"BUT LOVE WAS NEVER CONSIDERED AN ELEMENT IN CLASSICAL THOUGHT..."

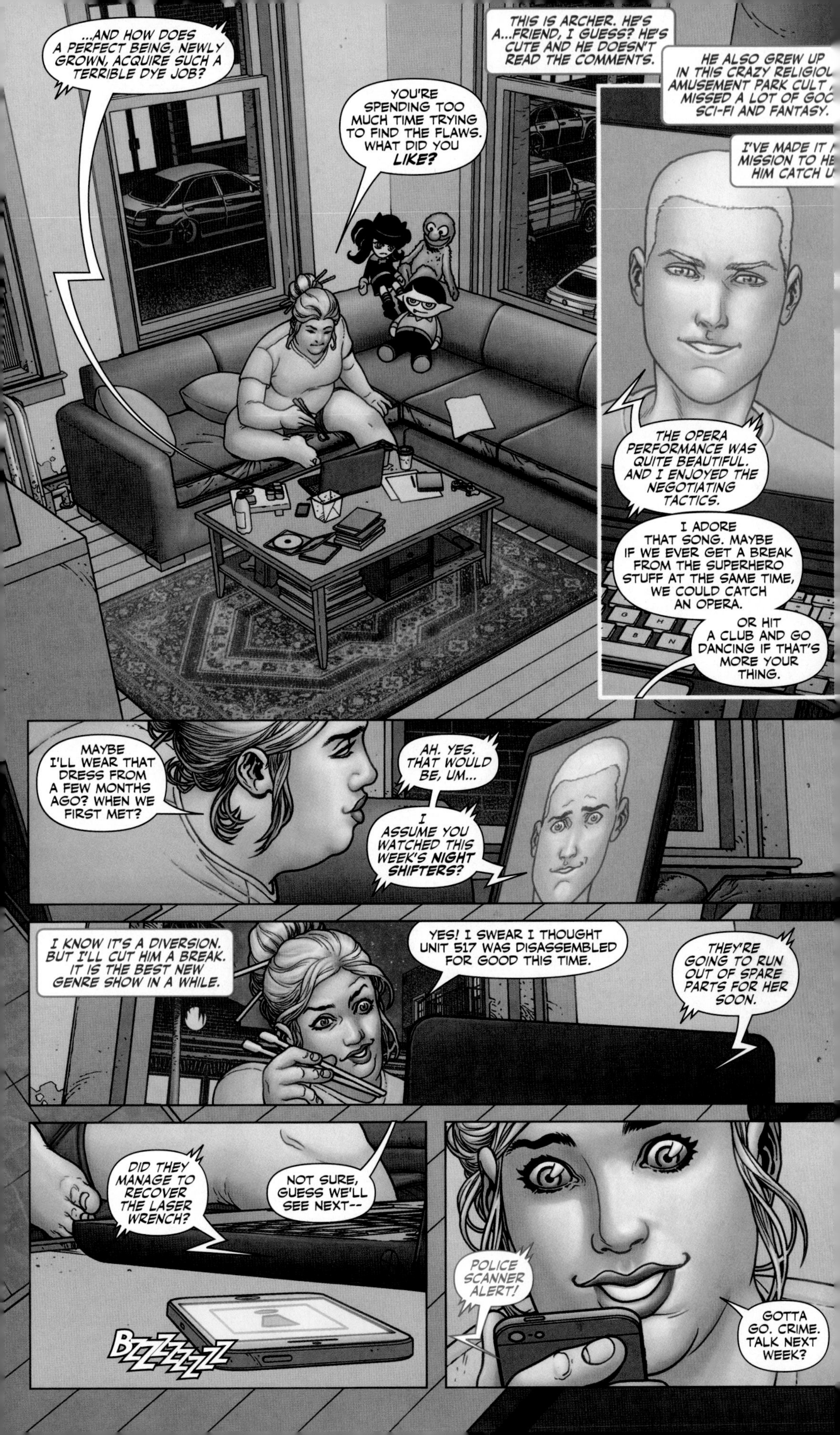
...AND HOW DOES A PERFECT BEING, NEWLY GROWN, ACQUIRE SUCH A TERRIBLE DYE JOB?
YOU'RE SPENDING TOO MUCH TIME TRYING TO FIND THE FLAWS. WHAT DID YOU LIKE?
THIS IS ARCHER. HE'S A...FRIEND, I GUESS? HE'S CUTE AND HE DOESN'T READ THE COMMENTS.
HE ALSO GREW UP IN THIS CRAZY RELIGIOU AMUSEMENT PARK CULT MISSED A LOT OF GOO SCI-FI AND FANTASY.
I'VE MADE IT M MISSION TO HE HIM CATCH U
THE OPERA PERFORMANCE WAS QUITE BEAUTIFUL. AND I ENJOYED THE NEGOTIATING TACTICS.
I ADORE THAT SONG. MAYBE IF WE EVER GET A BREAK FROM THE SUPERHERO STUFF AT THE SAME TIME, WE COULD CATCH AN OPERA.
OR HIT A CLUB AND GO DANCING IF THAT'S MORE YOUR THING.
MAYBE I'LL WEAR THAT DRESS FROM A FEW MONTHS AGO? WHEN WE FIRST MET?
AH. YES. THAT WOULD BE, UM...
I ASSUME YOU WATCHED THIS WEEK'S NIGHT SHIFTERS?
I KNOW IT'S A DIVERSION. BUT I'LL CUT HIM A BREAK. IT IS THE BEST NEW GENRE SHOW IN A WHILE.
YES! I SWEAR I THOUGHT UNIT 517 WAS DISASSEMBLED FOR GOOD THIS TIME.
THEY'RE GOING TO RUN OUT OF SPARE PARTS FOR HER SOON.
DID THEY MANAGE TO RECOVER THE LASER WRENCH?
NOT SURE, GUESS WE'LL SEE NEXT--
BZZZZZZZ
POLICE SCANNER ALERT!
GOTTA GO. CRIME. TALK NEXT WEEK?

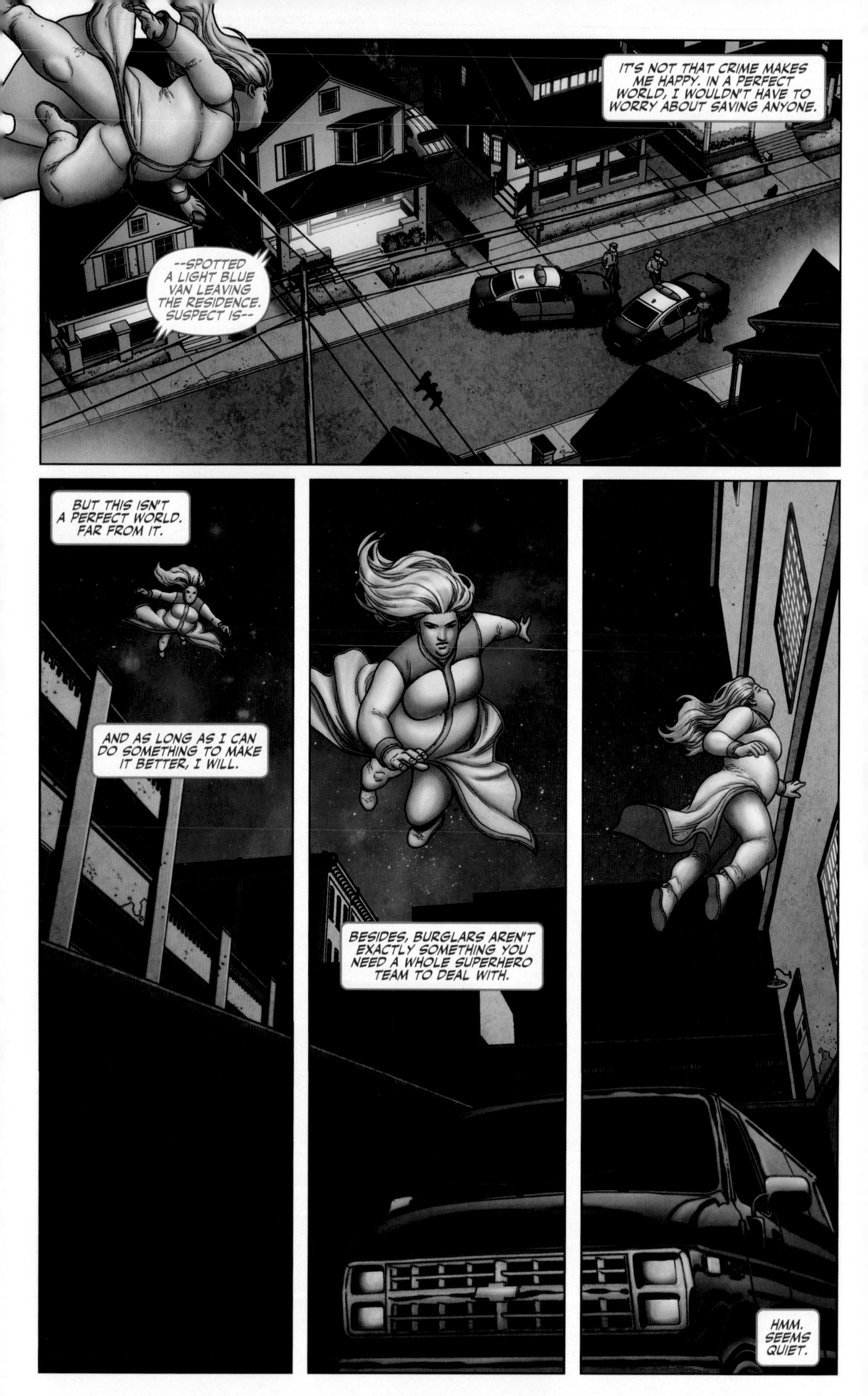
IT'S NOT THAT CRIME MAKES ME HAPPY. IN A PERFECT WORLD, I WOULDN'T HAVE TO WORRY ABOUT SAVING ANYONE.
--SPOTTED A LIGHT BLUE VAN LEAVING THE RESIDENCE. SUSPECT IS--
BUT THIS ISN'T A PERFECT WORLD. FAR FROM IT.
AND AS LONG AS I CAN DO SOMETHING TO MAKE IT BETTER, I WILL.
BESIDES, BURGLARS AREN'T EXACTLY SOMETHING YOU NEED A WHOLE SUPERHERO TEAM TO DEAL WITH.
HMM. SEEMS QUIET.

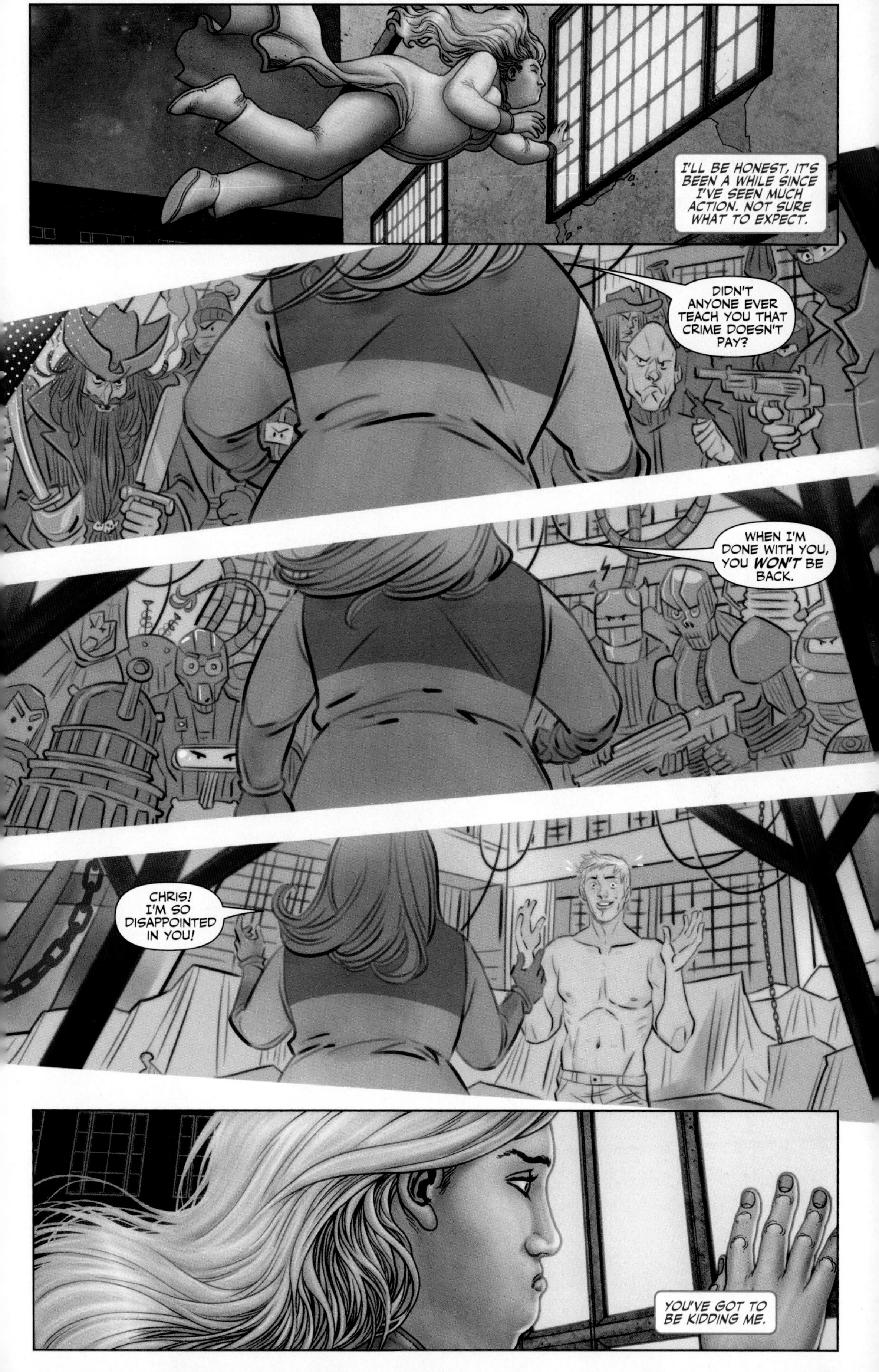
I'LL BE HONEST, IT'S BEEN A WHILE SINCE I'VE SEEN MUCH ACTION. NOT SURE WHAT TO EXPECT.
DIDN'T ANYONE EVER TEACH YOU THAT CRIME DOESN'T PAY?
WHEN I'M DONE WITH YOU, YOU **WON'T** BE BACK.
CHRIS! I'M SO DISAPPOINTED IN YOU!
YOU'VE GOT TO BE KIDDING ME.

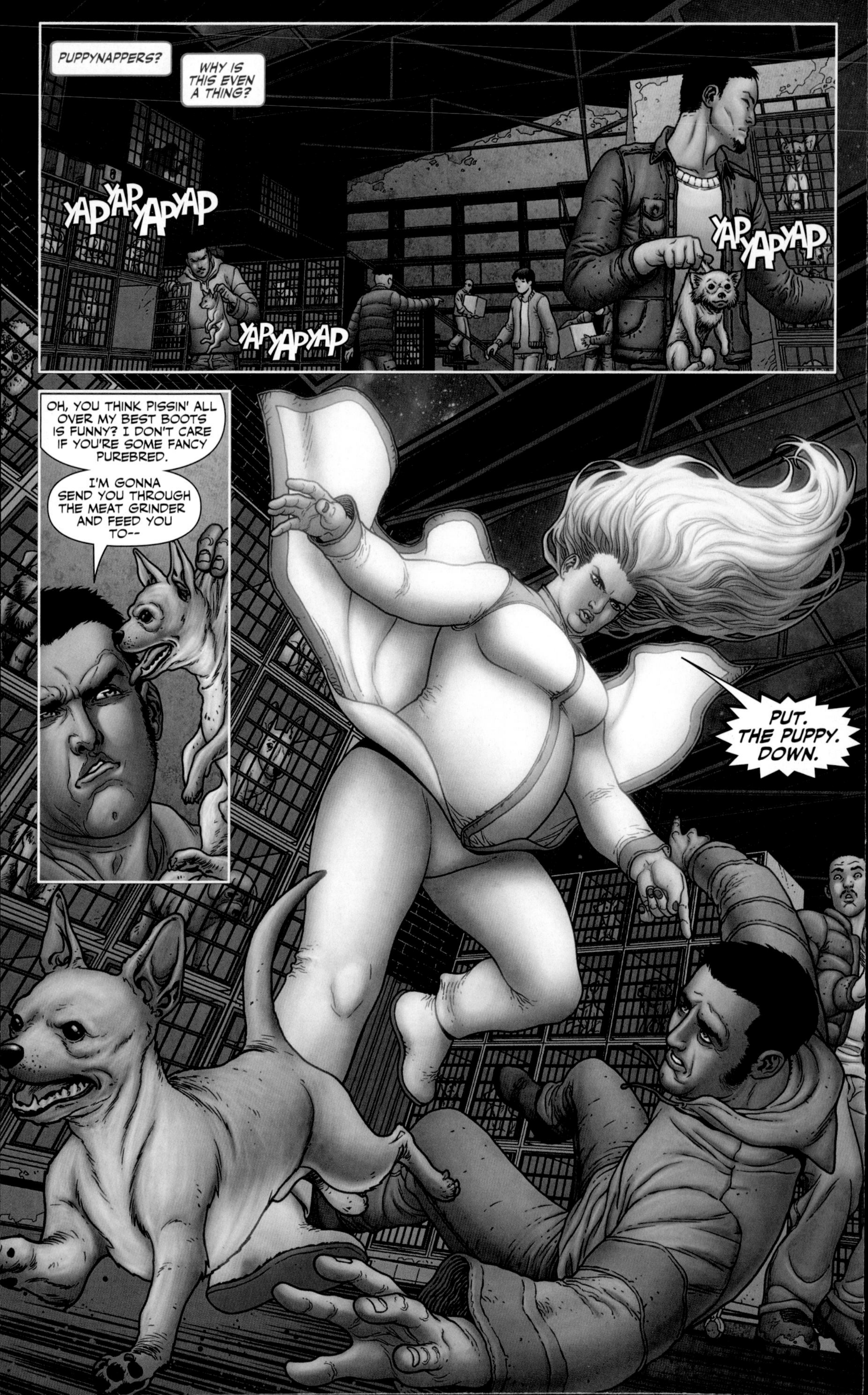

PUPPYNAPPERS?
WHY IS THIS EVEN A THING?
YAPYAPYAPYAP
YAPYAPYAP
YAPYAPYAP
OH, YOU THINK PISSIN' ALL OVER MY BEST BOOTS IS FUNNY? I DON'T CARE IF YOU'RE SOME FANCY PUREBRED.
I'M GONNA SEND YOU THROUGH THE MEAT GRINDER AND FEED YOU TO--
PUT. THE PUPPY. DOWN.

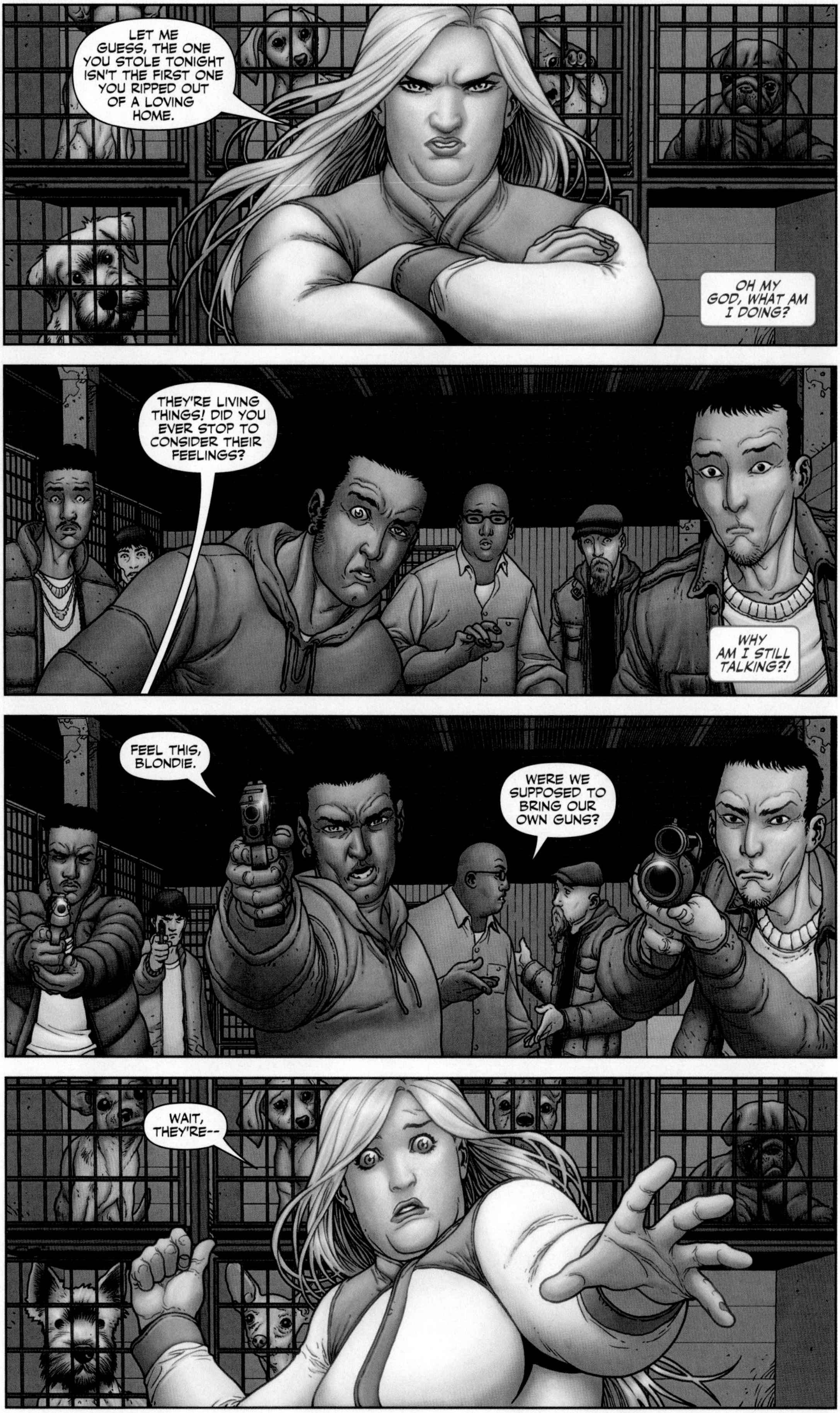
LET ME GUESS, THE ONE YOU STOLE TONIGHT ISN'T THE FIRST ONE YOU RIPPED OUT OF A LOVING HOME.
OH MY GOD, WHAT AM I DOING?
THEY'RE LIVING THINGS! DID YOU EVER STOP TO CONSIDER THEIR FEELINGS?
WHY AM I STILL TALKING?!
FEEL THIS, BLONDIE.
WERE WE SUPPOSED TO BRING OUR OWN GUNS?
WAIT, THEY'RE--

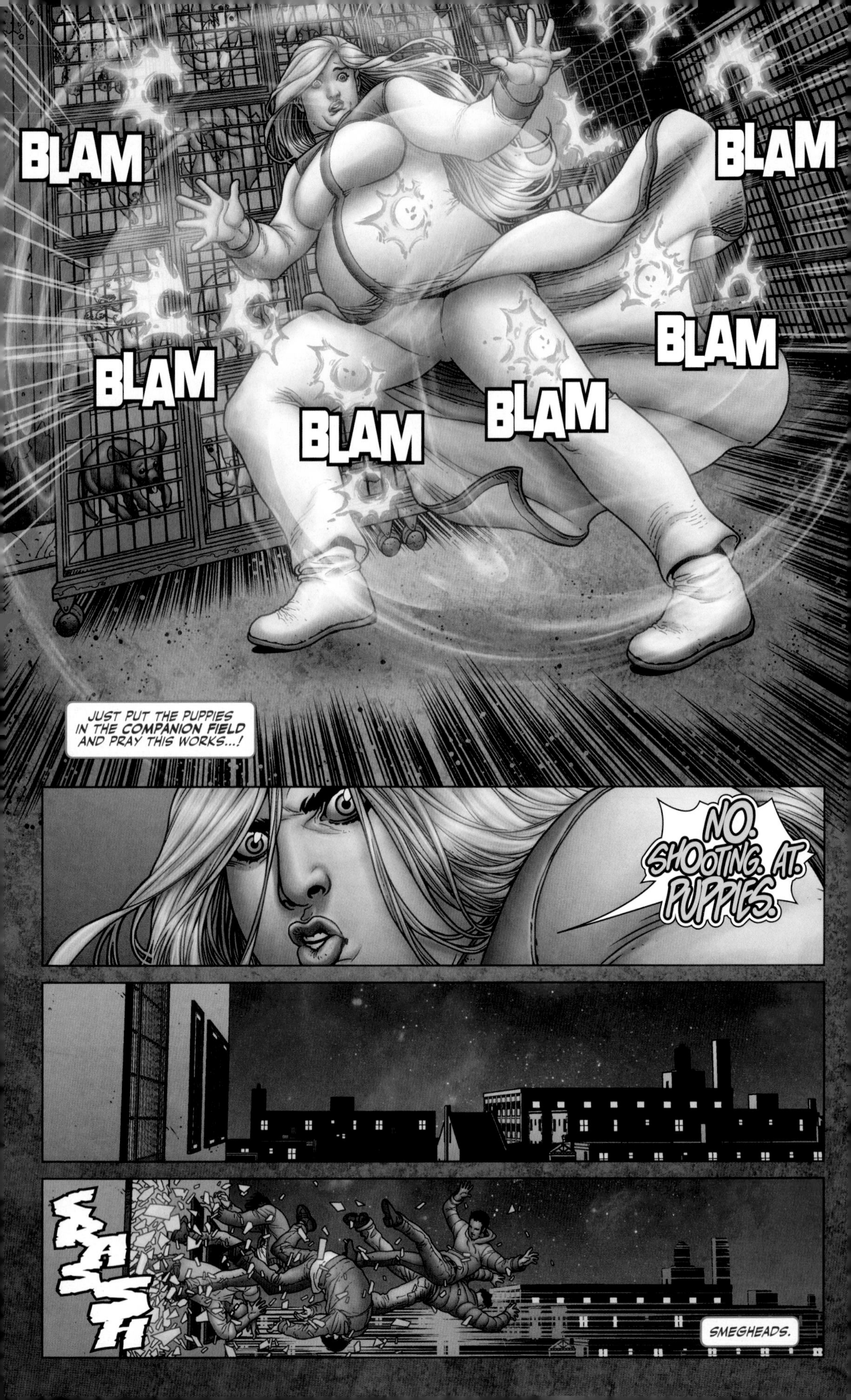
BLAM
BLAM
BLAM
BLAM
BLAM
BLAM
JUST PUT THE PUPPIES IN THE COMPANION FIELD AND PRAY THIS WORKS...!
NO. SHOOTING. AT. PUPPIES.
CRASH
SMEGHEADS.

puppynappers. srsly.

you have to have something for an old teammate to look into. pleeeeeaaaaaase @x? ._.

no names

may have something tho

remember the hack that exposed harada

duh, we kicked his butt and saved the world

THAT MAKES IT SOUND SO EASY. LIKE PEOPLE DIDN'T GET HURT. LIKE WE DIDN'T LOSE A FRIEND.

BUT WE HAD TO FIGHT AND WE HAD TO WIN. AND THAT'S THE THING TO REMEMBER.

tried to scrub the names of the potential psiots he'd been tracking

innocents who couldn't help what they are.

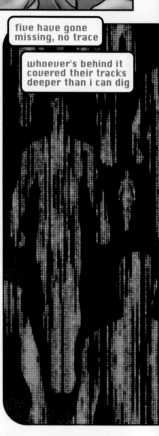

five have gone missing, no trace

whoever's behind it covered their tracks deeper than i can dig

WHOA. @X KNOWS WHAT HE'S DOING. BUILT THE WHOLE SUMMER SMITH IDENTITY FOR ME. IF HE HIT A DEAD END...

any clues??

last ping from missing kid's phone

sam bradshaw. sixteen.

worth checking but be careful

obvs!

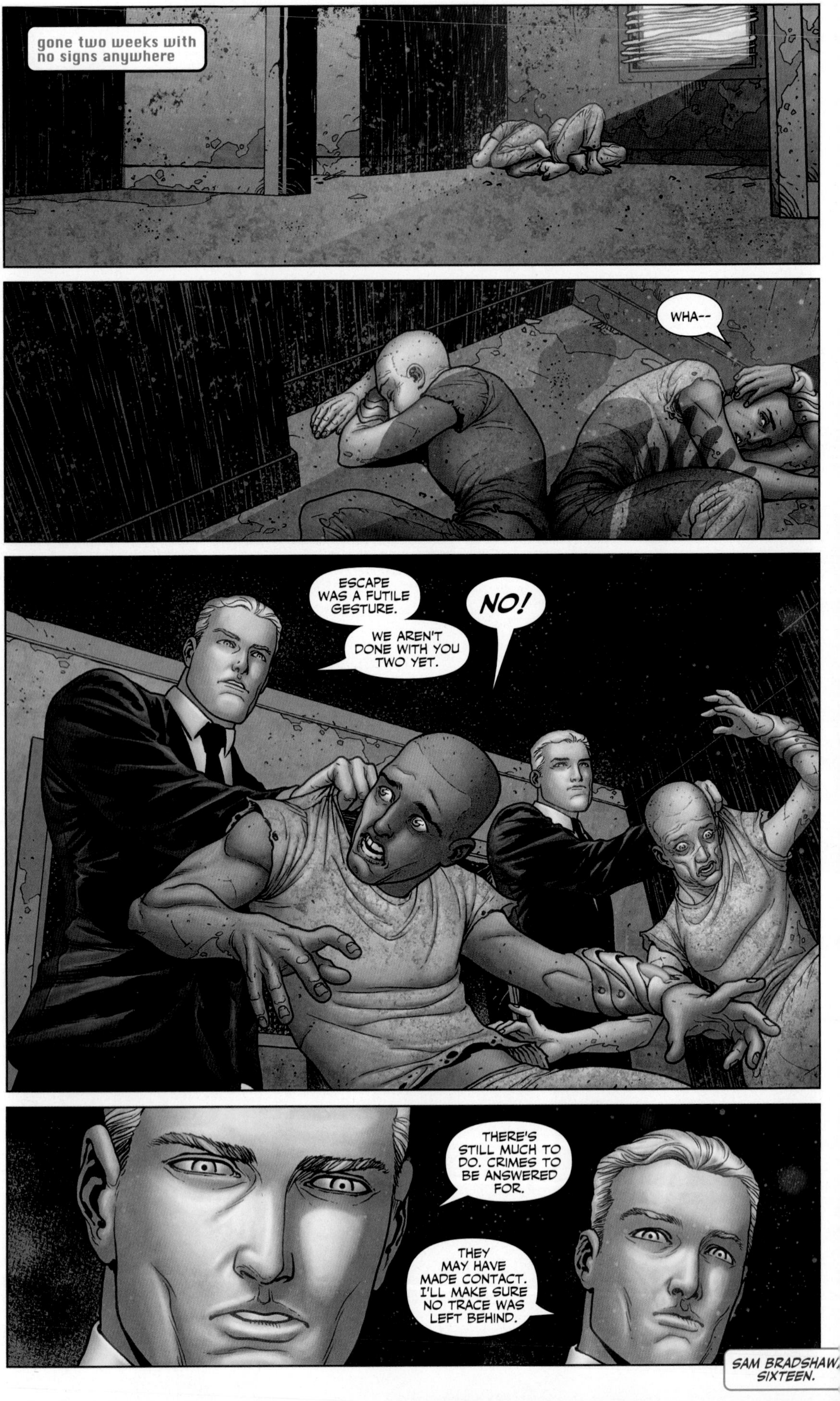
gone two weeks with no signs anywhere
WHA--
ESCAPE WAS A FUTILE GESTURE.
WE AREN'T DONE WITH YOU TWO YET.
NO!
THERE'S STILL MUCH TO DO. CRIMES TO BE ANSWERED FOR.
THEY MAY HAVE MADE CONTACT. I'LL MAKE SURE NO TRACE WAS LEFT BEHIND.
SAM BRADSHAW, SIXTEEN.

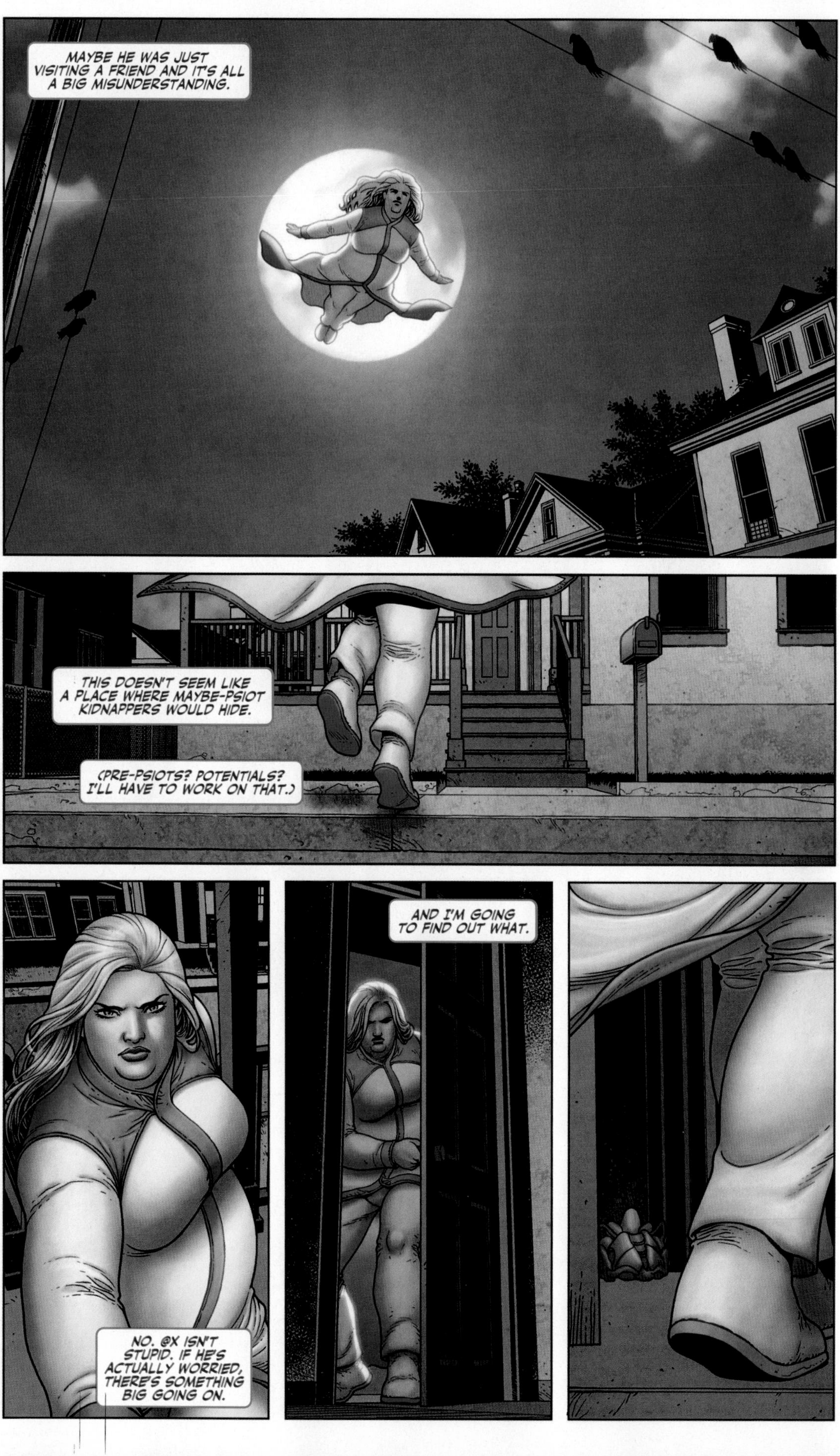
MAYBE HE WAS JUST VISITING A FRIEND AND IT'S ALL A BIG MISUNDERSTANDING.
THIS DOESN'T SEEM LIKE A PLACE WHERE MAYBE-PSIOT KIDNAPPERS WOULD HIDE.
(PRE-PSIOTS? POTENTIALS? I'LL HAVE TO WORK ON THAT.)
NO. @X ISN'T STUPID. IF HE'S ACTUALLY WORRIED, THERE'S SOMETHING BIG GOING ON.
AND I'M GOING TO FIND OUT WHAT.

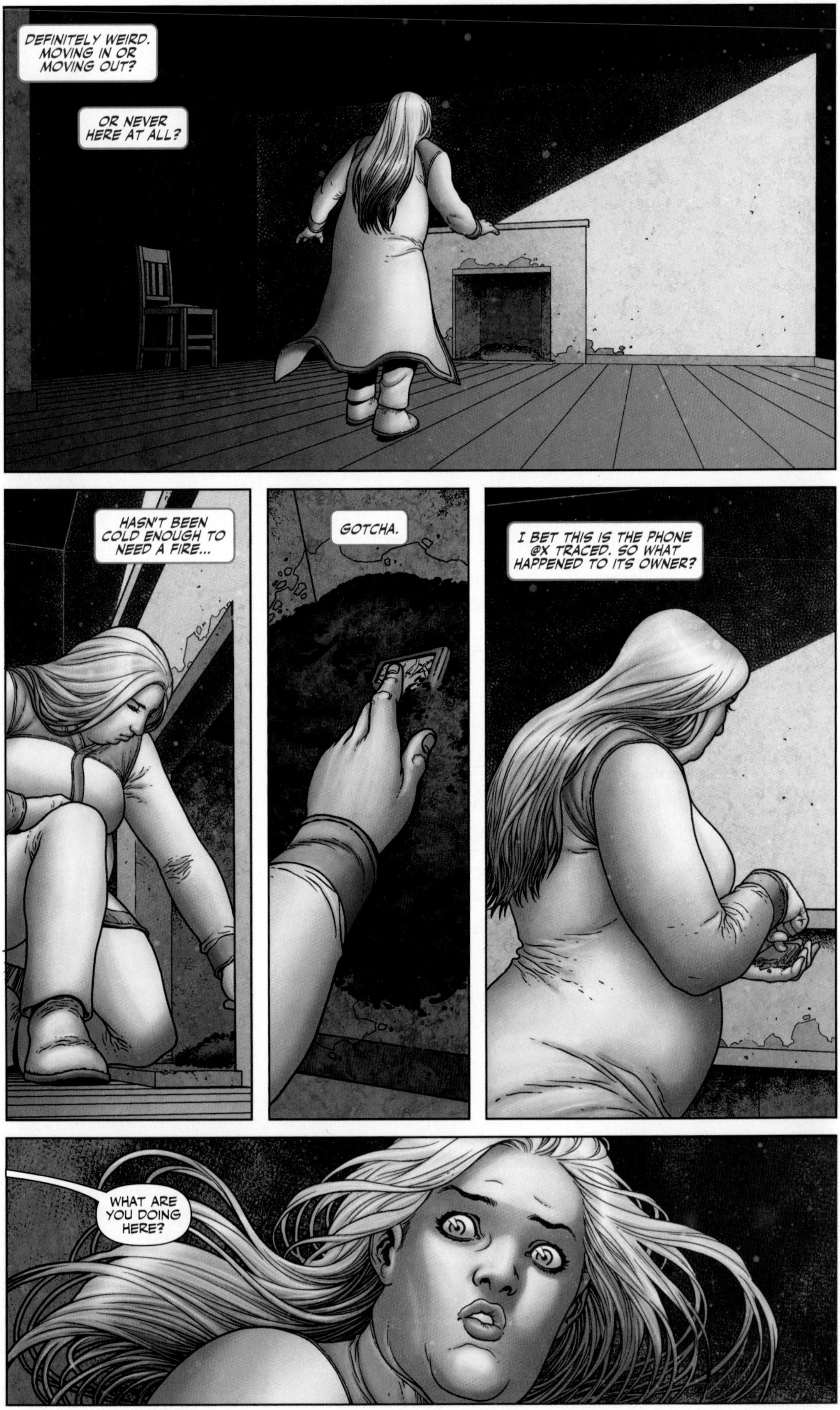
DEFINITELY WEIRD. MOVING IN OR MOVING OUT?
OR NEVER HERE AT ALL?
HASN'T BEEN COLD ENOUGH TO NEED A FIRE...
GOTCHA.
I BET THIS IS THE PHONE @X TRACED. SO WHAT HAPPENED TO ITS OWNER?
WHAT ARE YOU DOING HERE?

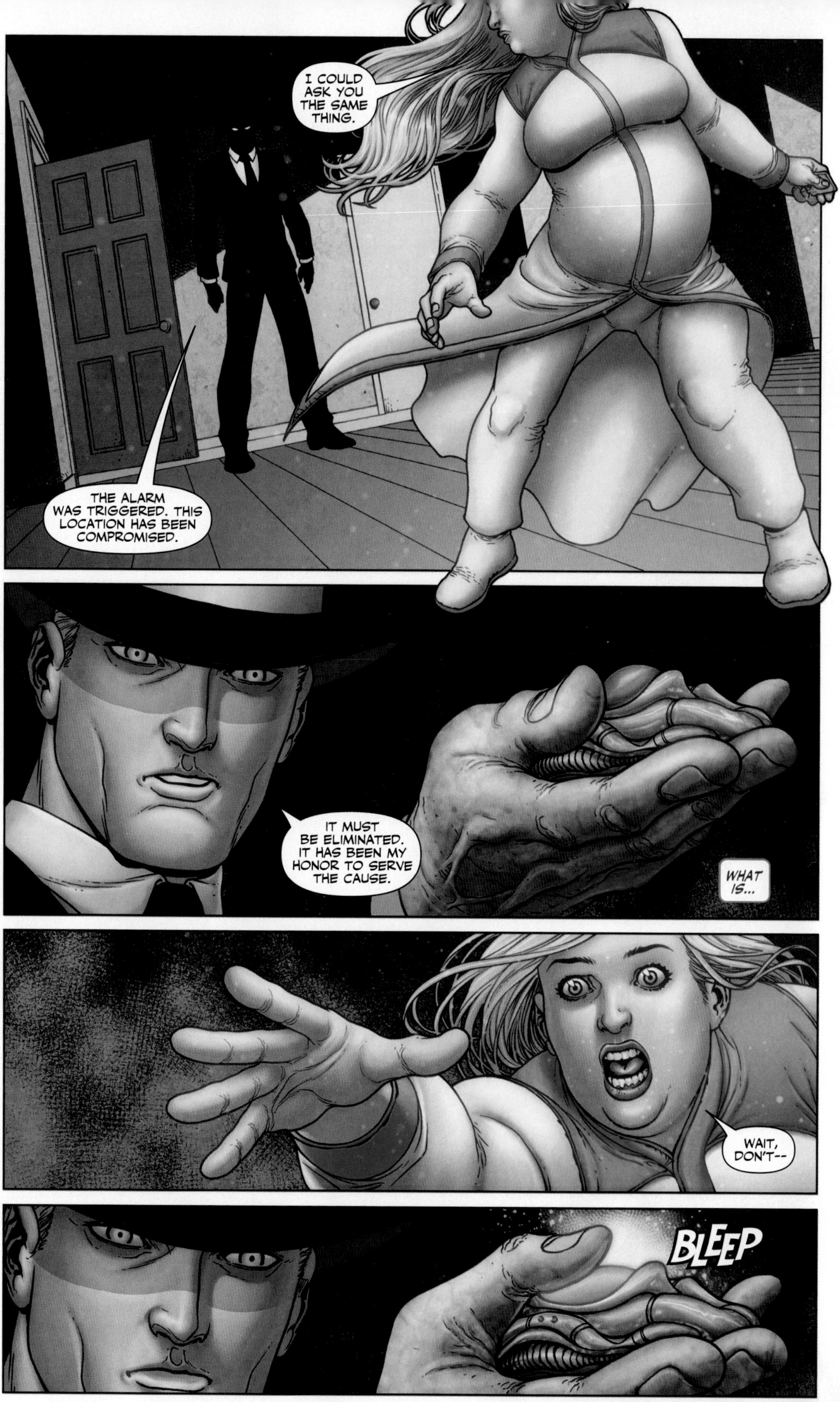
I COULD ASK YOU THE SAME THING.
THE ALARM WAS TRIGGERED. THIS LOCATION HAS BEEN COMPROMISED.
IT MUST BE ELIMINATED. IT HAS BEEN MY HONOR TO SERVE THE CAUSE.
WHAT IS...
WAIT, DON'T--
BLEEP

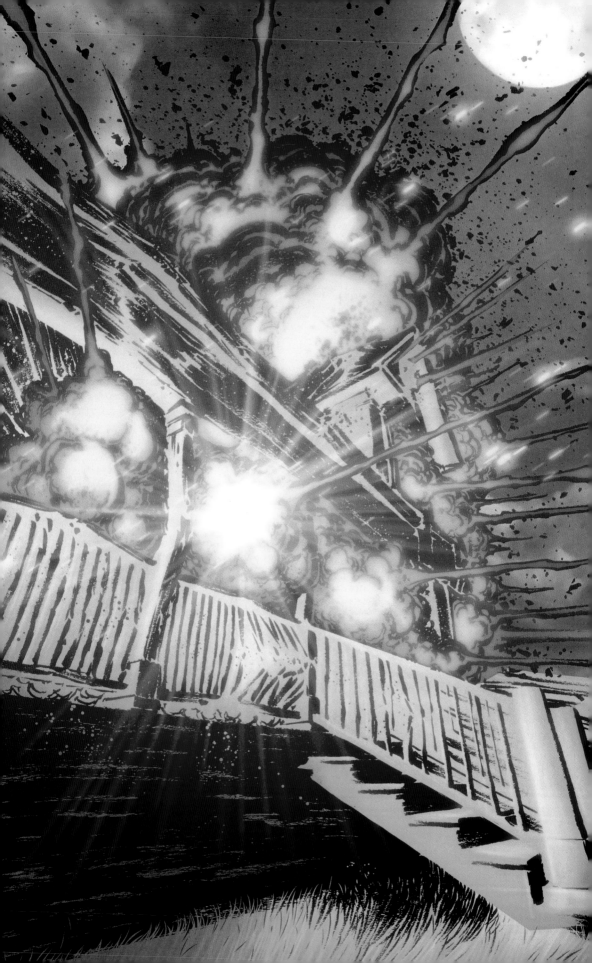

VALIANT

JODY HOUSER | FRANCIS PORTELA
MARGUERITE SAUVAGE

#2

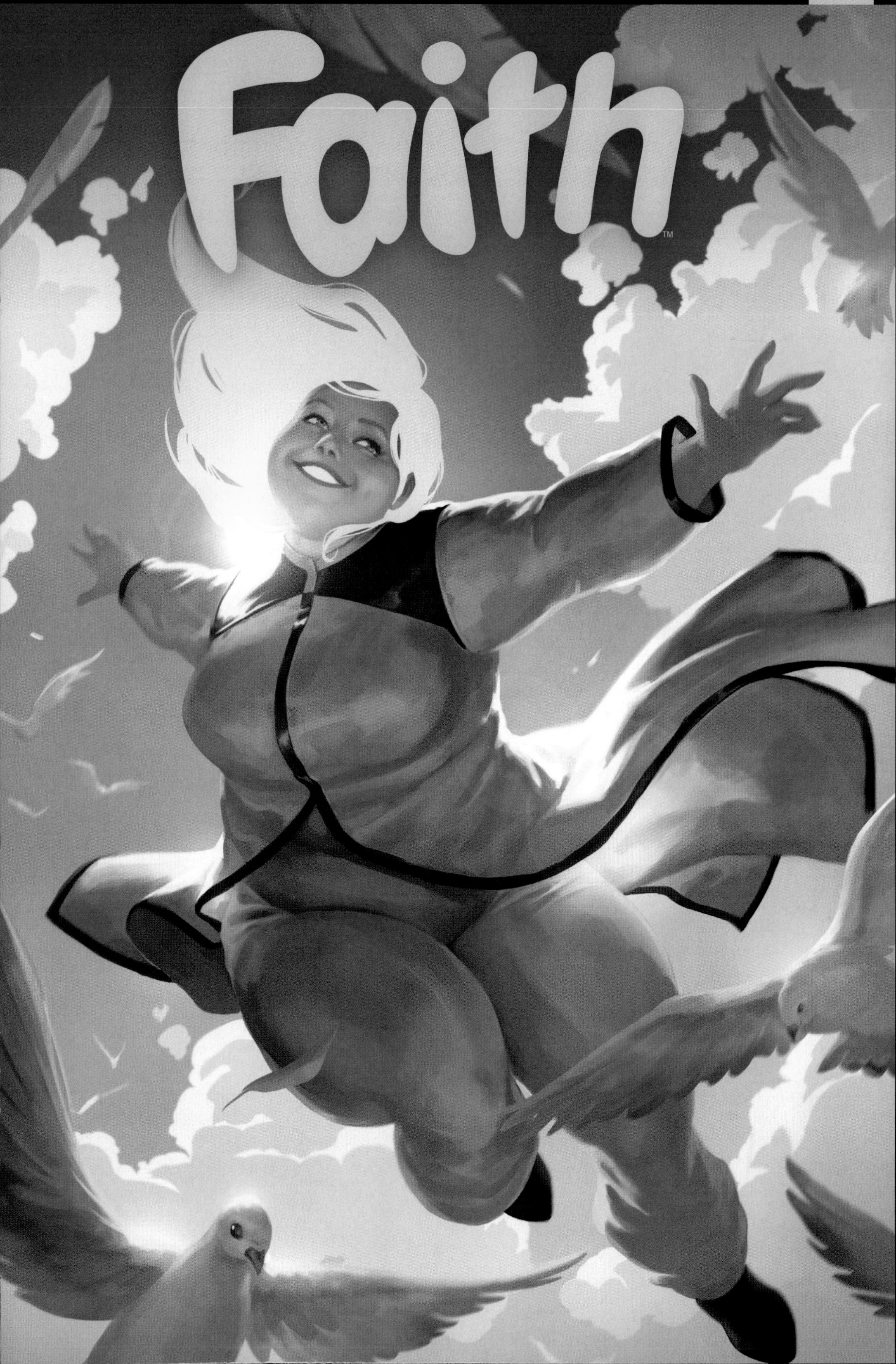
Faith™

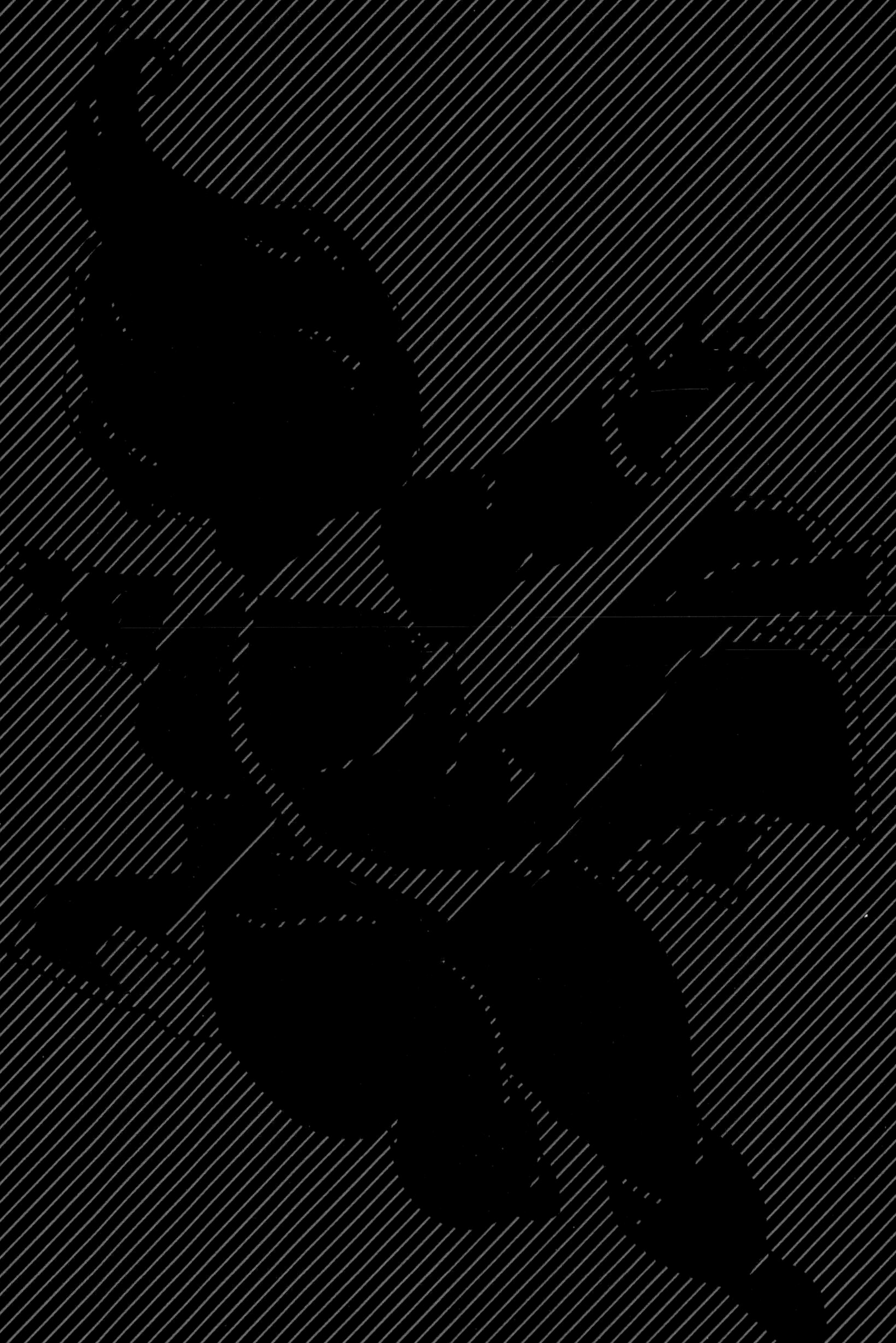

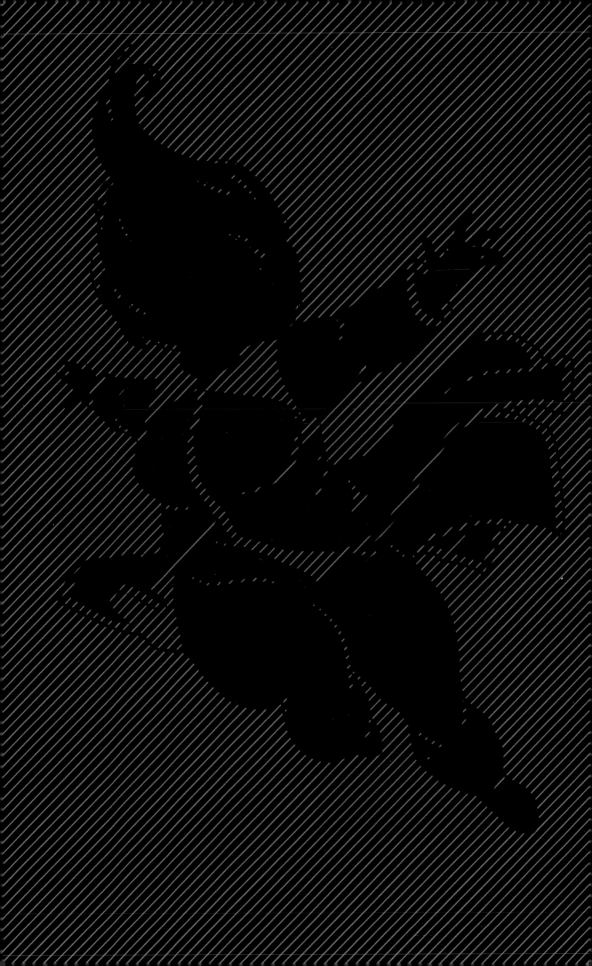

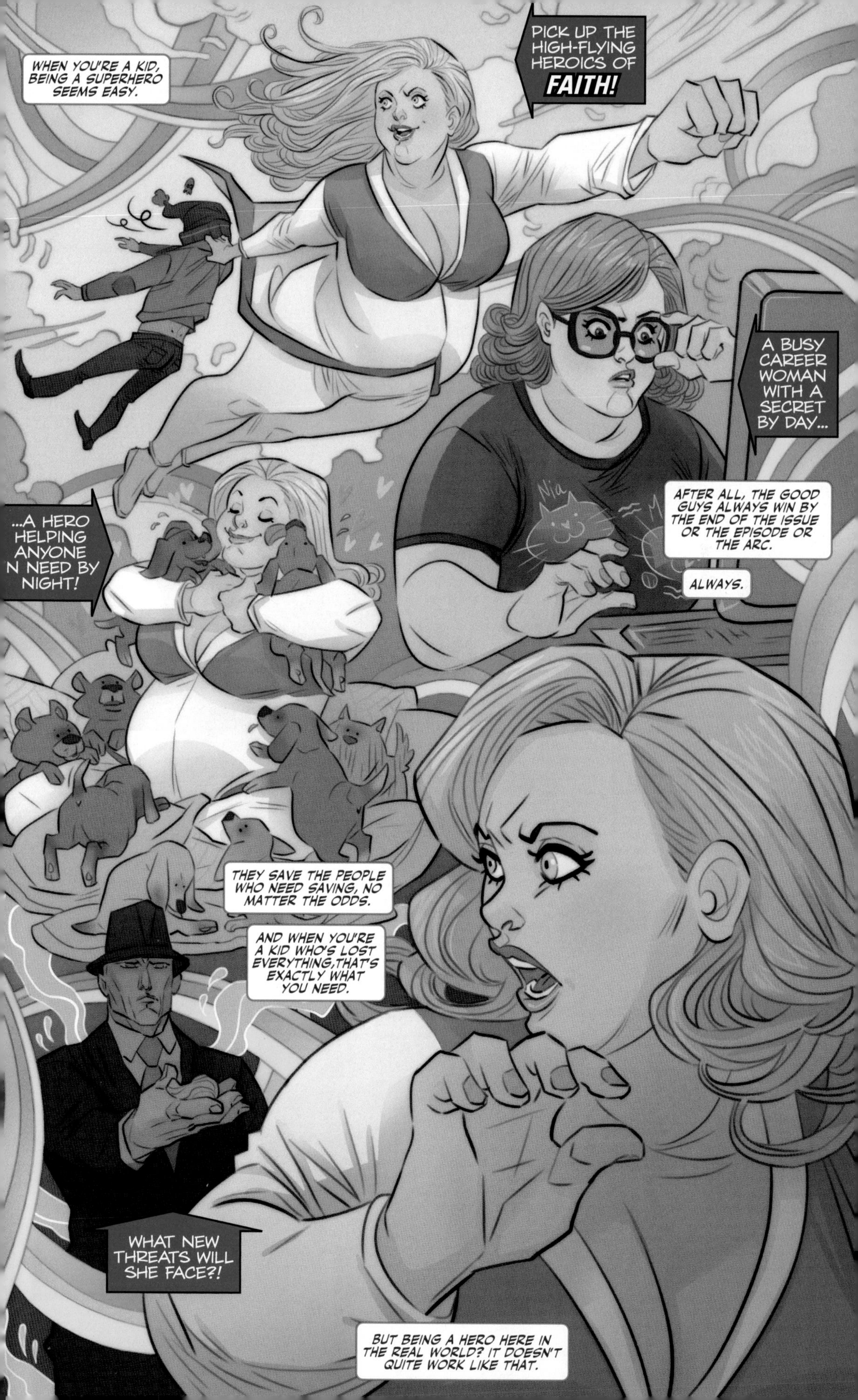
WHEN YOU'RE A KID, BEING A SUPERHERO SEEMS EASY.
PICK UP THE HIGH-FLYING HEROICS OF FAITH!
A BUSY CAREER WOMAN WITH A SECRET BY DAY...
...A HERO HELPING ANYONE N NEED BY NIGHT!
AFTER ALL, THE GOOD GUYS ALWAYS WIN BY THE END OF THE ISSUE OR THE EPISODE OR THE ARC.
ALWAYS.
THEY SAVE THE PEOPLE WHO NEED SAVING, NO MATTER THE ODDS.
AND WHEN YOU'RE A KID WHO'S LOST EVERYTHING, THAT'S EXACTLY WHAT YOU NEED.
WHAT NEW THREATS WILL SHE FACE?!
BUT BEING A HERO HERE IN THE REAL WORLD? IT DOESN'T QUITE WORK LIKE THAT.

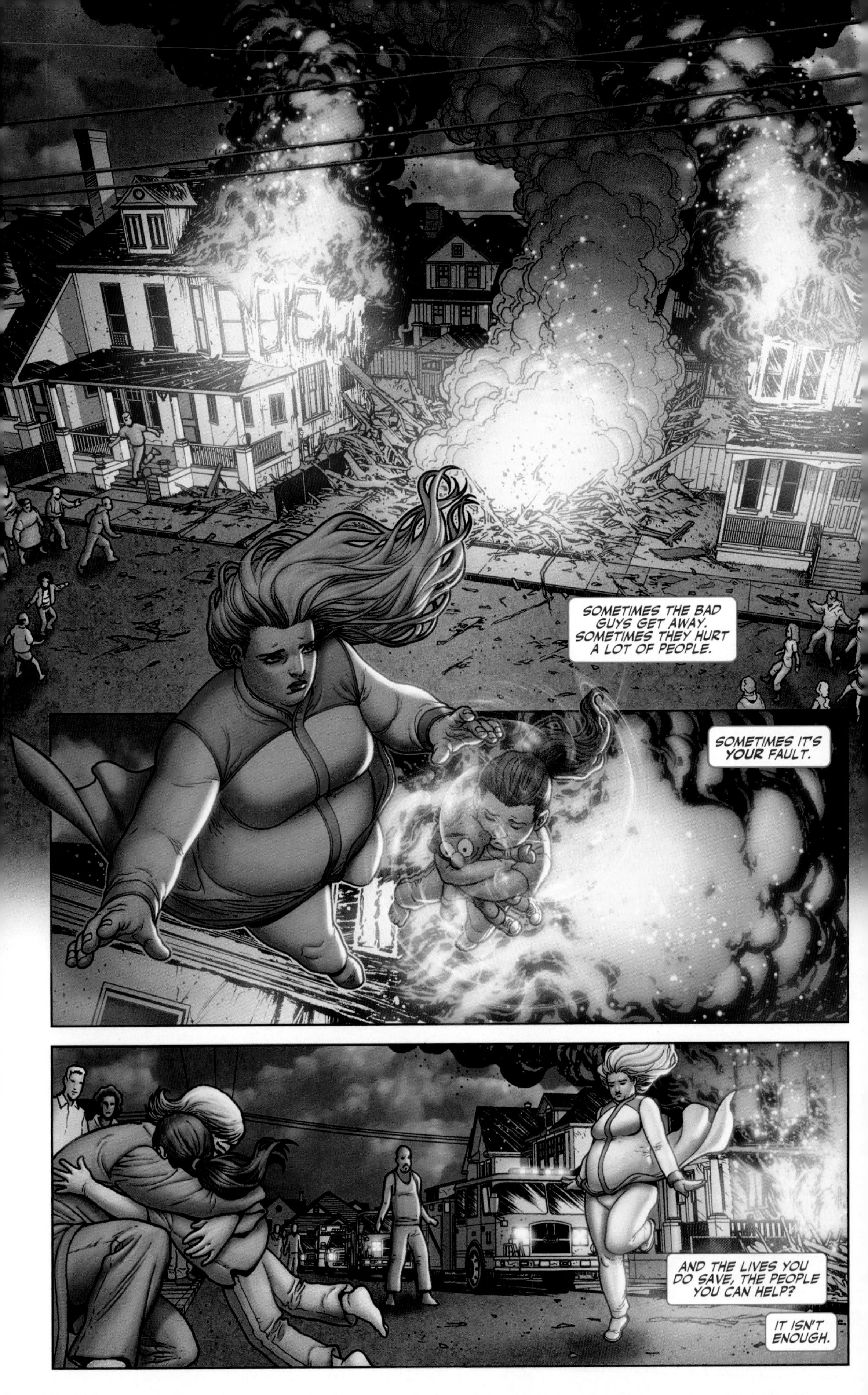
SOMETIMES THE BAD GUYS GET AWAY. SOMETIMES THEY HURT A LOT OF PEOPLE.
SOMETIMES IT'S *YOUR* FAULT.
AND THE LIVES YOU DO SAVE, THE PEOPLE YOU CAN HELP?
IT ISN'T ENOUGH.

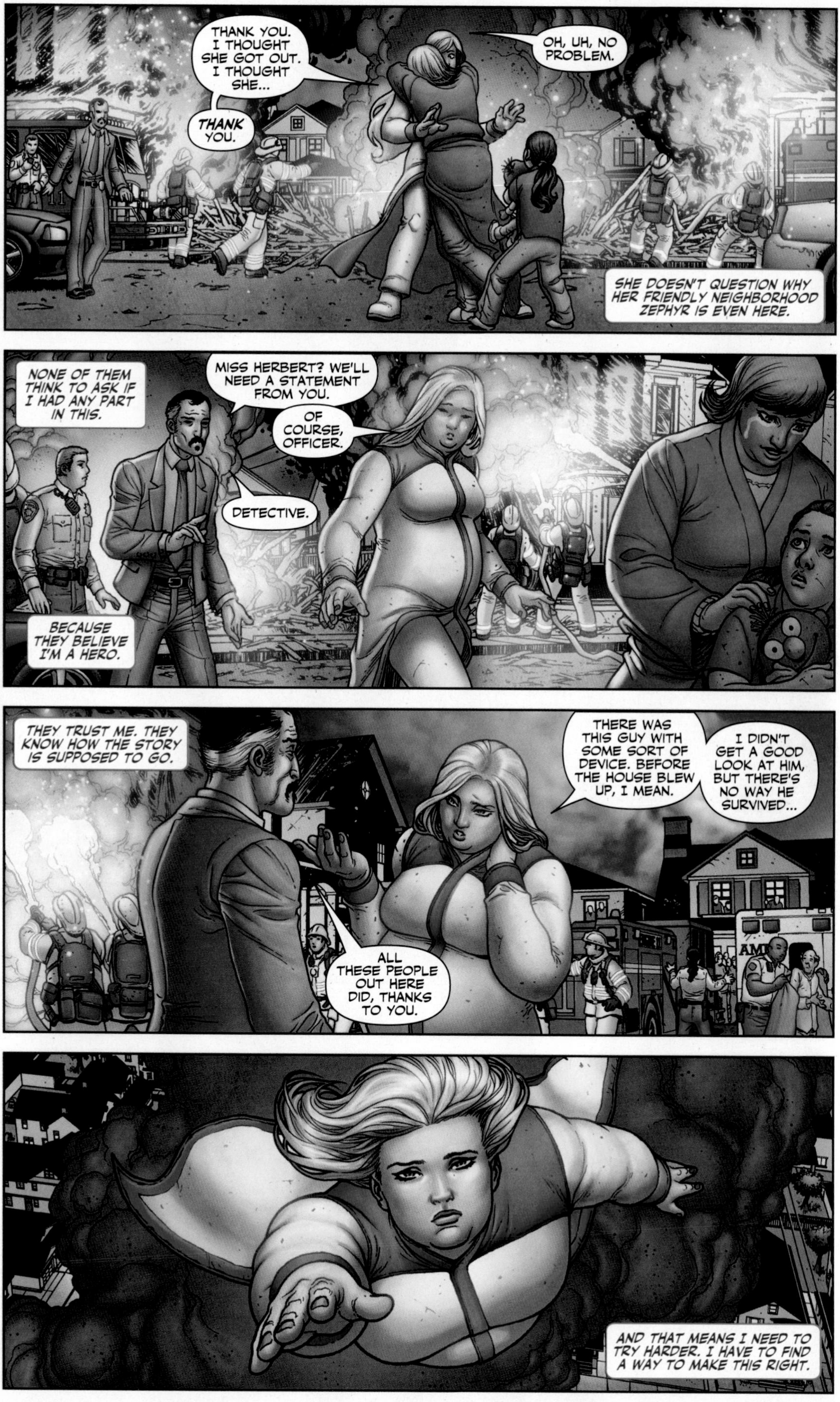

THANK YOU. I THOUGHT SHE GOT OUT. I THOUGHT SHE...
THANK YOU.
OH, UH, NO PROBLEM.
SHE DOESN'T QUESTION WHY HER FRIENDLY NEIGHBORHOOD ZEPHYR IS EVEN HERE.
NONE OF THEM THINK TO ASK IF I HAD ANY PART IN THIS.
MISS HERBERT? WE'LL NEED A STATEMENT FROM YOU.
OF COURSE, OFFICER.
DETECTIVE.
BECAUSE THEY BELIEVE I'M A HERO.
THEY TRUST ME. THEY KNOW HOW THE STORY IS SUPPOSED TO GO.
THERE WAS THIS GUY WITH SOME SORT OF DEVICE. BEFORE THE HOUSE BLEW UP, I MEAN.
I DIDN'T GET A GOOD LOOK AT HIM, BUT THERE'S NO WAY HE SURVIVED...
ALL THESE PEOPLE OUT HERE DID, THANKS TO YOU.
AND THAT MEANS I NEED TO TRY HARDER. I HAVE TO FIND A WAY TO MAKE THIS RIGHT.

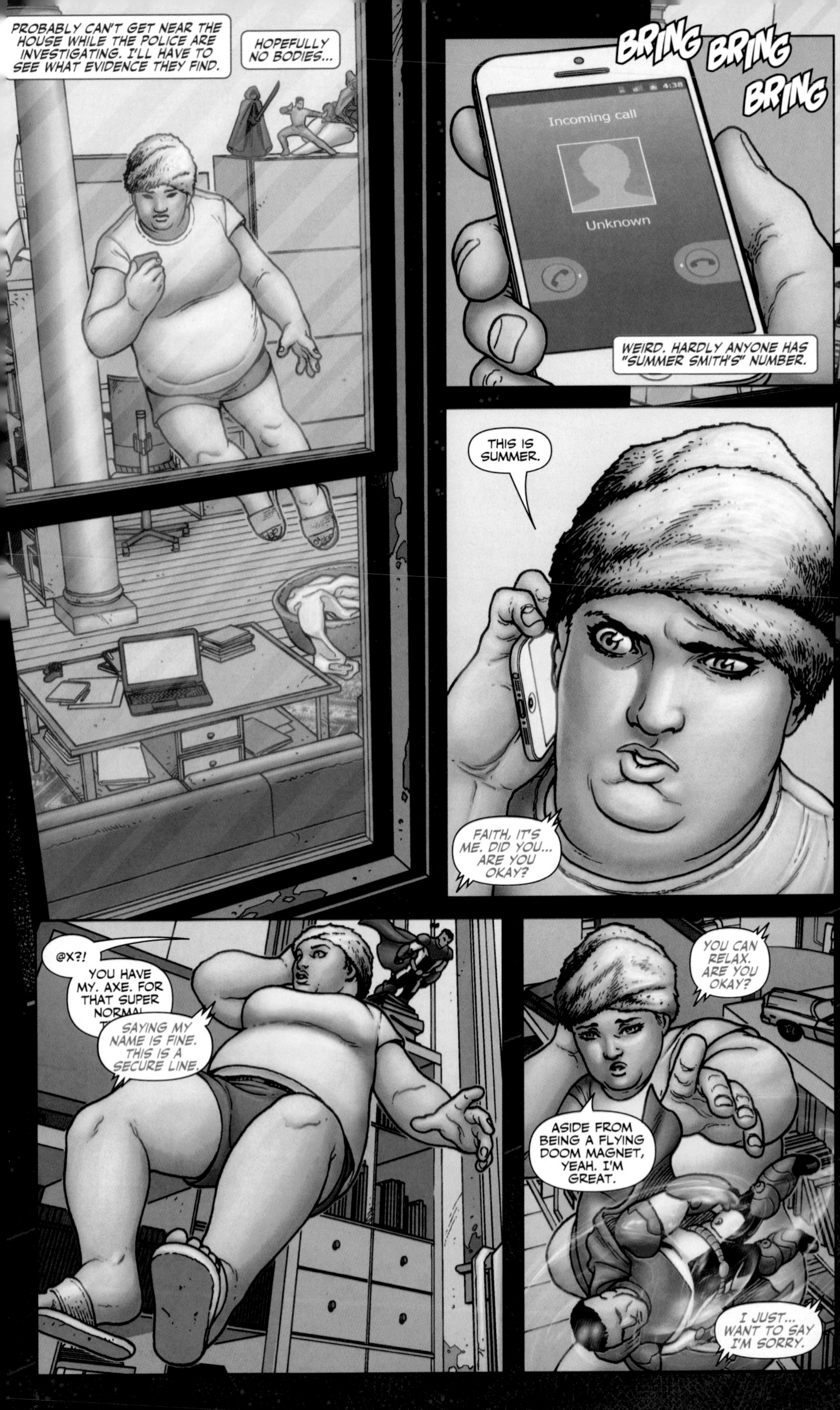
PROBABLY CAN'T GET NEAR THE HOUSE WHILE THE POLICE ARE INVESTIGATING. I'LL HAVE TO SEE WHAT EVIDENCE THEY FIND.
HOPEFULLY NO BODIES...
BRING BRING BRING
4:38
Incoming call
Unknown
WEIRD. HARDLY ANYONE HAS "SUMMER SMITH'S" NUMBER.
THIS IS SUMMER.
FAITH, IT'S ME. DID YOU... ARE YOU OKAY?
@X?!
YOU HAVE MY. AXE. FOR THAT SUPER
SAYING MY NAME IS FINE. THIS IS A SECURE LINE.
YOU CAN RELAX. ARE YOU OKAY?
ASIDE FROM BEING A FLYING DOOM MAGNET, YEAH. I'M GREAT.
I JUST... WANT TO SAY I'M SORRY.

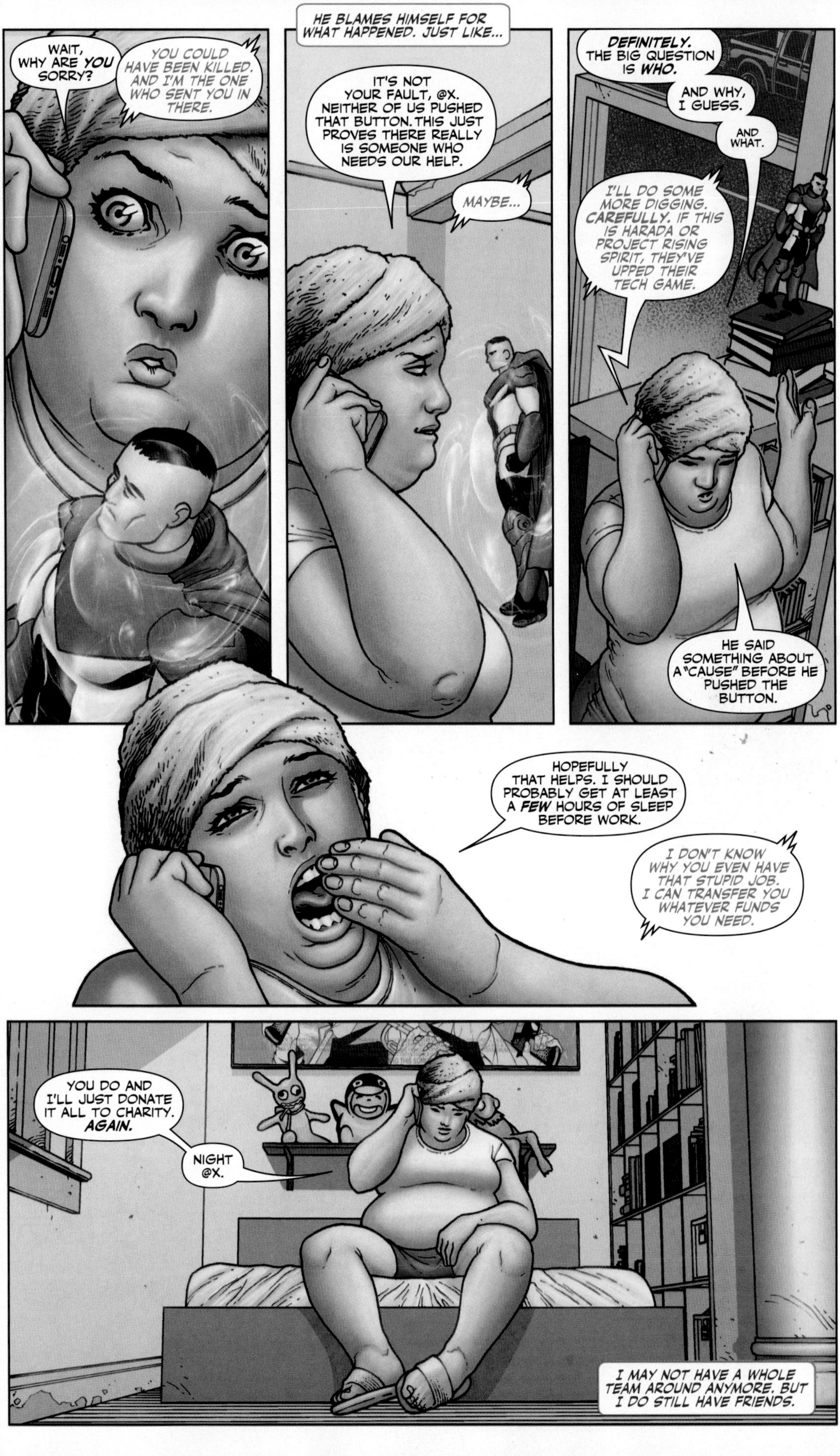
WAIT, WHY ARE *YOU* SORRY?
YOU COULD HAVE BEEN KILLED. AND I'M THE ONE WHO SENT YOU IN THERE.
HE BLAMES HIMSELF FOR WHAT HAPPENED. JUST LIKE...
IT'S NOT YOUR FAULT, @X. NEITHER OF US PUSHED THAT BUTTON. THIS JUST PROVES THERE REALLY IS SOMEONE WHO NEEDS OUR HELP.
MAYBE...
DEFINITELY. THE BIG QUESTION IS *WHO.*
AND WHY, I GUESS.
AND WHAT.
I'LL DO SOME MORE DIGGING. *CAREFULLY.* IF THIS IS HARADA OR PROJECT RISING SPIRIT, THEY'VE UPPED THEIR TECH GAME.
HE SAID SOMETHING ABOUT A "CAUSE" BEFORE HE PUSHED THE BUTTON.
HOPEFULLY THAT HELPS. I SHOULD PROBABLY GET AT LEAST A *FEW* HOURS OF SLEEP BEFORE WORK.
I DON'T KNOW WHY YOU EVEN HAVE THAT STUPID JOB. I CAN TRANSFER YOU WHATEVER FUNDS YOU NEED.
YOU DO AND I'LL JUST DONATE IT ALL TO CHARITY. *AGAIN.*
NIGHT @X.
I MAY NOT HAVE A WHOLE TEAM AROUND ANYMORE. BUT I DO STILL HAVE FRIENDS.

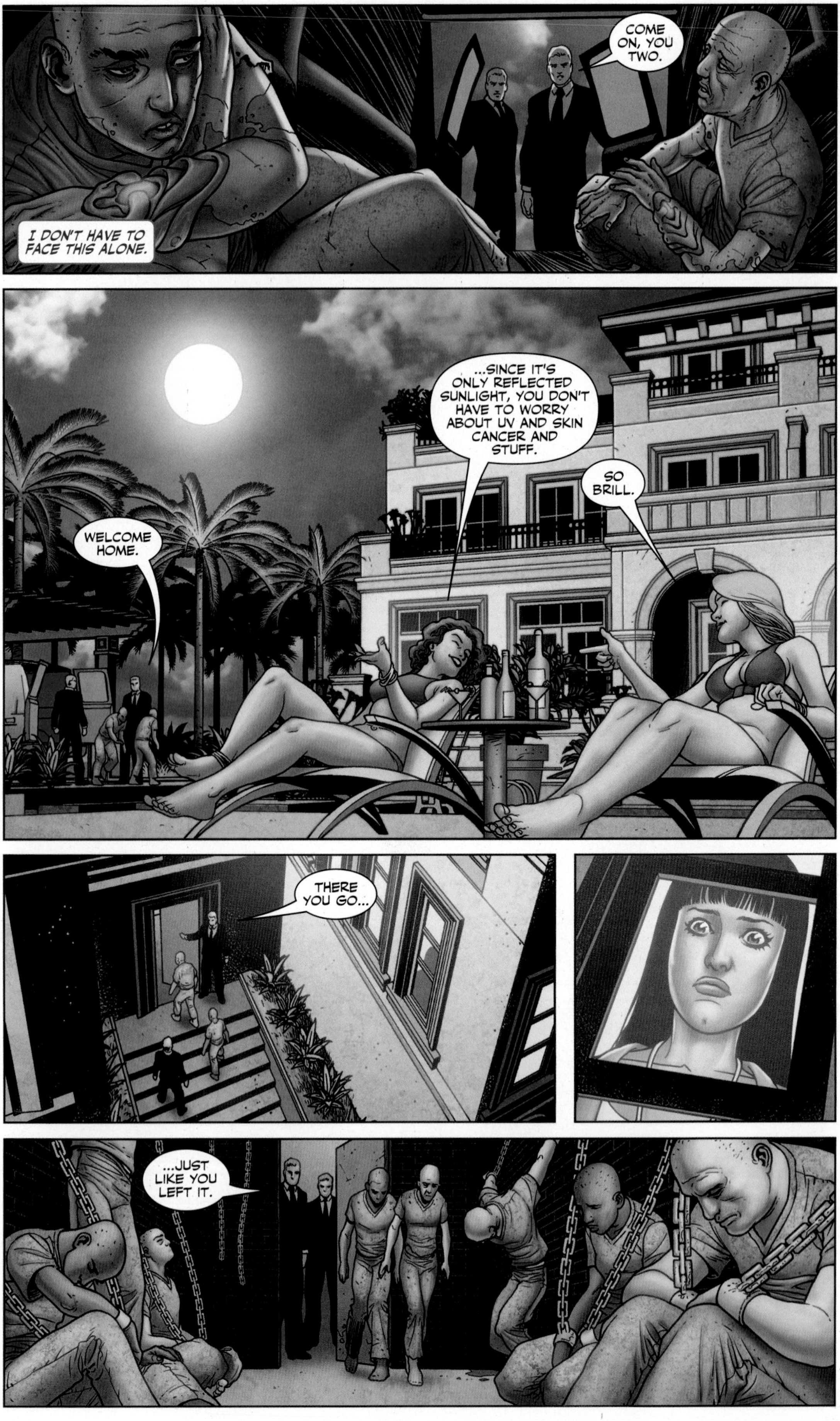
COME ON, YOU TWO.
I DON'T HAVE TO FACE THIS ALONE.
WELCOME HOME.
...SINCE IT'S ONLY REFLECTED SUNLIGHT, YOU DON'T HAVE TO WORRY ABOUT UV AND SKIN CANCER AND STUFF.
SO BRILL.
THERE YOU GO...
...JUST LIKE YOU LEFT IT.

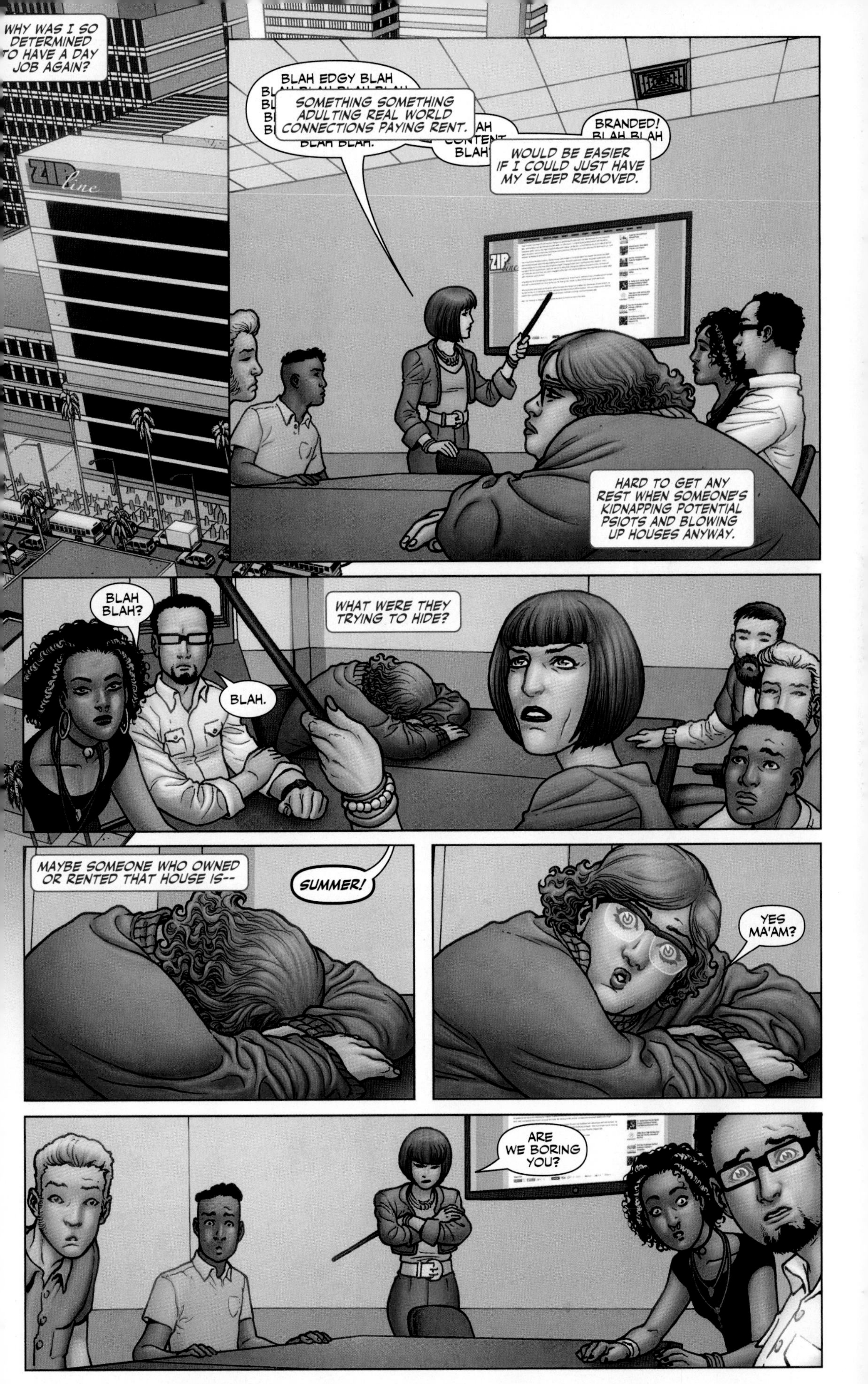
WHY WAS I SO DETERMINED TO HAVE A DAY JOB AGAIN?
ZIP line
BLAH EDGY BLAH
BLAH BLAH.
SOMETHING SOMETHING ADULTING REAL WORLD CONNECTIONS PAYING RENT.
BRANDED!
WOULD BE EASIER IF I COULD JUST HAVE MY SLEEP REMOVED.
HARD TO GET ANY REST WHEN SOMEONE'S KIDNAPPING POTENTIAL PSIOTS AND BLOWING UP HOUSES ANYWAY.
BLAH BLAH?
BLAH.
WHAT WERE THEY TRYING TO HIDE?
MAYBE SOMEONE WHO OWNED OR RENTED THAT HOUSE IS--
SUMMER!
YES MA'AM?
ARE WE BORING YOU?

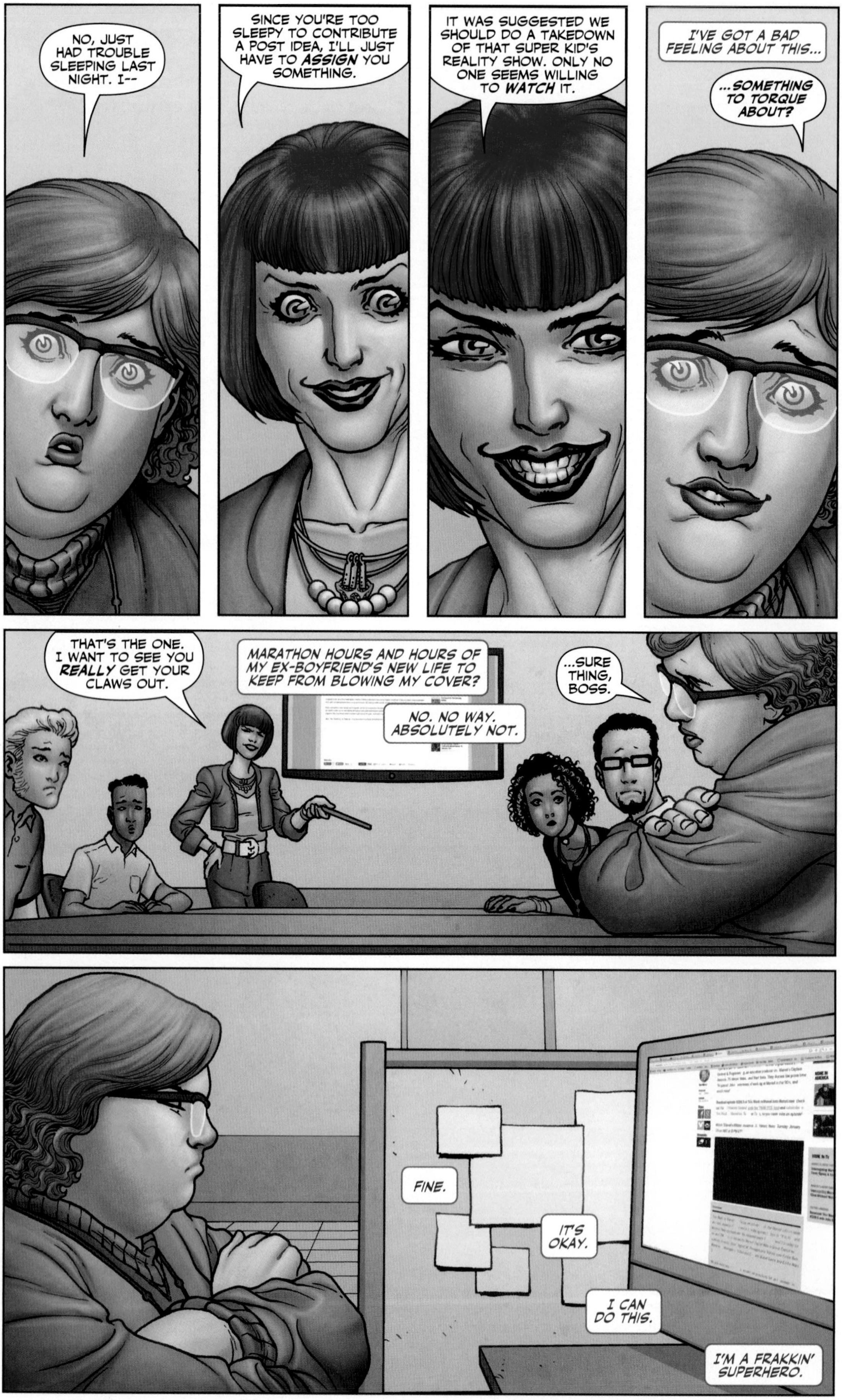
NO, JUST HAD TROUBLE SLEEPING LAST NIGHT. I--
SINCE YOU'RE TOO SLEEPY TO CONTRIBUTE A POST IDEA, I'LL JUST HAVE TO ASSIGN YOU SOMETHING.
IT WAS SUGGESTED WE SHOULD DO A TAKEDOWN OF THAT SUPER KID'S REALITY SHOW. ONLY NO ONE SEEMS WILLING TO WATCH IT.
I'VE GOT A BAD FEELING ABOUT THIS...
...SOMETHING TO TORQUE ABOUT?
THAT'S THE ONE. I WANT TO SEE YOU REALLY GET YOUR CLAWS OUT.
MARATHON HOURS AND HOURS OF MY EX-BOYFRIEND'S NEW LIFE TO KEEP FROM BLOWING MY COVER?
NO. NO WAY. ABSOLUTELY NOT.
...SURE THING, BOSS.
FINE.
IT'S OKAY.
I CAN DO THIS.
I'M A FRAKKIN' SUPERHERO.

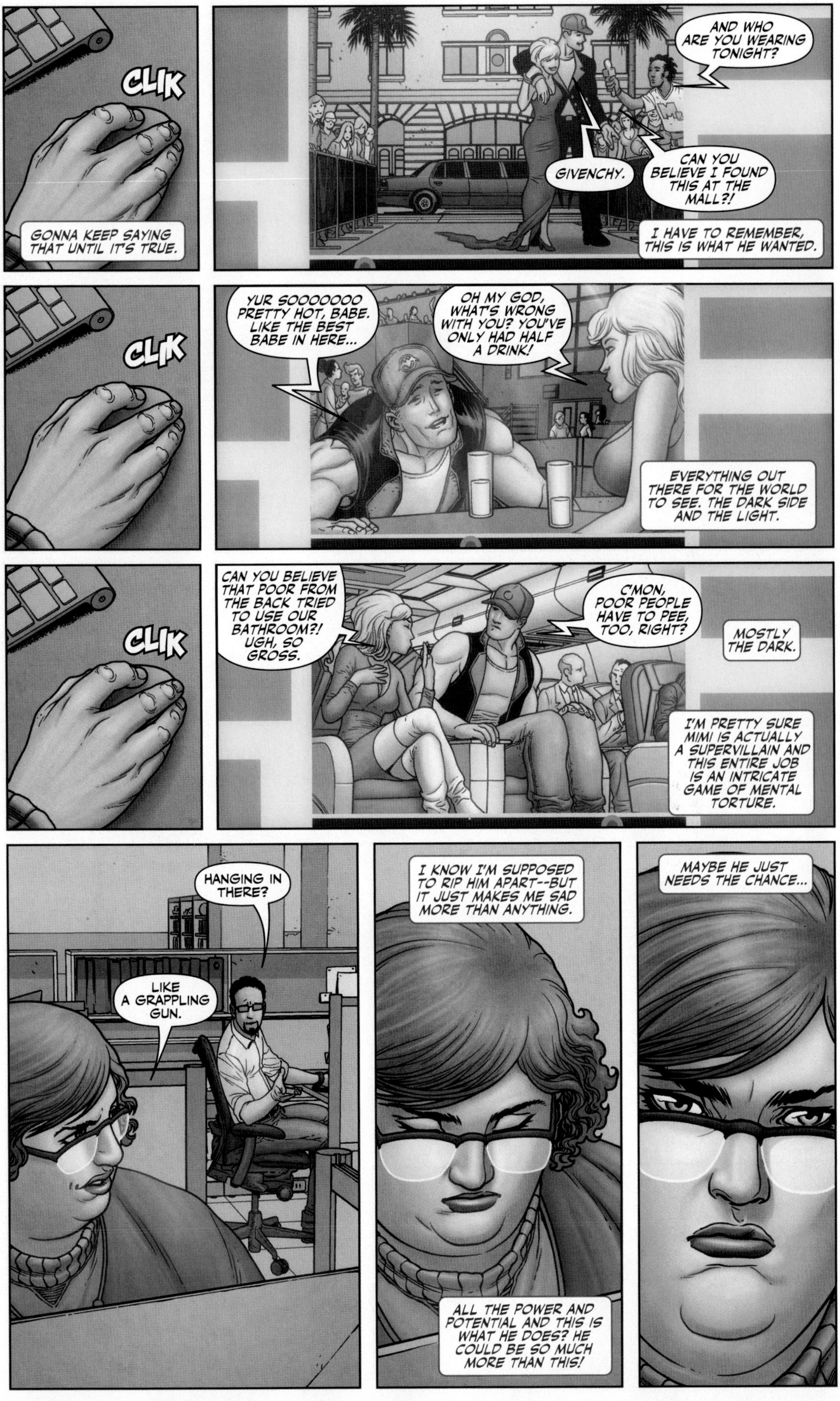
CLIK
GONNA KEEP SAYING THAT UNTIL IT'S TRUE.
AND WHO ARE YOU WEARING TONIGHT?
GIVENCHY.
CAN YOU BELIEVE I FOUND THIS AT THE MALL?!
I HAVE TO REMEMBER, THIS IS WHAT HE WANTED.
CLIK
YUR SOOOOOOO PRETTY HOT, BABE. LIKE THE BEST BABE IN HERE...
OH MY GOD, WHAT'S WRONG WITH YOU? YOU'VE ONLY HAD HALF A DRINK!
EVERYTHING OUT THERE FOR THE WORLD TO SEE. THE DARK SIDE AND THE LIGHT.
CLIK
CAN YOU BELIEVE THAT POOR FROM THE BACK TRIED TO USE OUR BATHROOM?! UGH, SO GROSS.
C'MON, POOR PEOPLE HAVE TO PEE, TOO, RIGHT?
MOSTLY THE DARK.
I'M PRETTY SURE MIMI IS ACTUALLY A SUPERVILLAIN AND THIS ENTIRE JOB IS AN INTRICATE GAME OF MENTAL TORTURE.
HANGING IN THERE?
LIKE A GRAPPLING GUN.
I KNOW I'M SUPPOSED TO RIP HIM APART--BUT IT JUST MAKES ME SAD MORE THAN ANYTHING.
ALL THE POWER AND POTENTIAL AND THIS IS WHAT HE DOES? HE COULD BE SO MUCH MORE THAN THIS!
MAYBE HE JUST NEEDS THE CHANCE...

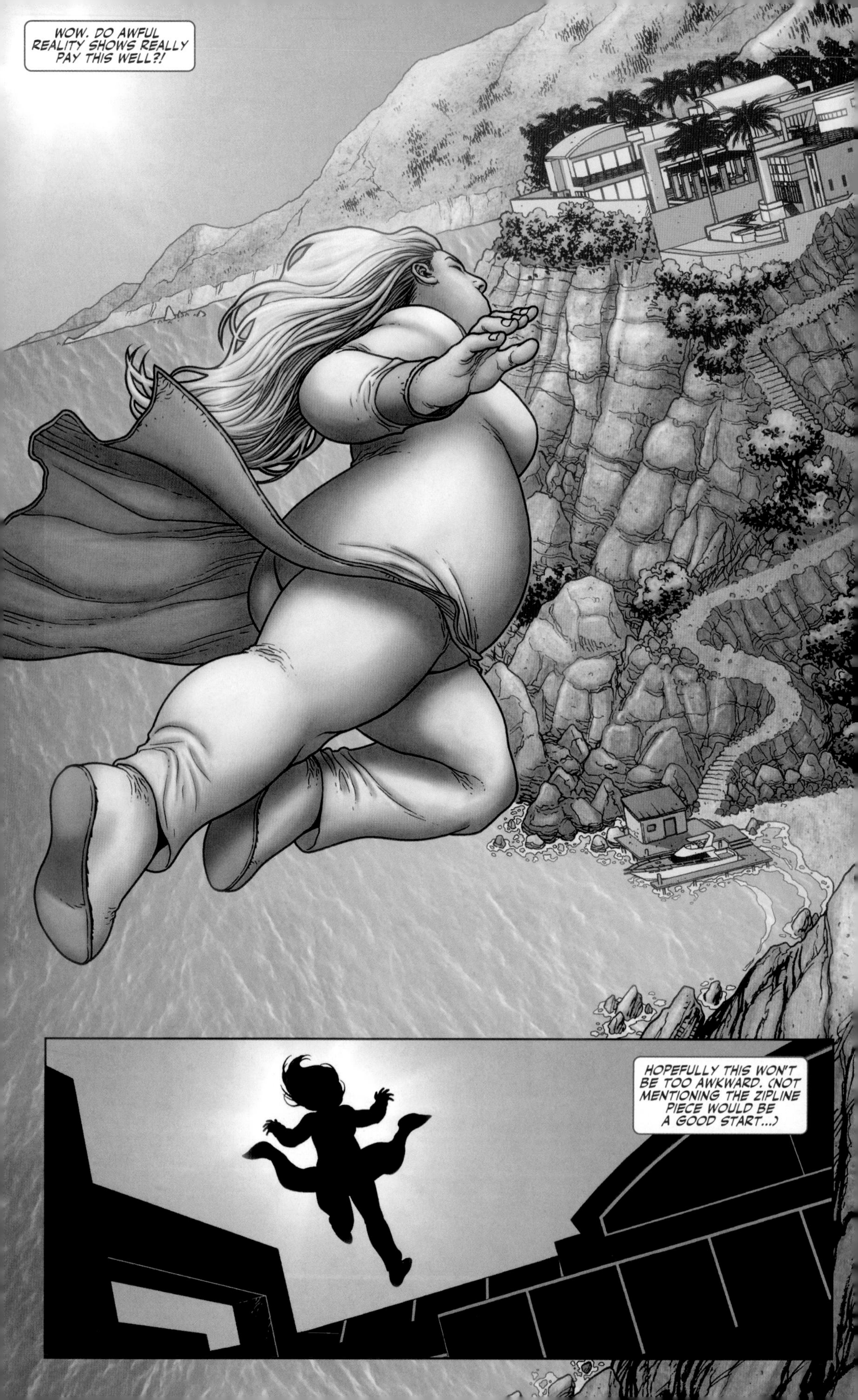
WOW. DO AWFUL REALITY SHOWS REALLY PAY THIS WELL?!
HOPEFULLY THIS WON'T BE TOO AWKWARD. (NOT MENTIONING THE ZIPLINE PIECE WOULD BE A GOOD START...)

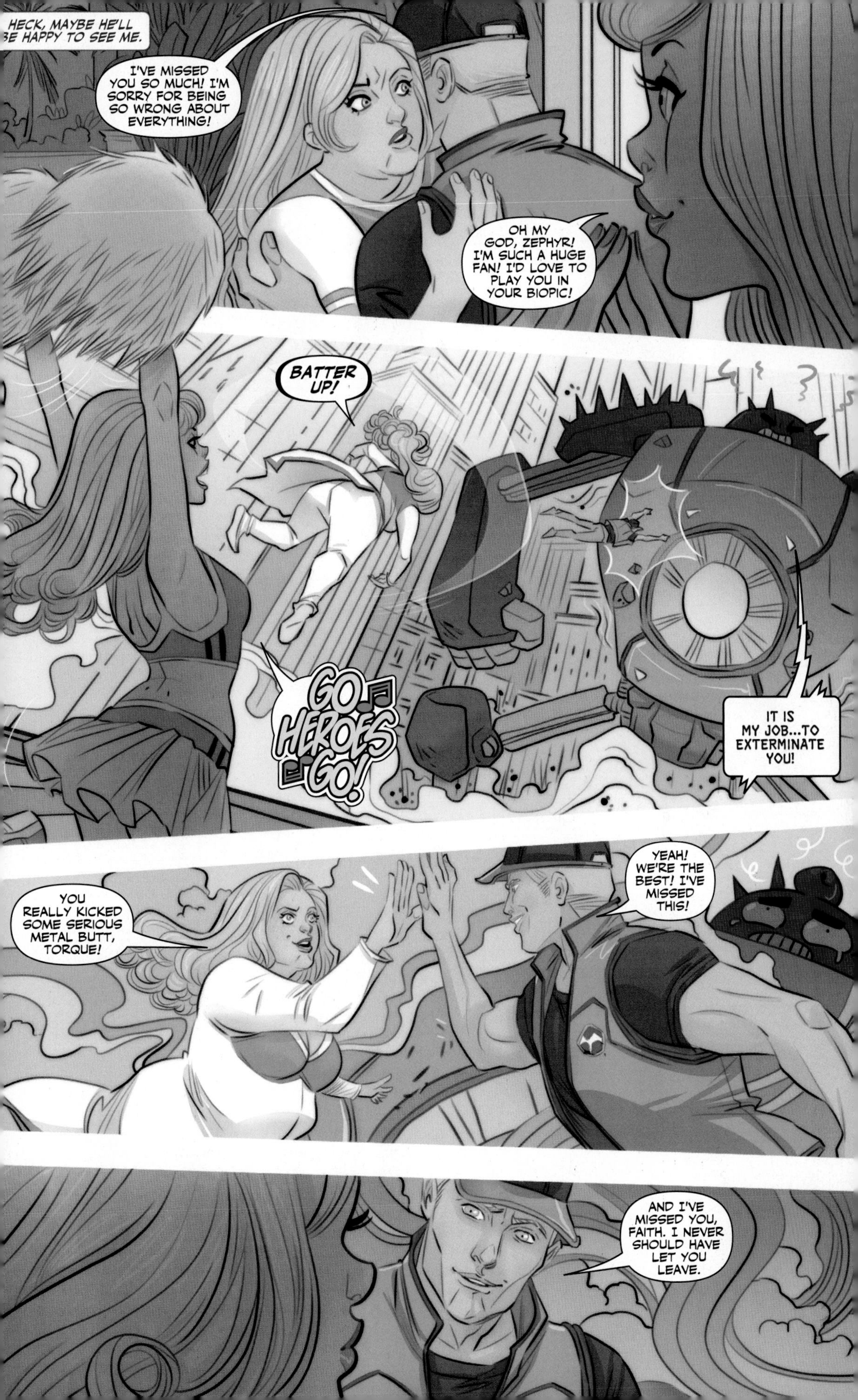
HECK, MAYBE HE'LL BE HAPPY TO SEE ME.
I'VE MISSED YOU SO MUCH! I'M SORRY FOR BEING SO WRONG ABOUT EVERYTHING!
OH MY GOD, ZEPHYR! I'M SUCH A HUGE FAN! I'D LOVE TO PLAY YOU IN YOUR BIOPIC!
BATTER UP!
GO HEROES GO!
IT IS MY JOB...TO EXTERMINATE YOU!
YOU REALLY KICKED SOME SERIOUS METAL BUTT, TORQUE!
YEAH! WE'RE THE BEST! I'VE MISSED THIS!
AND I'VE MISSED YOU, FAITH. I NEVER SHOULD HAVE LET YOU LEAVE.

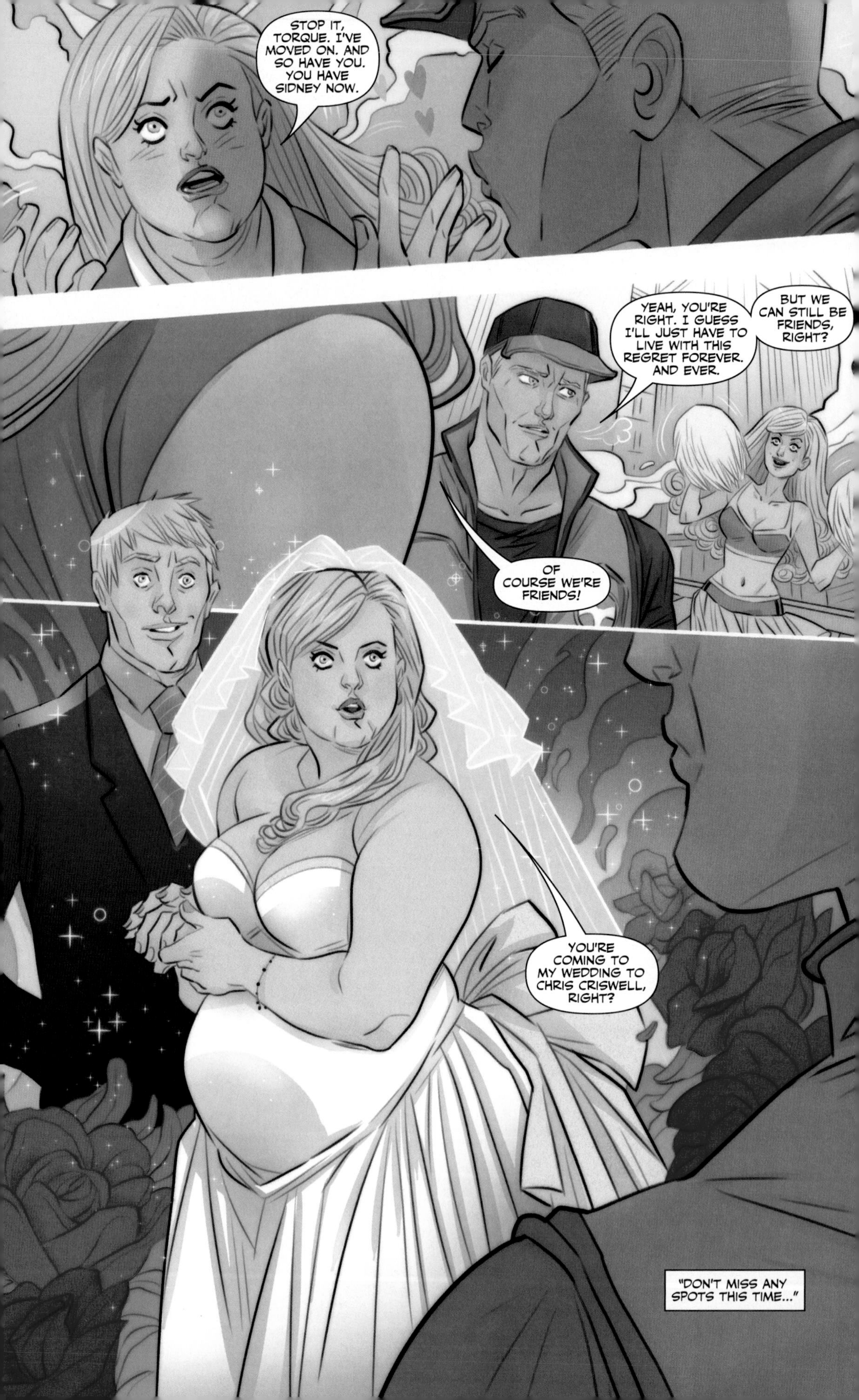
STOP IT, TORQUE. I'VE MOVED ON. AND SO HAVE YOU. YOU HAVE SIDNEY NOW.
YEAH, YOU'RE RIGHT. I GUESS I'LL JUST HAVE TO LIVE WITH THIS REGRET FOREVER. AND EVER.
BUT WE CAN STILL BE FRIENDS, RIGHT?
OF COURSE WE'RE FRIENDS!
YOU'RE COMING TO MY WEDDING TO CHRIS CRISWELL, RIGHT?
"DON'T MISS ANY SPOTS THIS TIME..."

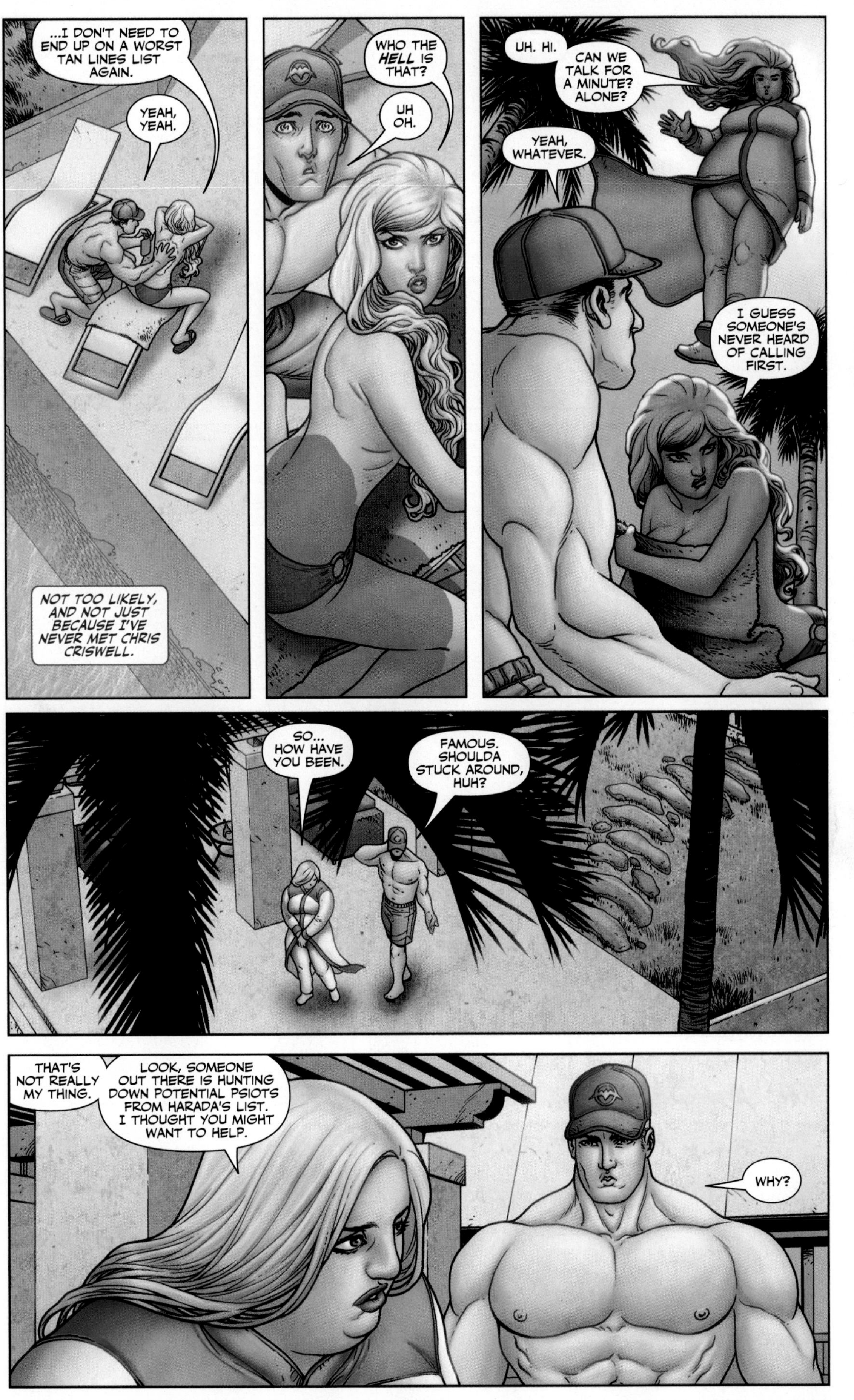
...I DON'T NEED TO END UP ON A WORST TAN LINES LIST AGAIN.
YEAH, YEAH.
NOT TOO LIKELY, AND NOT JUST BECAUSE I'VE NEVER MET CHRIS CRISWELL.
WHO THE *HELL* IS THAT?
UH OH.
UH. HI.
CAN WE TALK FOR A MINUTE? ALONE?
YEAH, WHATEVER.
I GUESS SOMEONE'S NEVER HEARD OF CALLING FIRST.
SO... HOW HAVE YOU BEEN.
FAMOUS. SHOULDA STUCK AROUND, HUH?
THAT'S NOT REALLY MY THING.
LOOK, SOMEONE OUT THERE IS HUNTING DOWN POTENTIAL PSIOTS FROM HARADA'S LIST. I THOUGHT YOU MIGHT WANT TO HELP.
WHY?

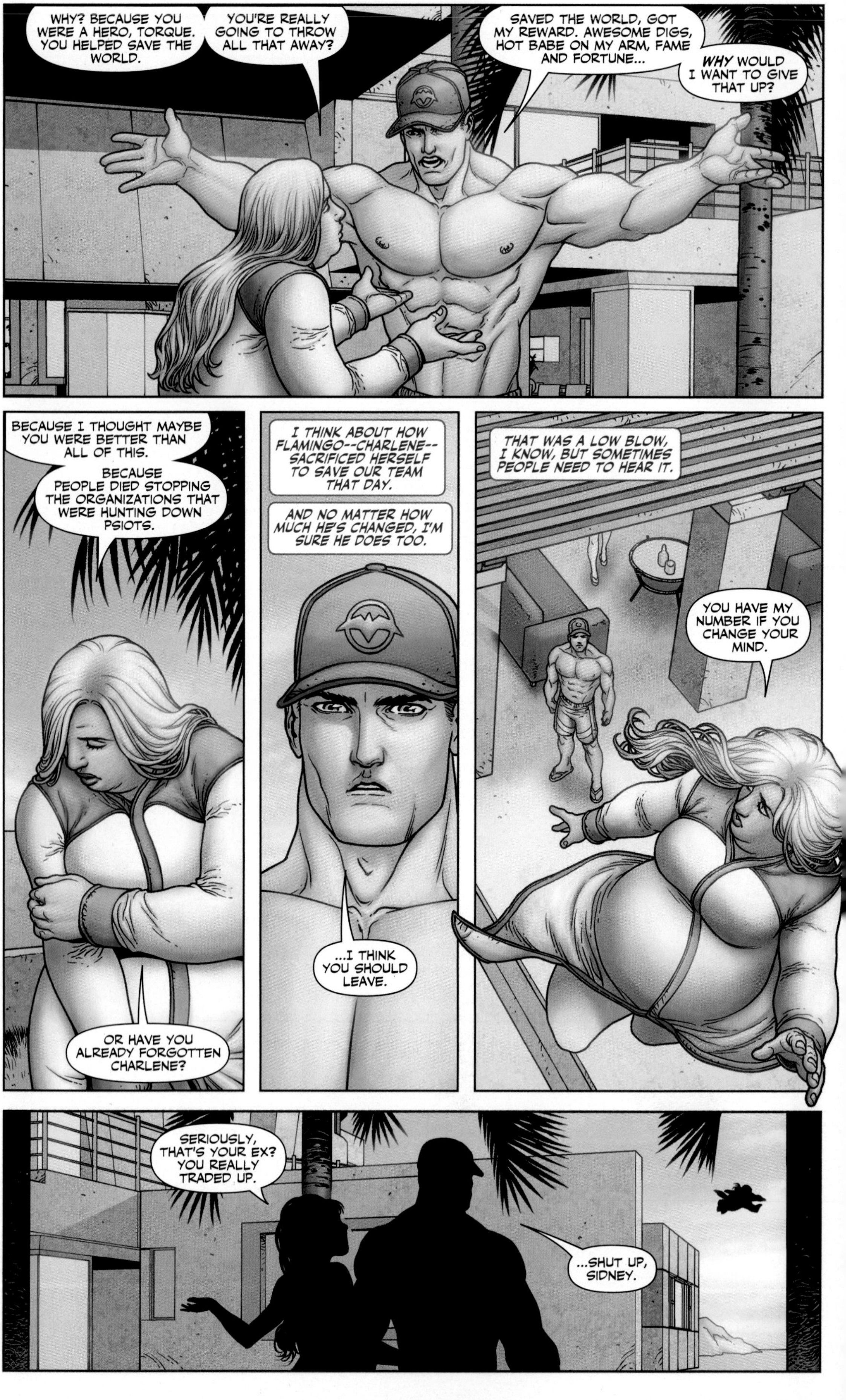
WHY? BECAUSE YOU WERE A HERO, TORQUE. YOU HELPED SAVE THE WORLD.
YOU'RE REALLY GOING TO THROW ALL THAT AWAY?
SAVED THE WORLD, GOT MY REWARD. AWESOME DIGS, HOT BABE ON MY ARM, FAME AND FORTUNE...
WHY WOULD I WANT TO GIVE THAT UP?
BECAUSE I THOUGHT MAYBE YOU WERE BETTER THAN ALL OF THIS.
BECAUSE PEOPLE DIED STOPPING THE ORGANIZATIONS THAT WERE HUNTING DOWN PSIOTS.
OR HAVE YOU ALREADY FORGOTTEN CHARLENE?
I THINK ABOUT HOW FLAMINGO--CHARLENE--SACRIFICED HERSELF TO SAVE OUR TEAM THAT DAY.
AND NO MATTER HOW MUCH HE'S CHANGED, I'M SURE HE DOES TOO.
...I THINK YOU SHOULD LEAVE.
THAT WAS A LOW BLOW, I KNOW, BUT SOMETIMES PEOPLE NEED TO HEAR IT.
YOU HAVE MY NUMBER IF YOU CHANGE YOUR MIND.
SERIOUSLY, THAT'S YOUR EX? YOU REALLY TRADED UP.
...SHUT UP, SIDNEY.

SO, THAT DIDN'T GO WELL.

I GUESS I'M ALONE IN THE FIELD FOR NOW.

@X IS GREAT, BUT HE'S MORE OF A "STAY IN THE CLOCK TOWER" GUY.

BESIDES, HE'S ALREADY DONE A BUNCH OF THE LEGWORK.

MAYBE IT'S TIME FOR ME TO PUT AWAY THE COSTUME AND PUT ON MY INVESTIGATOR HAT.

I SHOULD GET AN ACTUAL INVESTIGATOR HAT.

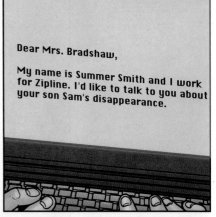

Dear Mrs. Bradshaw,

My name is Summer Smith and I work for Zipline. I'd like to talk to you about your son Sam's disappearance.

BUZZ

"THANK YOU FOR COMING, MISS SMITH."

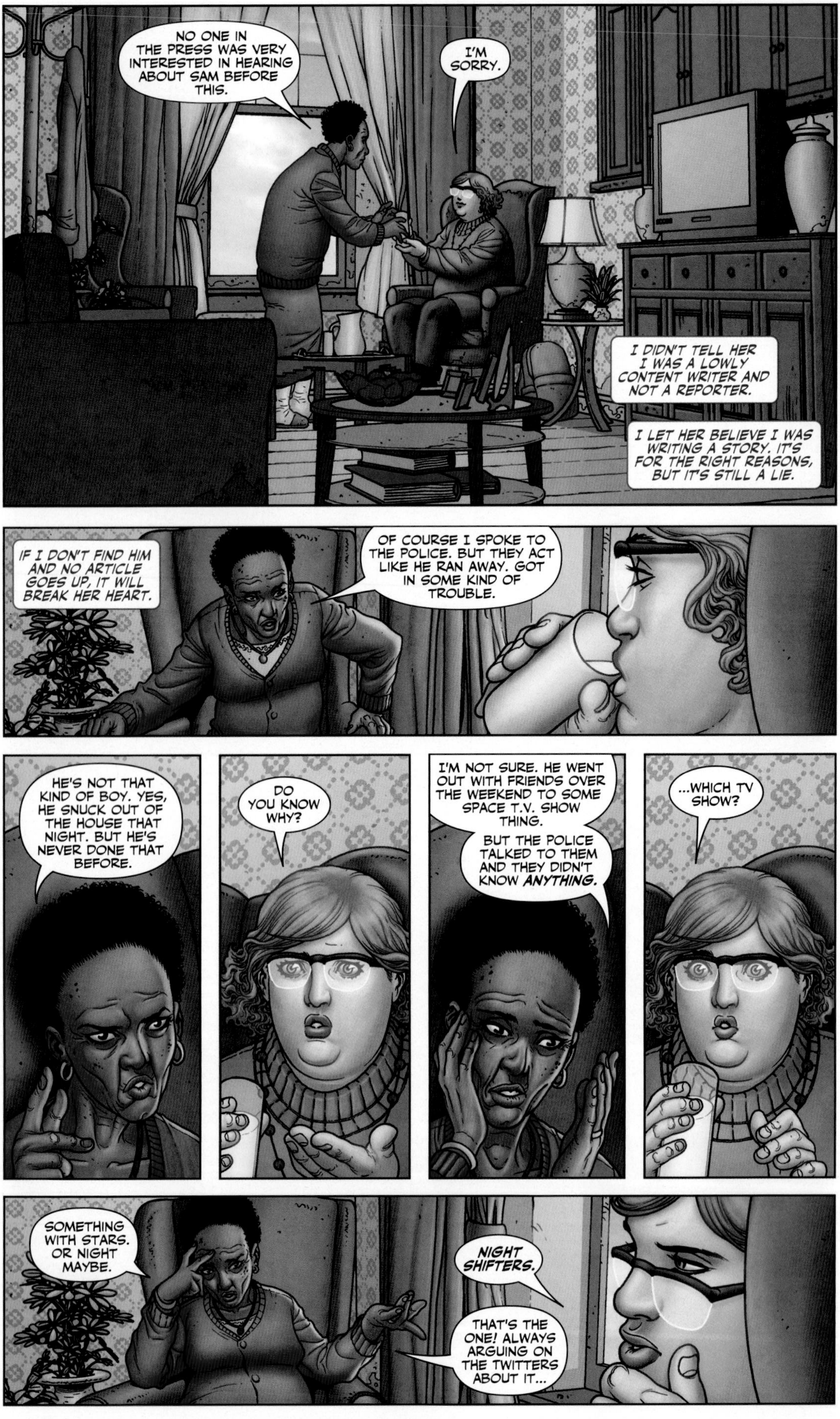
NO ONE IN THE PRESS WAS VERY INTERESTED IN HEARING ABOUT SAM BEFORE THIS.
I'M SORRY.
I DIDN'T TELL HER I WAS A LOWLY CONTENT WRITER AND NOT A REPORTER.
I LET HER BELIEVE I WAS WRITING A STORY. IT'S FOR THE RIGHT REASONS, BUT IT'S STILL A LIE.
IF I DON'T FIND HIM AND NO ARTICLE GOES UP, IT WILL BREAK HER HEART.
OF COURSE I SPOKE TO THE POLICE. BUT THEY ACT LIKE HE RAN AWAY. GOT IN SOME KIND OF TROUBLE.
HE'S NOT THAT KIND OF BOY. YES, HE SNUCK OUT OF THE HOUSE THAT NIGHT. BUT HE'S NEVER DONE THAT BEFORE.
DO YOU KNOW WHY?
I'M NOT SURE. HE WENT OUT WITH FRIENDS OVER THE WEEKEND TO SOME SPACE T.V. SHOW THING.
BUT THE POLICE TALKED TO THEM AND THEY DIDN'T KNOW *ANYTHING.*
...WHICH TV SHOW?
SOMETHING WITH STARS. OR NIGHT MAYBE.
NIGHT SHIFTERS.
THAT'S THE ONE! ALWAYS ARGUING ON THE TWITTERS ABOUT IT...

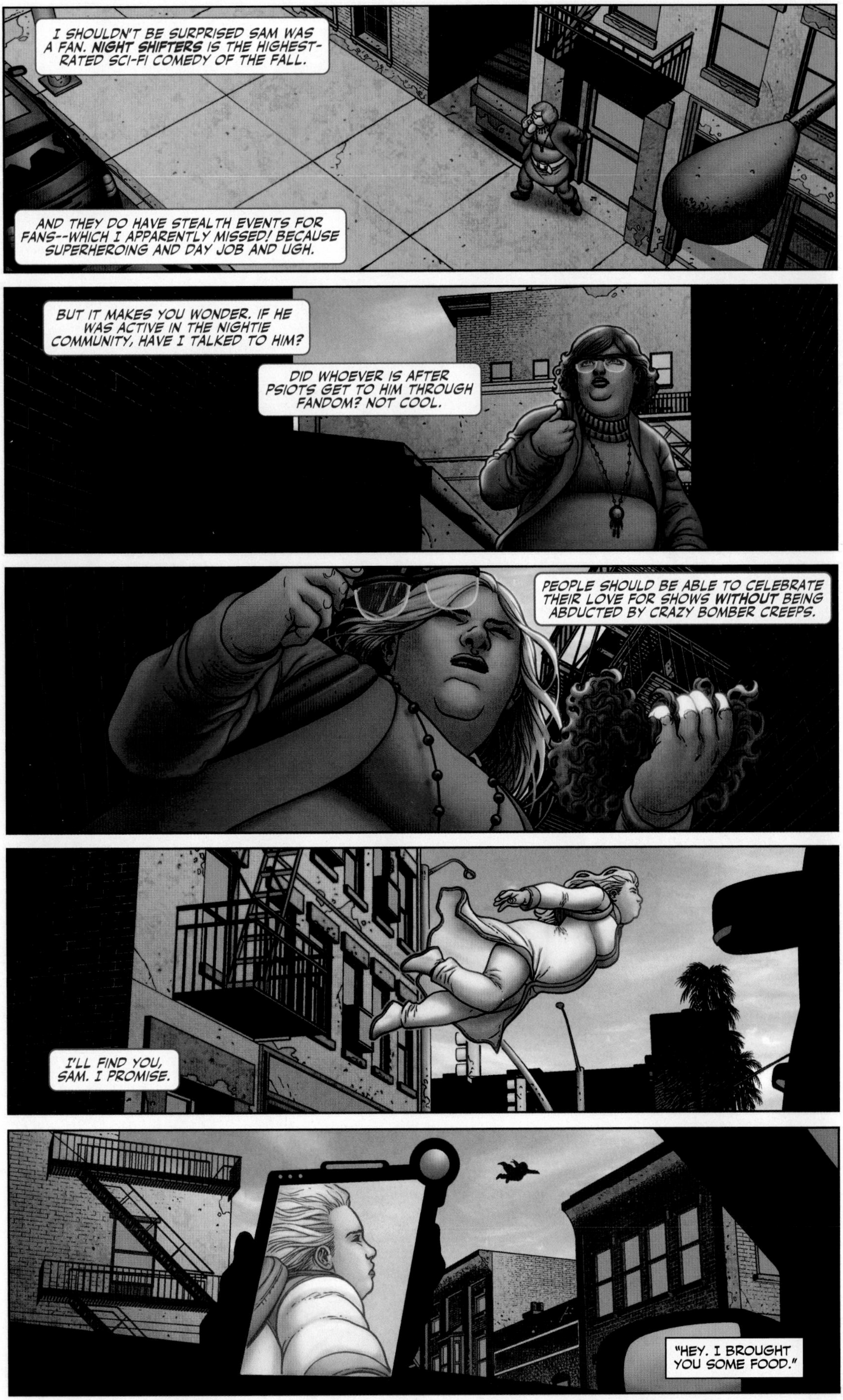
I SHOULDN'T BE SURPRISED SAM WAS A FAN. NIGHT SHIFTERS IS THE HIGHEST-RATED SCI-FI COMEDY OF THE FALL.
AND THEY DO HAVE STEALTH EVENTS FOR FANS--WHICH I APPARENTLY MISSED! BECAUSE SUPERHEROING AND DAY JOB AND UGH.
BUT IT MAKES YOU WONDER. IF HE WAS ACTIVE IN THE NIGHTIE COMMUNITY, HAVE I TALKED TO HIM?
DID WHOEVER IS AFTER PSIOTS GET TO HIM THROUGH FANDOM? NOT COOL.
PEOPLE SHOULD BE ABLE TO CELEBRATE THEIR LOVE FOR SHOWS WITHOUT BEING ABDUCTED BY CRAZY BOMBER CREEPS.
I'LL FIND YOU, SAM. I PROMISE.
"HEY. I BROUGHT YOU SOME FOOD."

TO EAT.

LEAVE ME ALONE.

ARE YOU OKAY? DID THEY--

STOP PRETENDING YOU CARE!

OF COURSE I CARE, SAM! IF I COULD DO SOMETHING, I WOULD.

BUT IF YOU GET OUT AGAIN, THEY'LL KNOW. THEY'LL EXECUTE ME.

JUST GO AWAY.

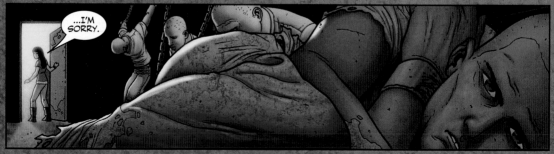

...I'M SORRY.

THE DIRECTOR IS GOING TO WANT TO SEE THIS...

SIR, THERE'S BEEN A COMPLICATION.

WE HAVE SOMEONE POKING AROUND.

AND NOT JUST ANYONE. ONE OF THE PSIOTS.

WELL, IF *FAITH'S* SO EAGER TO FIND US, YOU MAY AS WELL BRING HER IN.

HEY SUMMER! AMAZING TAKEDOWN OF *TORQUE*. DIDN'T KNOW YOU HAD IT IN YOU.

UM, THANKS?

ZIP li

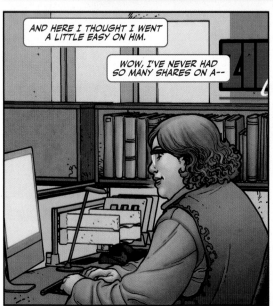

AND HERE I THOUGHT I WENT A LITTLE EASY ON HIM.

WOW, I'VE NEVER HAD SO MANY SHARES ON A--

WAIT. "WATCHING TORQUE FUMBLE HIS WAY THROUGH EXISTENCE IS LIKE FINGERNAILS ON THE CHALKBOARD OF YOUR SOUL"?! I DIDN'T WRITE THAT.

(WHAT DOES "CHALKBOARD OF YOUR SOUL" EVEN MEAN?!)

SOMEONE REWROTE MY WHOLE PIECE. SOMEONE...

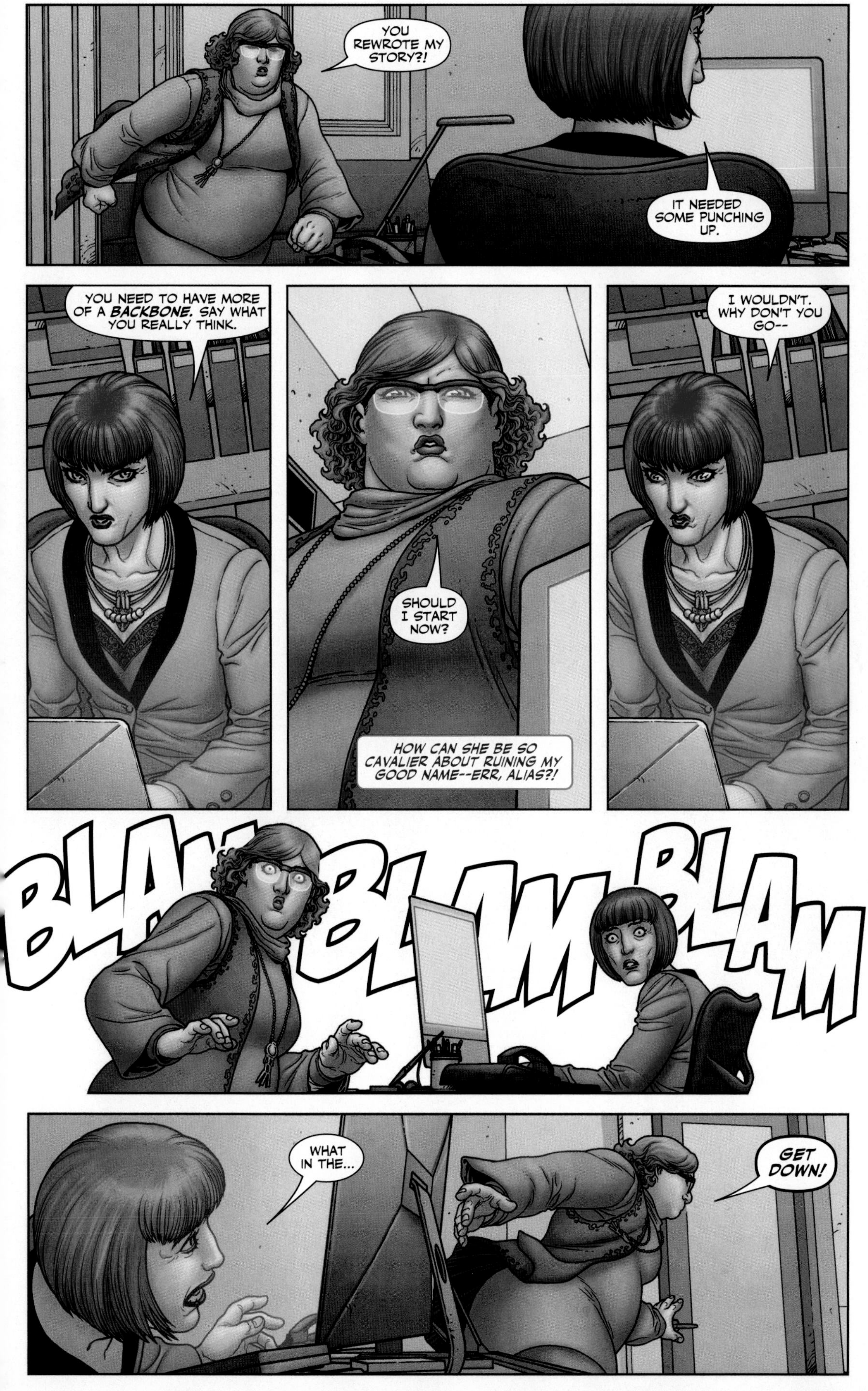
YOU REWROTE MY STORY?!
IT NEEDED SOME PUNCHING UP.
YOU NEED TO HAVE MORE OF A BACKBONE. SAY WHAT YOU REALLY THINK.
SHOULD I START NOW?
HOW CAN SHE BE SO CAVALIER ABOUT RUINING MY GOOD NAME--ERR, ALIAS?!
I WOULDN'T. WHY DON'T YOU GO--
BLAM
BLAM
BLAM
WHAT IN THE...
GET DOWN!

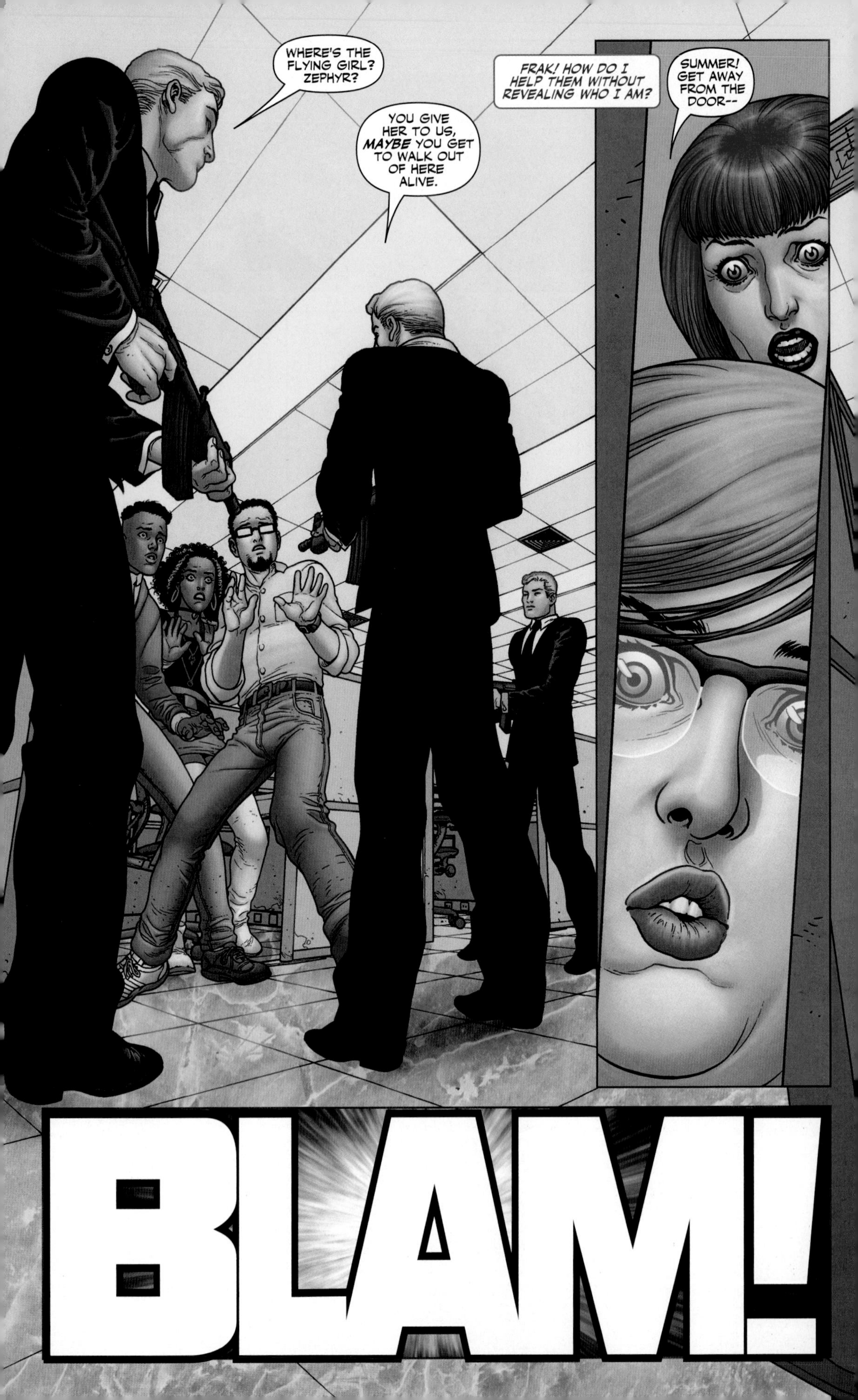
WHERE'S THE FLYING GIRL? ZEPHYR?
YOU GIVE HER TO US, *MAYBE* YOU GET TO WALK OUT OF HERE ALIVE.
FRAK! HOW DO I HELP THEM WITHOUT REVEALING WHO I AM?
SUMMER! GET AWAY FROM THE DOOR--
BLAM!

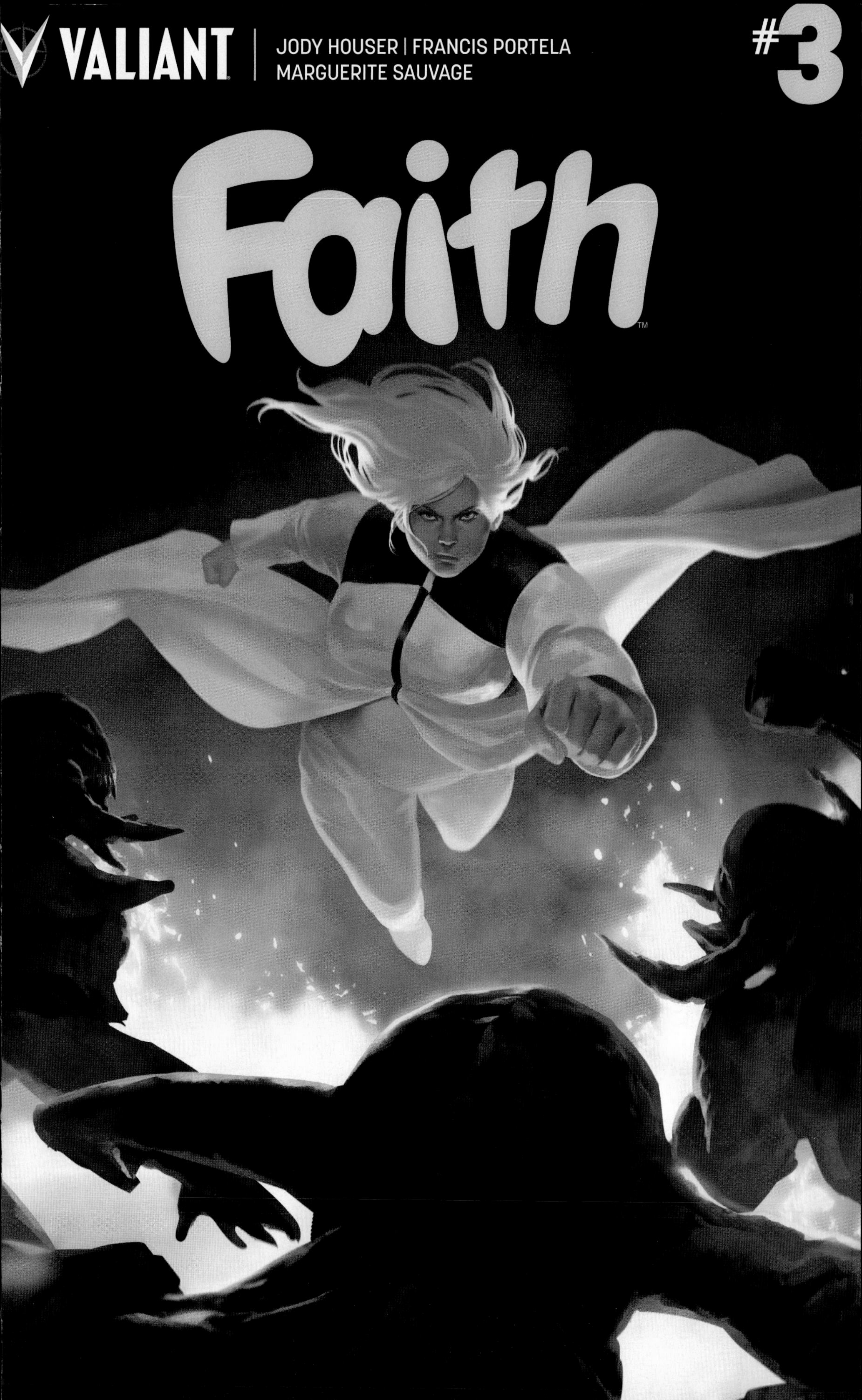
VALIANT
JODY HOUSER | FRANCIS PORTELA
MARGUERITE SAUVAGE
#3
Faith™

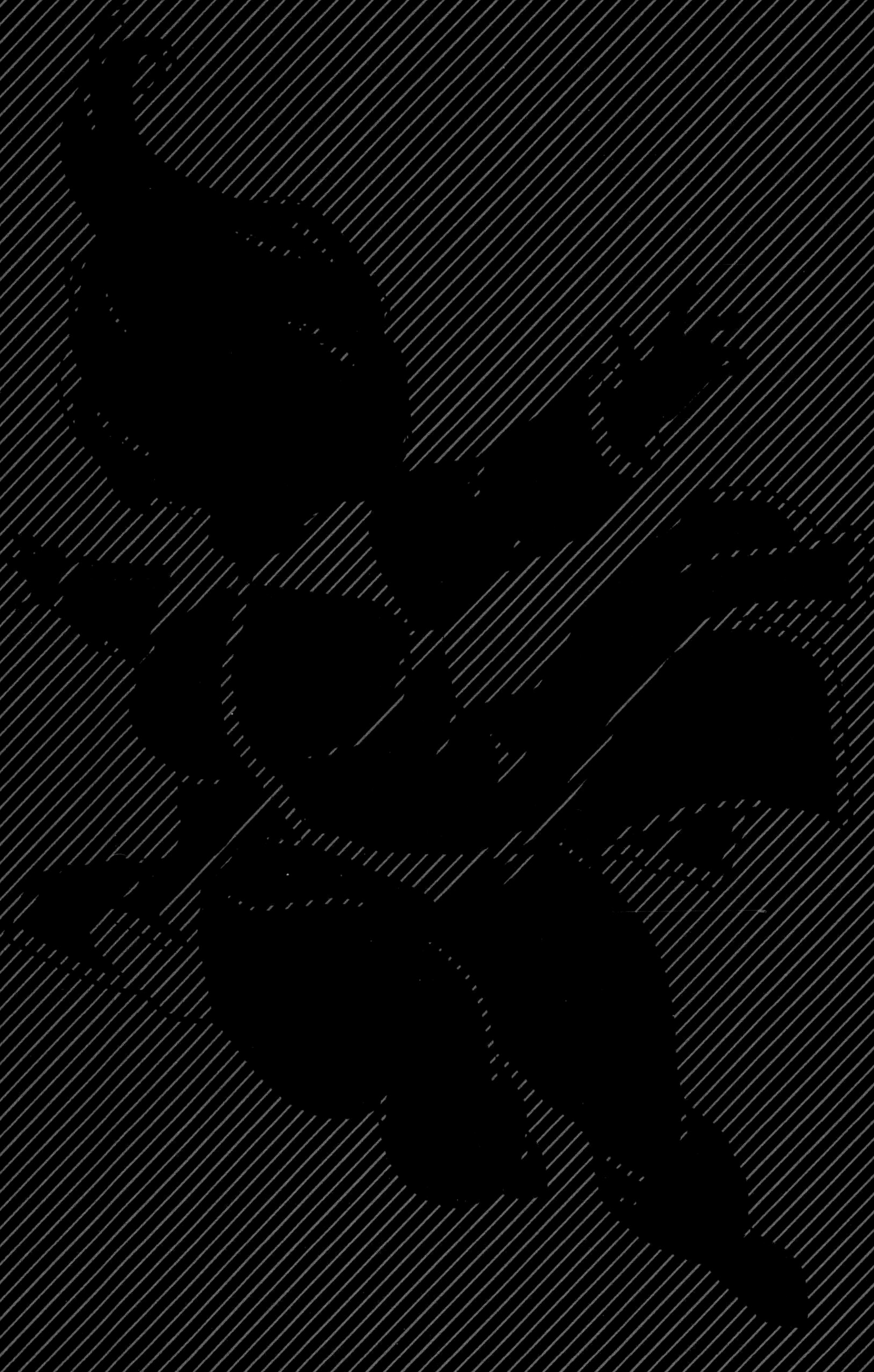

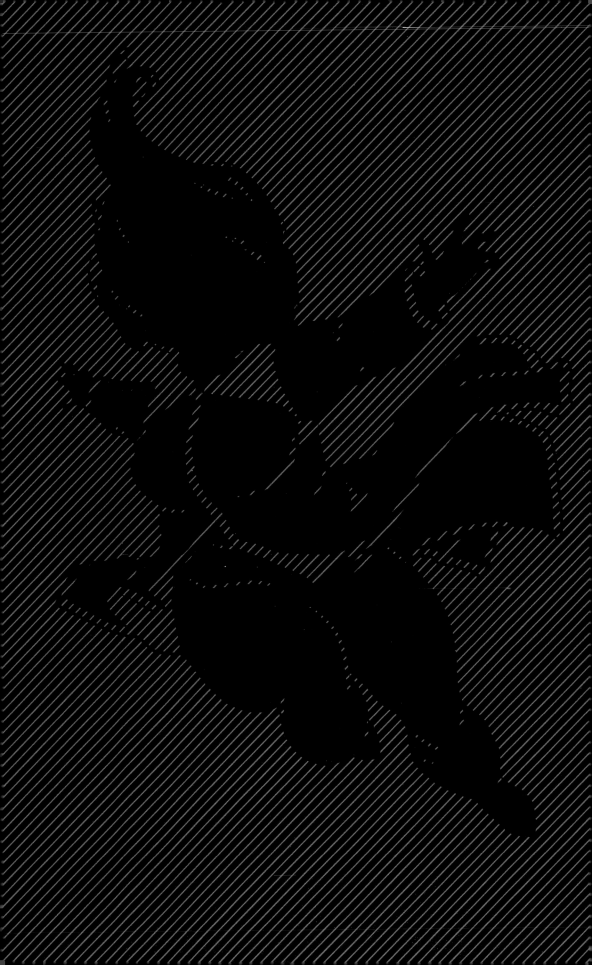

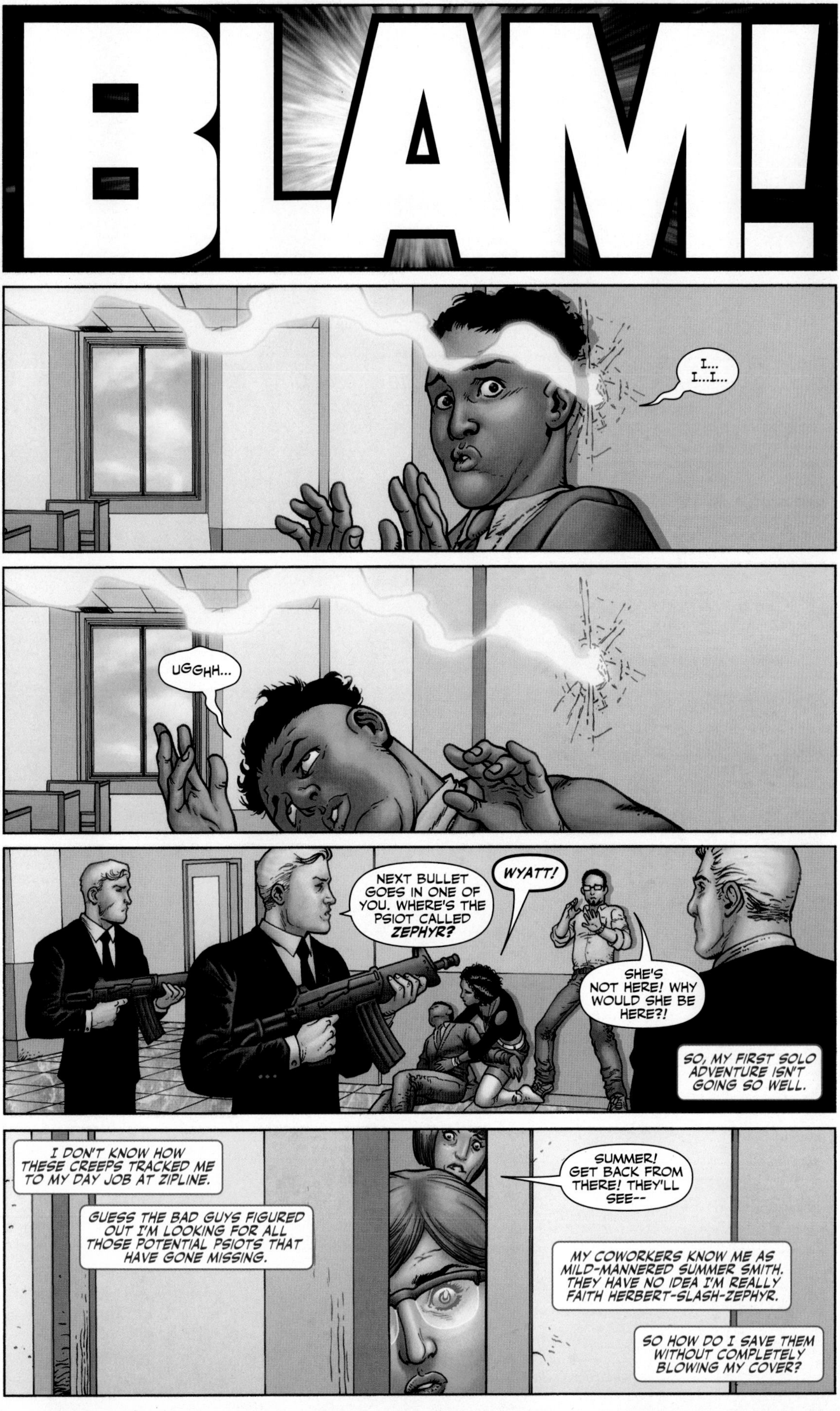
BLAM!
I...
I...I...
UGGHH...
NEXT BULLET GOES IN ONE OF YOU. WHERE'S THE PSIOT CALLED ZEPHYR?
WYATT!
SHE'S NOT HERE! WHY WOULD SHE BE HERE?!
SO, MY FIRST SOLO ADVENTURE ISN'T GOING SO WELL.
I DON'T KNOW HOW THESE CREEPS TRACKED ME TO MY DAY JOB AT ZIPLINE.
GUESS THE BAD GUYS FIGURED OUT I'M LOOKING FOR ALL THOSE POTENTIAL PSIOTS THAT HAVE GONE MISSING.
SUMMER! GET BACK FROM THERE! THEY'LL SEE--
MY COWORKERS KNOW ME AS MILD-MANNERED SUMMER SMITH. THEY HAVE NO IDEA I'M REALLY FAITH HERBERT-SLASH-ZEPHYR.
SO HOW DO I SAVE THEM WITHOUT COMPLETELY BLOWING MY COVER?

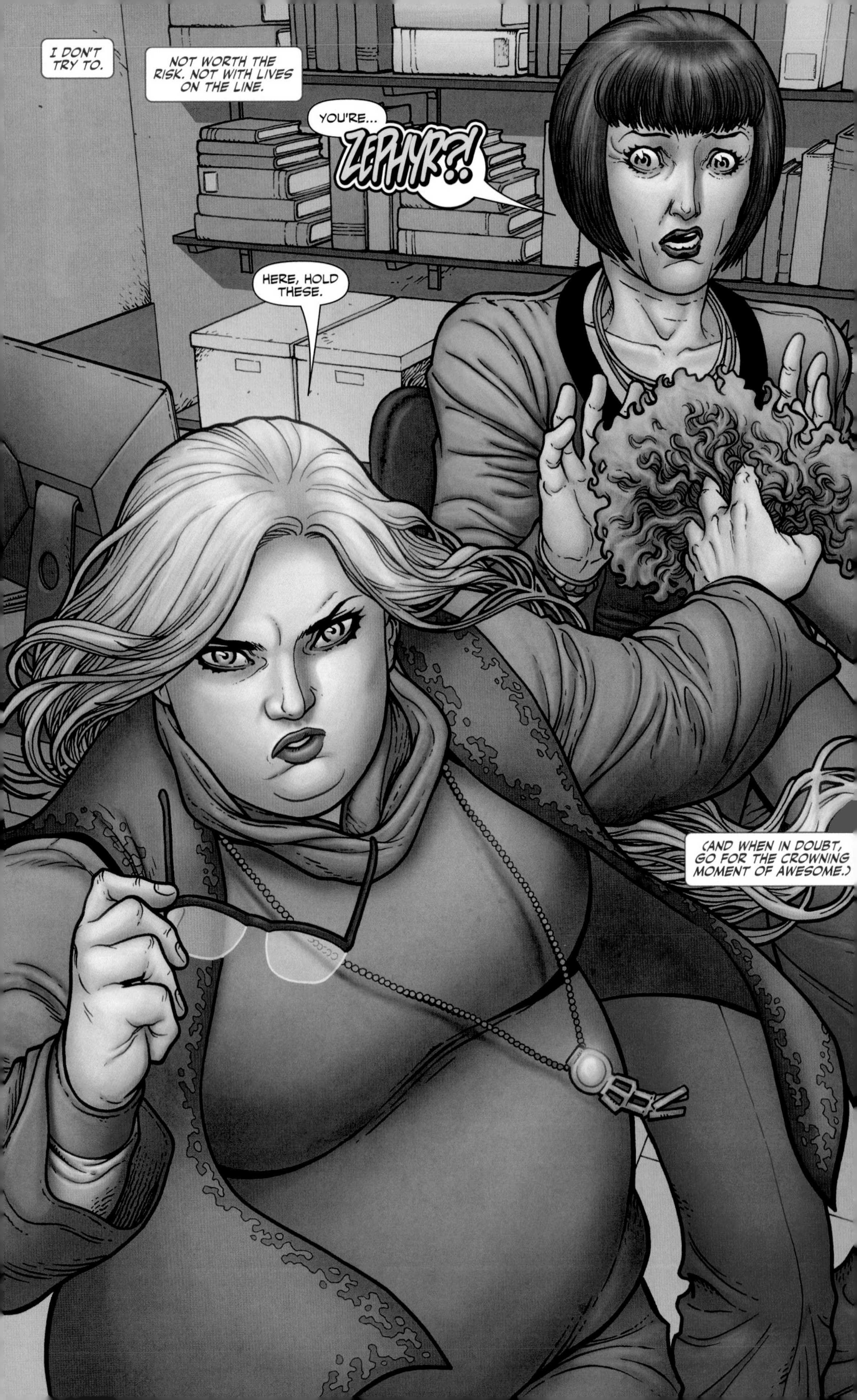
I DON'T TRY TO.
NOT WORTH THE RISK. NOT WITH LIVES ON THE LINE.
YOU'RE...
ZEPHYR?!
HERE, HOLD THESE.
(AND WHEN IN DOUBT, GO FOR THE CROWNING MOMENT OF AWESOME.)

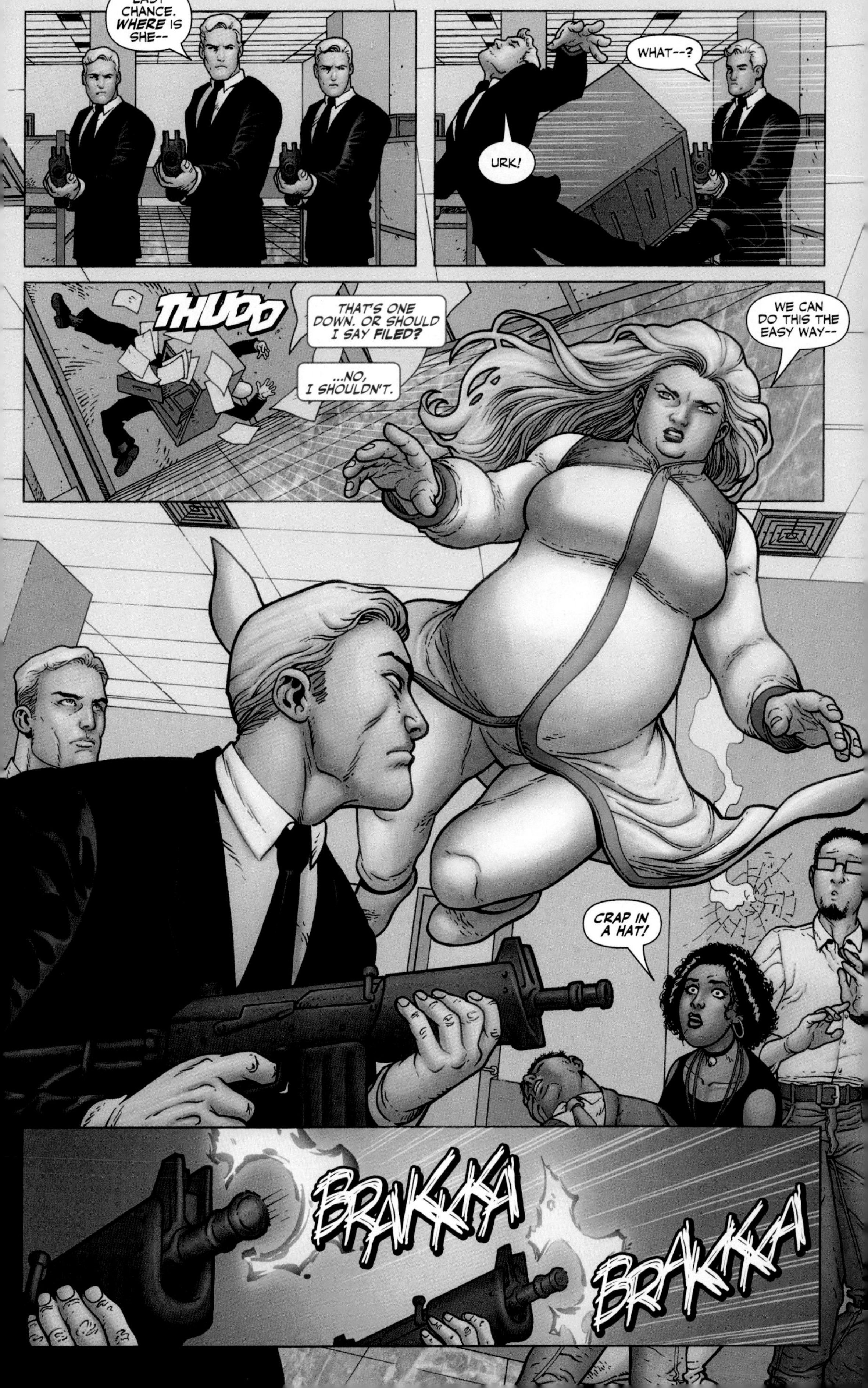
LAST CHANCE. WHERE IS SHE--
WHAT--?
URK!
THUDD
THAT'S ONE DOWN. OR SHOULD I SAY FILED?
...NO, I SHOULDN'T.
WE CAN DO THIS THE EASY WAY--
CRAP IN A HAT!
BRAKKA
BRAKKA

FINE. THE HARD WAY.

POK POK POK POK POK POK POK POK

PROBABLY SHOULD HAVE FIGURED OUT WHAT THE HARD WAY IS FIRST...

THESE GUYS DIDN'T HESITATE. A LOT MORE PROFESSIONAL THAN THOSE PUPPY THIEVES I TOOK DOWN.

GO! HURRY!

POK

POK

ERAKKA ERAKKA

ERAKKA ERAKKA POK

POK POK

POK

POK

POK

POK POK

WHO SENT YOU?

GROZIT, WHAT WOULD A GRIMDARK, TOTALLY-INTIMIDATING HERO (WHO STILL HAS A STRONG MORAL CODE AGAINST KILLING) DO?

OH. RIGHT.

MAKE THE BAD GUYS THINK I DON'T HAVE A STRONG MORAL CODE AGAINST KILLING.

COME ON, BOYS. WHERE WE'RE GOING, WE DON'T NEED ROADS.

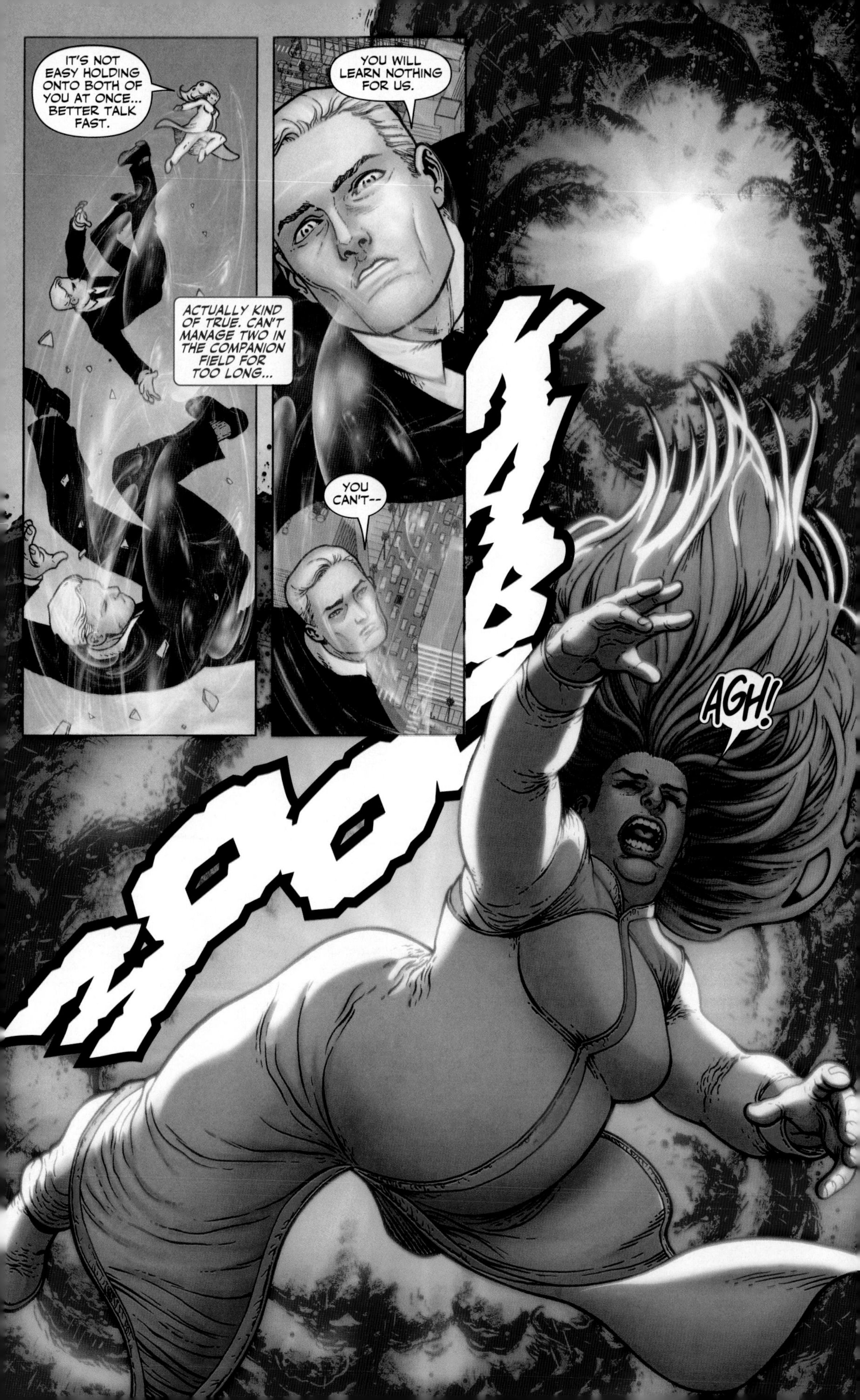
IT'S NOT EASY HOLDING ONTO BOTH OF YOU AT ONCE... BETTER TALK FAST.
ACTUALLY KIND OF TRUE. CAN'T MANAGE TWO IN THE COMPANION FIELD FOR TOO LONG...
YOU WILL LEARN NOTHING FOR US.
YOU CAN'T--
KABOOM
AGH!

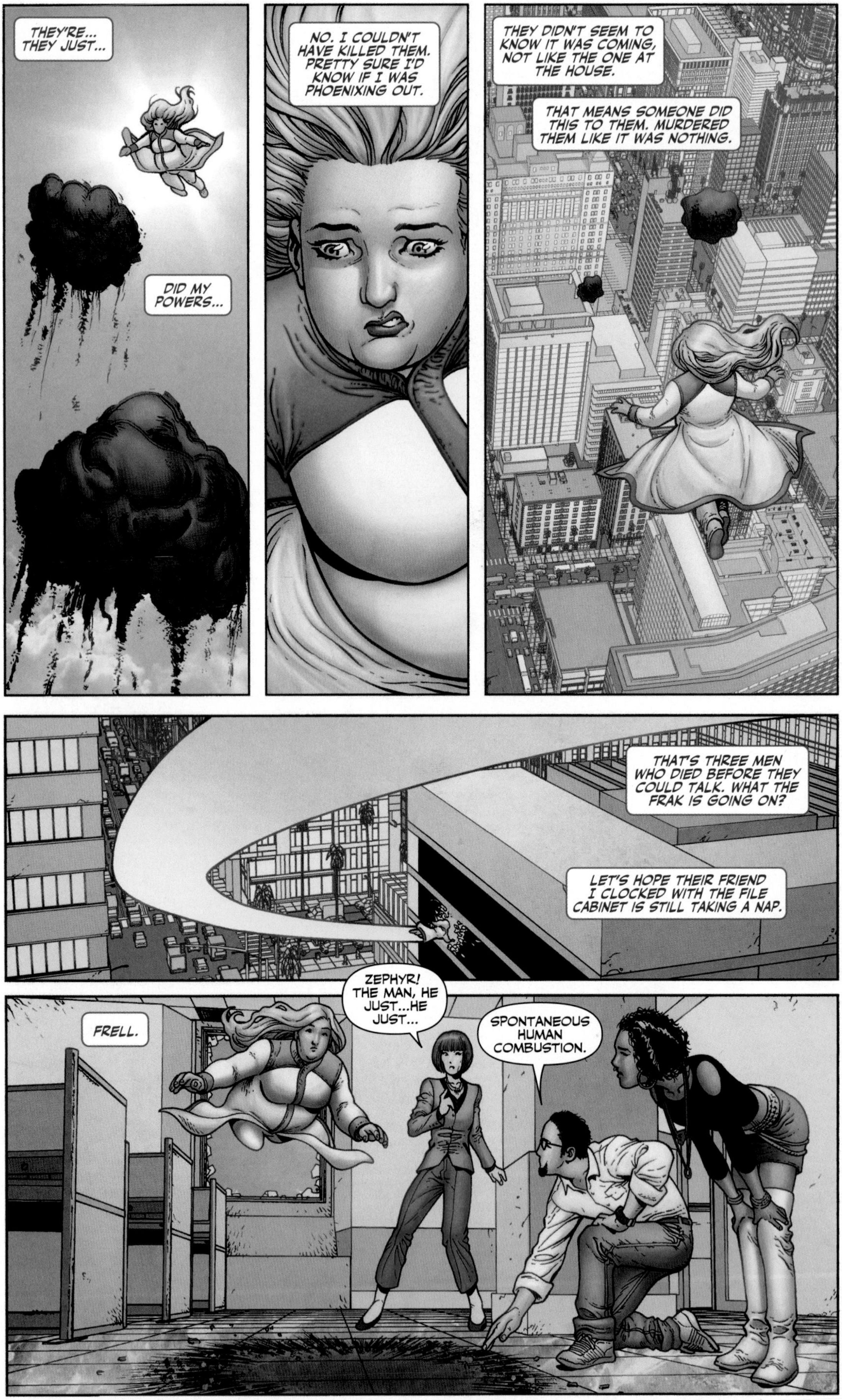
THEY'RE... THEY JUST...
DID MY POWERS...
NO. I COULDN'T HAVE KILLED THEM. PRETTY SURE I'D KNOW IF I WAS PHOENIXING OUT.
THEY DIDN'T SEEM TO KNOW IT WAS COMING, NOT LIKE THE ONE AT THE HOUSE.
THAT MEANS SOMEONE DID THIS TO THEM. MURDERED THEM LIKE IT WAS NOTHING.
THAT'S THREE MEN WHO DIED BEFORE THEY COULD TALK. WHAT THE FRAK IS GOING ON?
LET'S HOPE THEIR FRIEND I CLOCKED WITH THE FILE CABINET IS STILL TAKING A NAP.
FRELL.
ZEPHYR! THE MAN, HE JUST...HE JUST...
SPONTANEOUS HUMAN COMBUSTION.

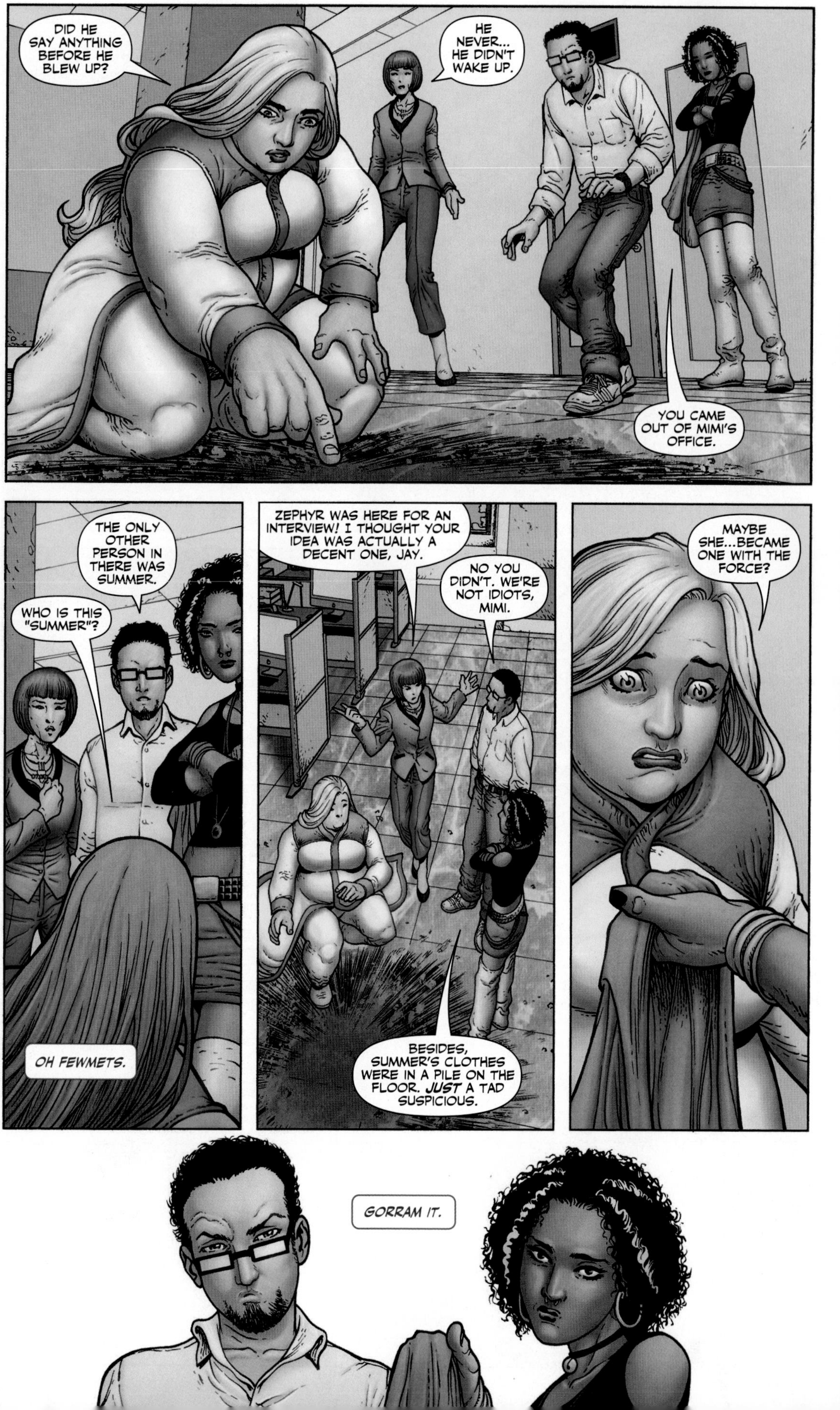
DID HE SAY ANYTHING BEFORE HE BLEW UP?
HE NEVER... HE DIDN'T WAKE UP.
YOU CAME OUT OF MIMI'S OFFICE.
THE ONLY OTHER PERSON IN THERE WAS SUMMER.
WHO IS THIS "SUMMER"?
OH FEWMETS.
ZEPHYR WAS HERE FOR AN INTERVIEW! I THOUGHT YOUR IDEA WAS ACTUALLY A DECENT ONE, JAY.
NO YOU DIDN'T. WE'RE NOT IDIOTS, MIMI.
BESIDES, SUMMER'S CLOTHES WERE IN A PILE ON THE FLOOR. JUST A TAD SUSPICIOUS.
MAYBE SHE...BECAME ONE WITH THE FORCE?
GORRAM IT.

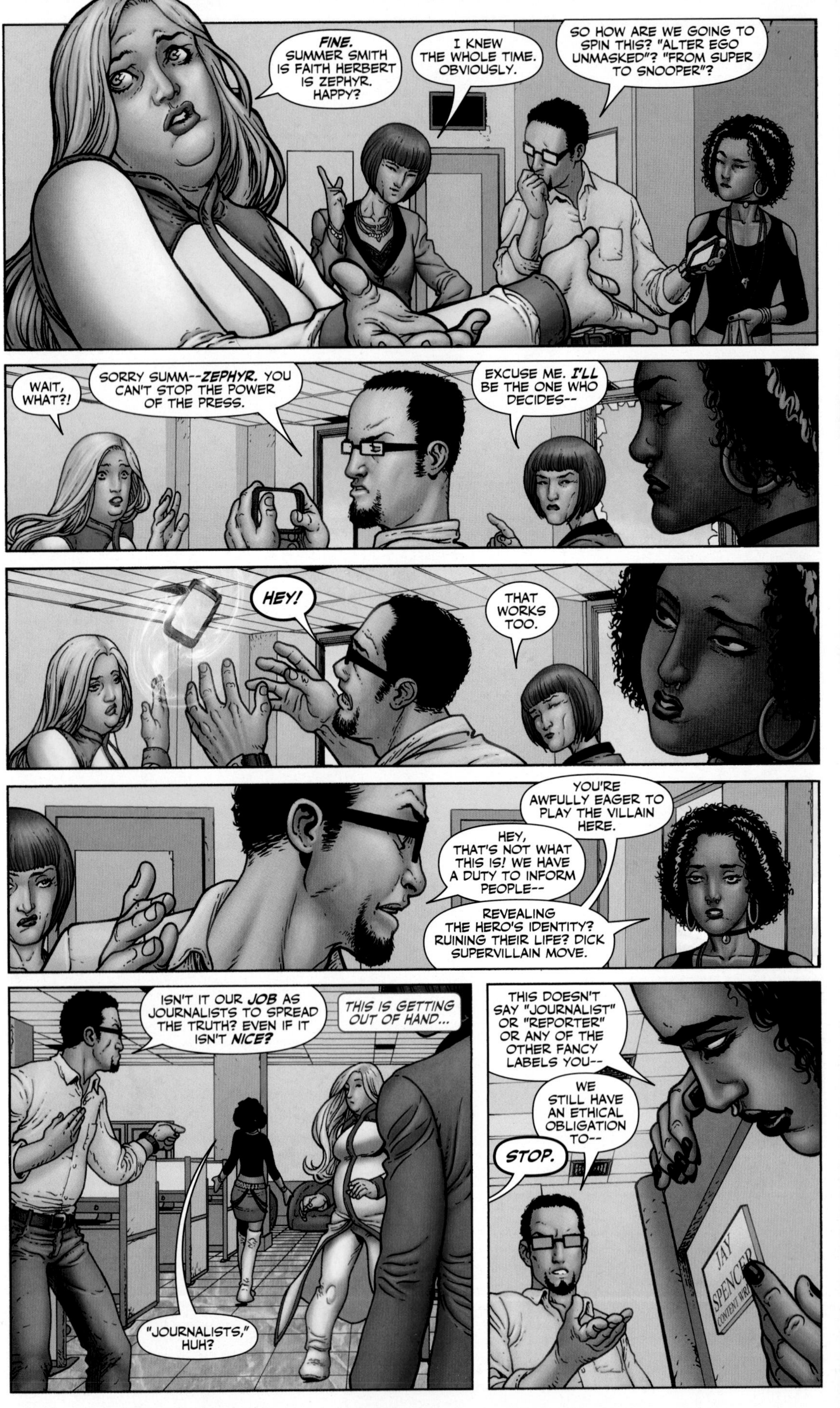
FINE. SUMMER SMITH IS FAITH HERBERT IS ZEPHYR. HAPPY?
I KNEW THE WHOLE TIME. OBVIOUSLY.
SO HOW ARE WE GOING TO SPIN THIS? "ALTER EGO UNMASKED"? "FROM SUPER TO SNOOPER"?
WAIT, WHAT?!
SORRY SUMM--ZEPHYR. YOU CAN'T STOP THE POWER OF THE PRESS.
EXCUSE ME. I'LL BE THE ONE WHO DECIDES--
HEY!
THAT WORKS TOO.
YOU'RE AWFULLY EAGER TO PLAY THE VILLAIN HERE.
HEY, THAT'S NOT WHAT THIS IS! WE HAVE A DUTY TO INFORM PEOPLE--
REVEALING THE HERO'S IDENTITY? RUINING THEIR LIFE? DICK SUPERVILLAIN MOVE.
ISN'T IT OUR JOB AS JOURNALISTS TO SPREAD THE TRUTH? EVEN IF IT ISN'T NICE?
THIS IS GETTING OUT OF HAND...
"JOURNALISTS," HUH?
THIS DOESN'T SAY "JOURNALIST" OR "REPORTER" OR ANY OF THE OTHER FANCY LABELS YOU--
WE STILL HAVE AN ETHICAL OBLIGATION TO--
STOP.
JAY

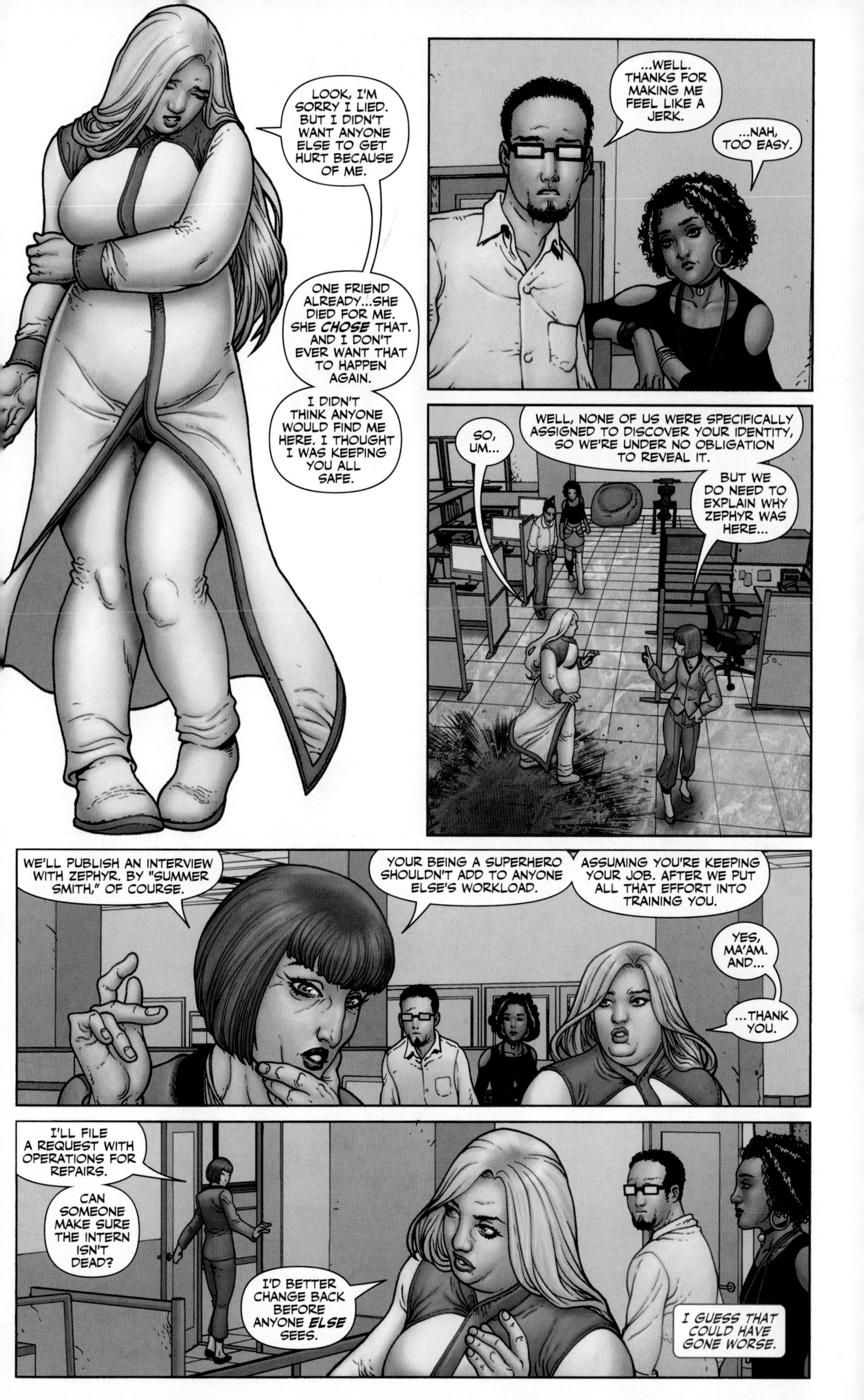
LOOK, I'M SORRY I LIED. BUT I DIDN'T WANT ANYONE ELSE TO GET HURT BECAUSE OF ME.
ONE FRIEND ALREADY...SHE DIED FOR ME. SHE *CHOSE* THAT. AND I DON'T EVER WANT THAT TO HAPPEN AGAIN.
I DIDN'T THINK ANYONE WOULD FIND ME HERE. I THOUGHT I WAS KEEPING YOU ALL SAFE.
...WELL. THANKS FOR MAKING ME FEEL LIKE A JERK.
...NAH, TOO EASY.
SO, UM...
WELL, NONE OF US WERE SPECIFICALLY ASSIGNED TO DISCOVER YOUR IDENTITY, SO WE'RE UNDER NO OBLIGATION TO REVEAL IT.
BUT WE DO NEED TO EXPLAIN WHY ZEPHYR WAS HERE...
WE'LL PUBLISH AN INTERVIEW WITH ZEPHYR. BY "SUMMER SMITH," OF COURSE.
YOUR BEING A SUPERHERO SHOULDN'T ADD TO ANYONE ELSE'S WORKLOAD.
ASSUMING YOU'RE KEEPING YOUR JOB. AFTER WE PUT ALL THAT EFFORT INTO TRAINING YOU.
YES, MA'AM. AND...
...THANK YOU.
I'LL FILE A REQUEST WITH OPERATIONS FOR REPAIRS.
CAN SOMEONE MAKE SURE THE INTERN ISN'T DEAD?
I'D BETTER CHANGE BACK BEFORE ANYONE *ELSE* SEES.
I GUESS THAT COULD HAVE GONE WORSE.

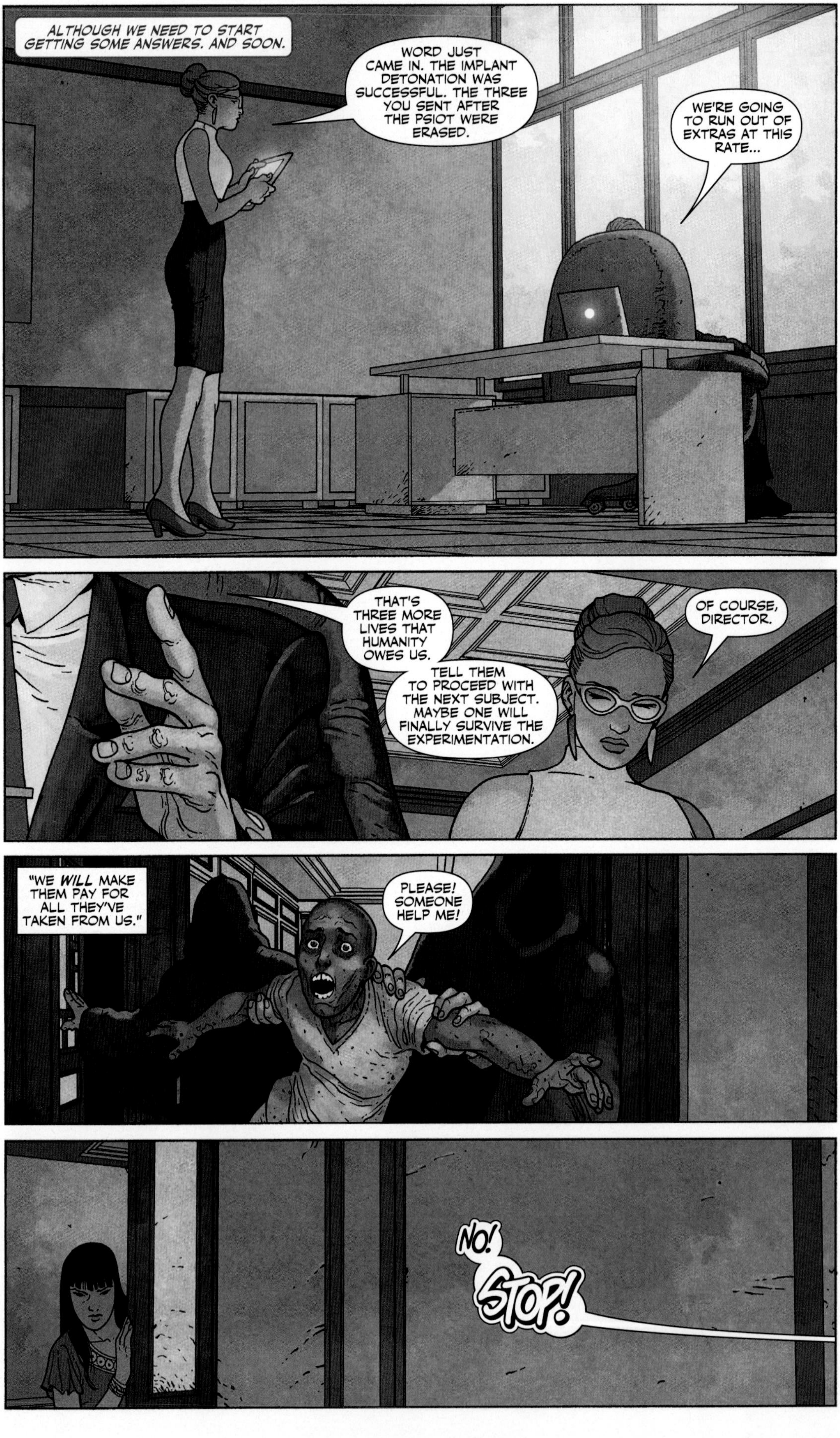

ALTHOUGH WE NEED TO START GETTING SOME ANSWERS. AND SOON.
WORD JUST CAME IN. THE IMPLANT DETONATION WAS SUCCESSFUL. THE THREE YOU SENT AFTER THE PSIOT WERE ERASED.
WE'RE GOING TO RUN OUT OF EXTRAS AT THIS RATE...
THAT'S THREE MORE LIVES THAT HUMANITY OWES US.
TELL THEM TO PROCEED WITH THE NEXT SUBJECT. MAYBE ONE WILL FINALLY SURVIVE THE EXPERIMENTATION.
OF COURSE, DIRECTOR.
"WE *WILL* MAKE THEM PAY FOR ALL THEY'VE TAKEN FROM US."
PLEASE! SOMEONE HELP ME!
NO!
STOP!

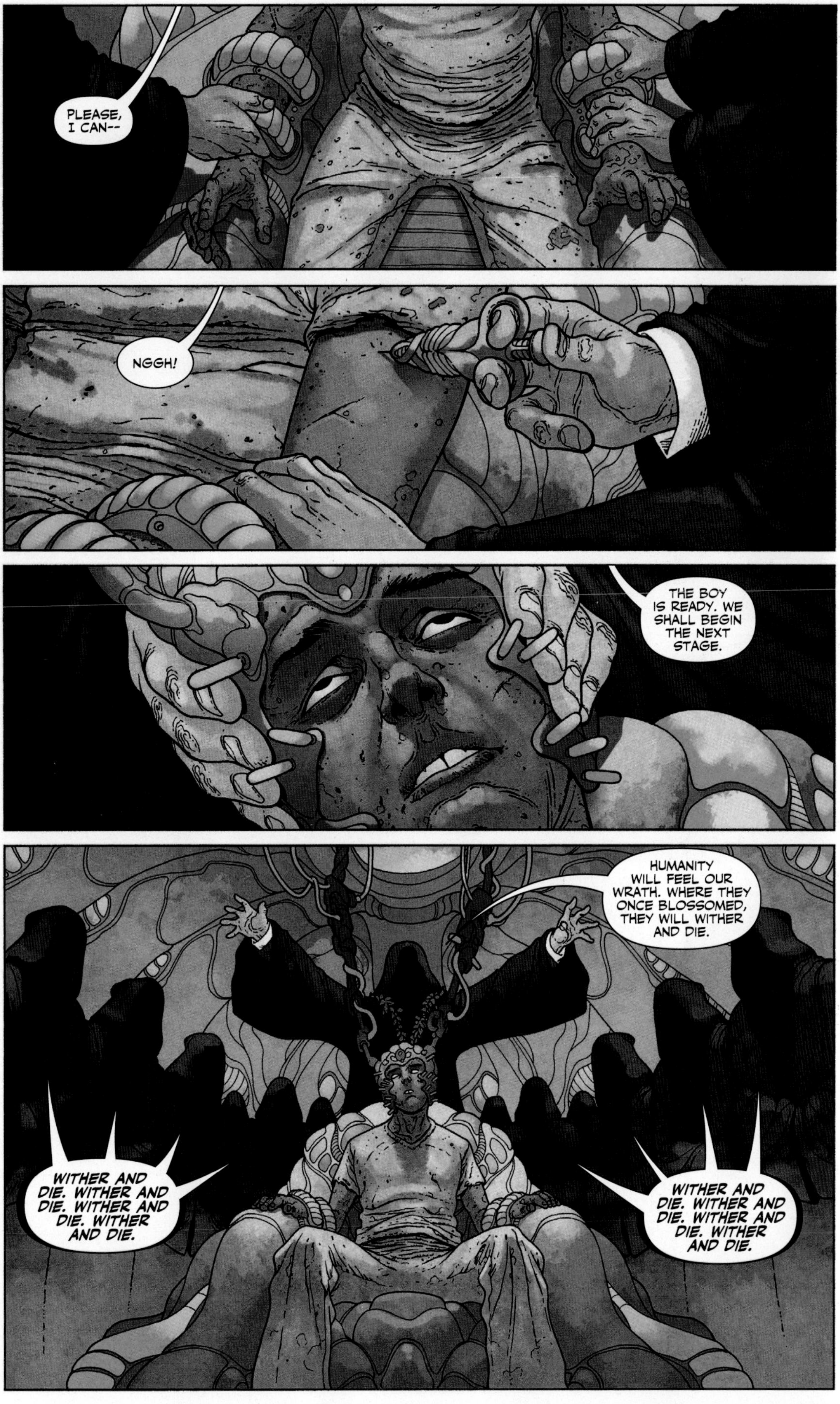
PLEASE, I CAN--
NGGH!
THE BOY IS READY. WE SHALL BEGIN THE NEXT STAGE.
HUMANITY WILL FEEL OUR WRATH. WHERE THEY ONCE BLOSSOMED, THEY WILL WITHER AND DIE.
WITHER AND DIE. WITHER AND DIE. WITHER AND DIE. WITHER AND DIE.
WITHER AND DIE. WITHER AND DIE. WITHER AND DIE. WITHER AND DIE.

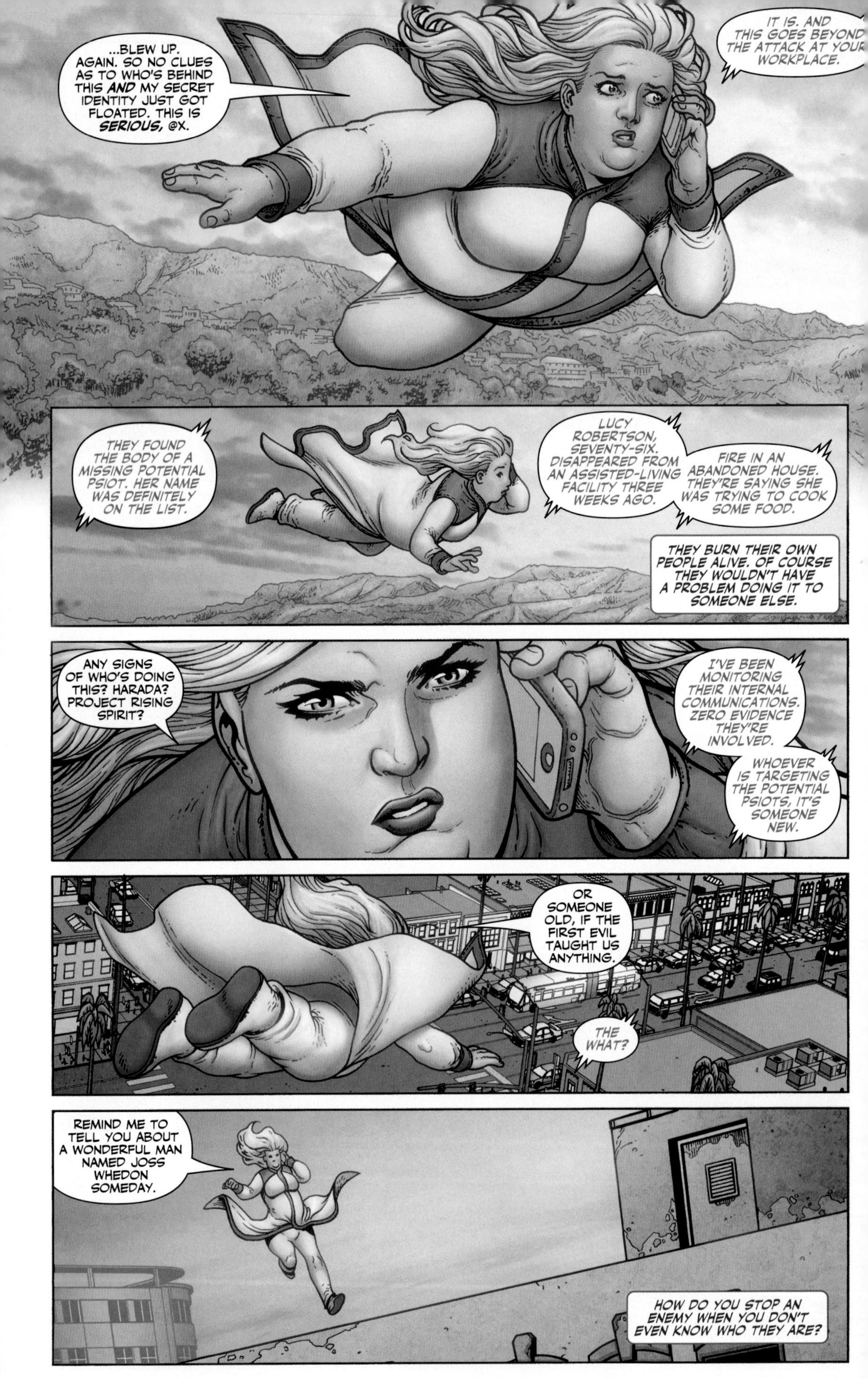
...BLEW UP. AGAIN. SO NO CLUES AS TO WHO'S BEHIND THIS AND MY SECRET IDENTITY JUST GOT FLOATED. THIS IS SERIOUS, @X.
IT IS. AND THIS GOES BEYOND THE ATTACK AT YOUR WORKPLACE.
THEY FOUND THE BODY OF A MISSING POTENTIAL PSIOT. HER NAME WAS DEFINITELY ON THE LIST.
LUCY ROBERTSON, SEVENTY-SIX. DISAPPEARED FROM AN ASSISTED-LIVING FACILITY THREE WEEKS AGO.
FIRE IN AN ABANDONED HOUSE. THEY'RE SAYING SHE WAS TRYING TO COOK SOME FOOD.
THEY BURN THEIR OWN PEOPLE ALIVE. OF COURSE THEY WOULDN'T HAVE A PROBLEM DOING IT TO SOMEONE ELSE.
ANY SIGNS OF WHO'S DOING THIS? HARADA? PROJECT RISING SPIRIT?
I'VE BEEN MONITORING THEIR INTERNAL COMMUNICATIONS. ZERO EVIDENCE THEY'RE INVOLVED.
WHOEVER IS TARGETING THE POTENTIAL PSIOTS, IT'S SOMEONE NEW.
OR SOMEONE OLD, IF THE FIRST EVIL TAUGHT US ANYTHING.
THE WHAT?
REMIND ME TO TELL YOU ABOUT A WONDERFUL MAN NAMED JOSS WHEDON SOMEDAY.
HOW DO YOU STOP AN ENEMY WHEN YOU DON'T EVEN KNOW WHO THEY ARE?

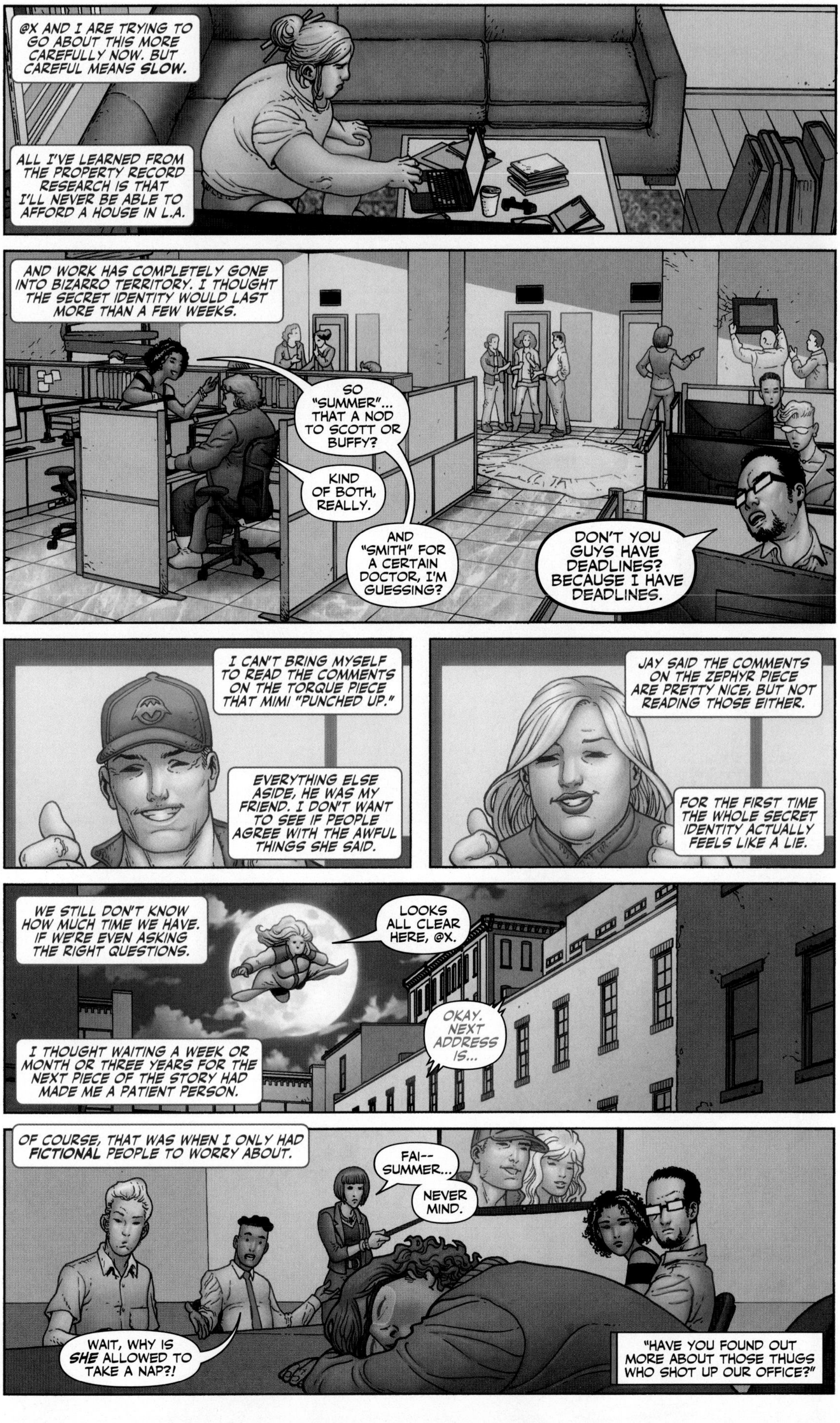
@X AND I ARE TRYING TO GO ABOUT THIS MORE CAREFULLY NOW. BUT CAREFUL MEANS SLOW.
ALL I'VE LEARNED FROM THE PROPERTY RECORD RESEARCH IS THAT I'LL NEVER BE ABLE TO AFFORD A HOUSE IN L.A.
AND WORK HAS COMPLETELY GONE INTO BIZARRO TERRITORY. I THOUGHT THE SECRET IDENTITY WOULD LAST MORE THAN A FEW WEEKS.
SO "SUMMER"... THAT A NOD TO SCOTT OR BUFFY?
KIND OF BOTH, REALLY.
AND "SMITH" FOR A CERTAIN DOCTOR, I'M GUESSING?
DON'T YOU GUYS HAVE DEADLINES? BECAUSE I HAVE DEADLINES.
I CAN'T BRING MYSELF TO READ THE COMMENTS ON THE TORQUE PIECE THAT MIMI "PUNCHED UP."
EVERYTHING ELSE ASIDE, HE WAS MY FRIEND. I DON'T WANT TO SEE IF PEOPLE AGREE WITH THE AWFUL THINGS SHE SAID.
JAY SAID THE COMMENTS ON THE ZEPHYR PIECE ARE PRETTY NICE, BUT NOT READING THOSE EITHER.
FOR THE FIRST TIME THE WHOLE SECRET IDENTITY ACTUALLY FEELS LIKE A LIE.
WE STILL DON'T KNOW HOW MUCH TIME WE HAVE. IF WE'RE EVEN ASKING THE RIGHT QUESTIONS.
LOOKS ALL CLEAR HERE, @X.
OKAY. NEXT ADDRESS IS...
I THOUGHT WAITING A WEEK OR MONTH OR THREE YEARS FOR THE NEXT PIECE OF THE STORY HAD MADE ME A PATIENT PERSON.
OF COURSE, THAT WAS WHEN I ONLY HAD FICTIONAL PEOPLE TO WORRY ABOUT.
FAI-- SUMMER...
NEVER MIND.
WAIT, WHY IS SHE ALLOWED TO TAKE A NAP?!
"HAVE YOU FOUND OUT MORE ABOUT THOSE THUGS WHO SHOT UP OUR OFFICE?"

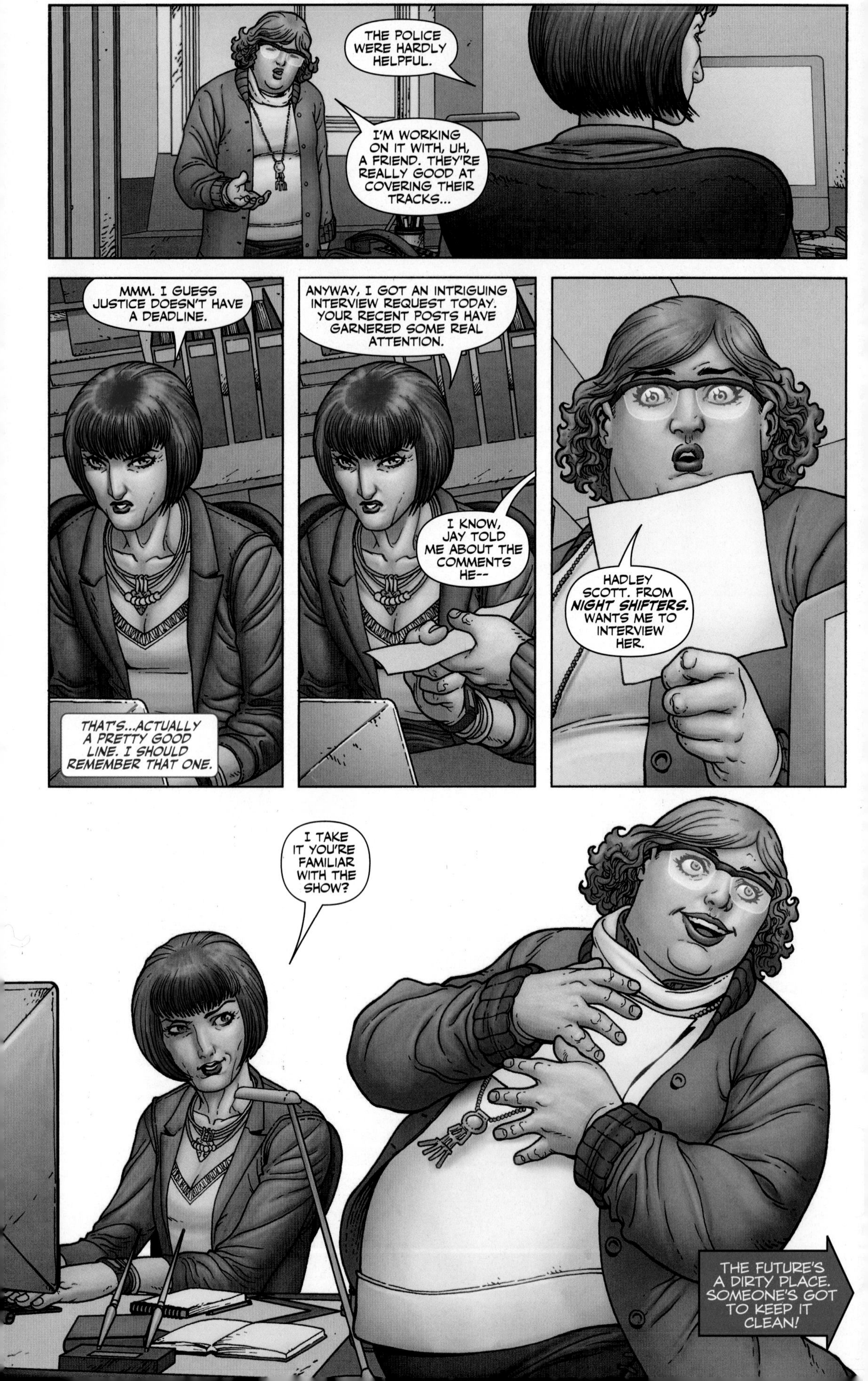
THE POLICE WERE HARDLY HELPFUL.
I'M WORKING ON IT WITH, UH, A FRIEND. THEY'RE REALLY GOOD AT COVERING THEIR TRACKS...
MMM. I GUESS JUSTICE DOESN'T HAVE A DEADLINE.
THAT'S...ACTUALLY A PRETTY GOOD LINE. I SHOULD REMEMBER THAT ONE.
ANYWAY, I GOT AN INTRIGUING INTERVIEW REQUEST TODAY. YOUR RECENT POSTS HAVE GARNERED SOME REAL ATTENTION.
I KNOW, JAY TOLD ME ABOUT THE COMMENTS HE--
HADLEY SCOTT. FROM NIGHT SHIFTERS. WANTS ME TO INTERVIEW HER.
I TAKE IT YOU'RE FAMILIAR WITH THE SHOW?
THE FUTURE'S A DIRTY PLACE. SOMEONE'S GOT TO KEEP IT CLEAN!

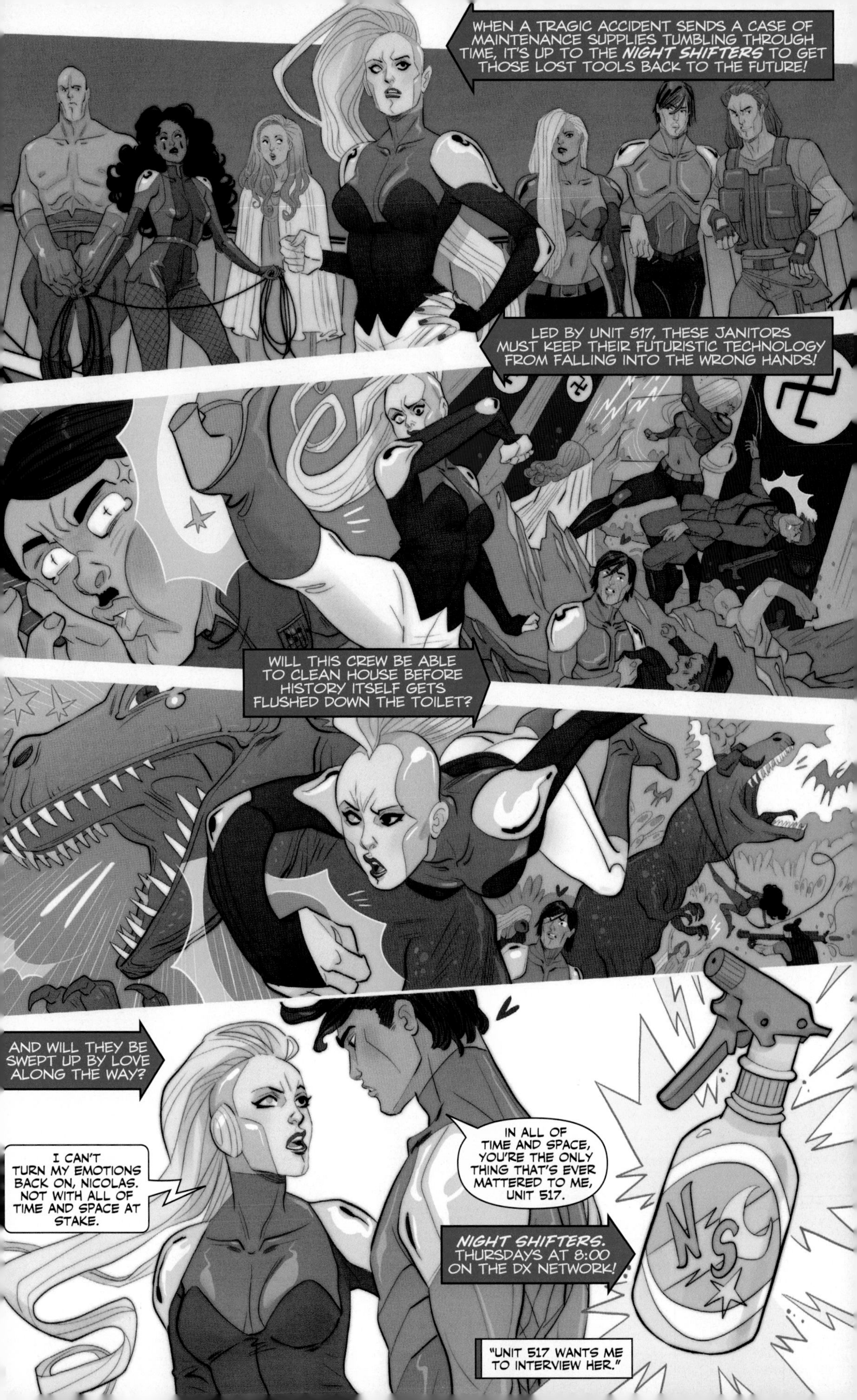
WHEN A TRAGIC ACCIDENT SENDS A CASE OF MAINTENANCE SUPPLIES TUMBLING THROUGH TIME, IT'S UP TO THE *NIGHT SHIFTERS* TO GET THOSE LOST TOOLS BACK TO THE FUTURE!
LED BY UNIT 517, THESE JANITORS MUST KEEP THEIR FUTURISTIC TECHNOLOGY FROM FALLING INTO THE WRONG HANDS!
WILL THIS CREW BE ABLE TO CLEAN HOUSE BEFORE HISTORY ITSELF GETS FLUSHED DOWN THE TOILET?
AND WILL THEY BE SWEPT UP BY LOVE ALONG THE WAY?
I CAN'T TURN MY EMOTIONS BACK ON, NICOLAS. NOT WITH ALL OF TIME AND SPACE AT STAKE.
IN ALL OF TIME AND SPACE, YOU'RE THE ONLY THING THAT'S EVER MATTERED TO ME, UNIT 517.
NIGHT SHIFTERS. THURSDAYS AT 8:00 ON THE DX NETWORK!
NSC
"UNIT 517 WANTS ME TO INTERVIEW HER."

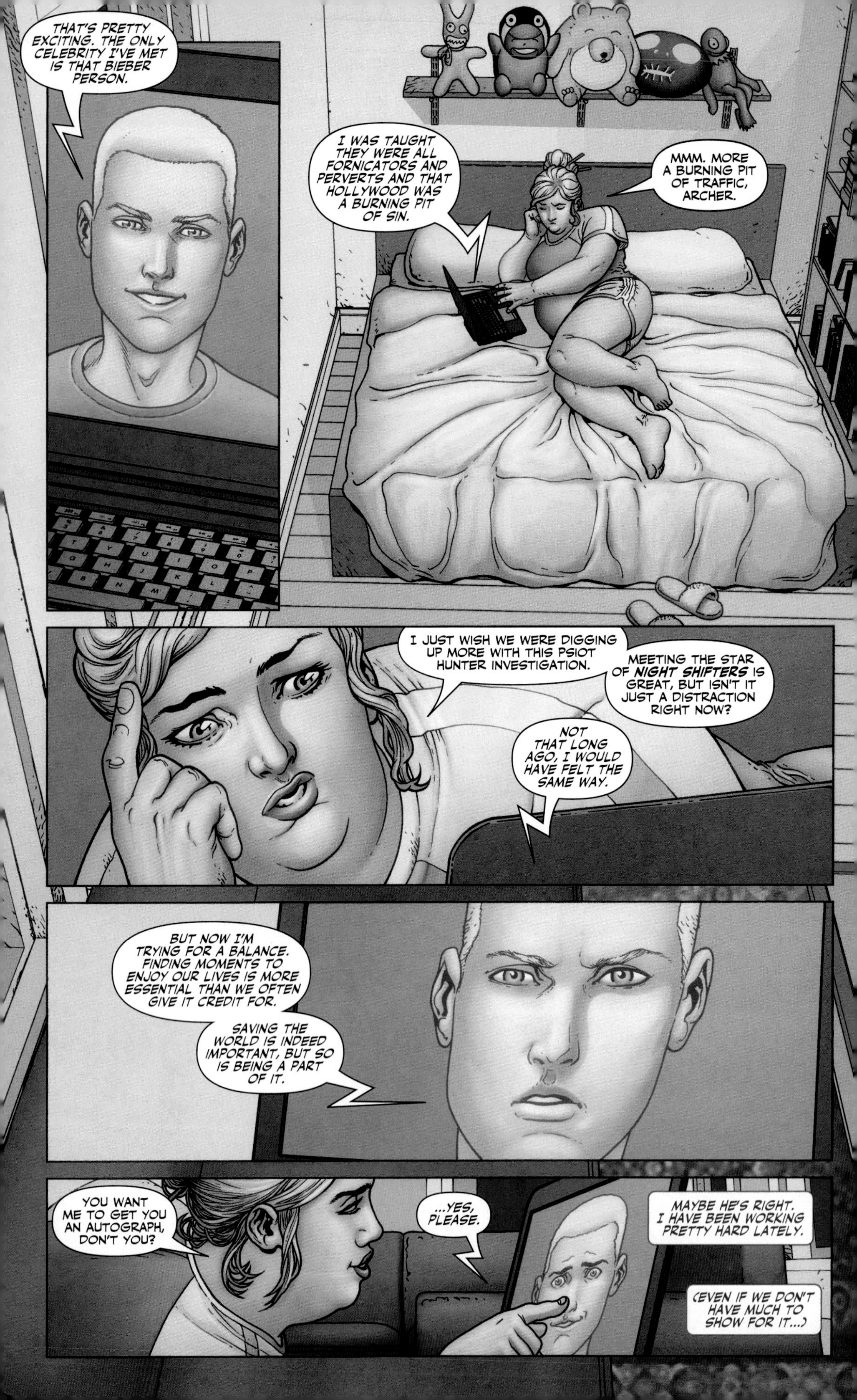
THAT'S PRETTY EXCITING. THE ONLY CELEBRITY I'VE MET IS THAT BIEBER PERSON.
I WAS TAUGHT THEY WERE ALL FORNICATORS AND PERVERTS AND THAT HOLLYWOOD WAS A BURNING PIT OF SIN.
MMM. MORE A BURNING PIT OF TRAFFIC, ARCHER.
I JUST WISH WE WERE DIGGING UP MORE WITH THIS PSIOT HUNTER INVESTIGATION.
MEETING THE STAR OF NIGHT SHIFTERS IS GREAT, BUT ISN'T IT JUST A DISTRACTION RIGHT NOW?
NOT THAT LONG AGO, I WOULD HAVE FELT THE SAME WAY.
BUT NOW I'M TRYING FOR A BALANCE. FINDING MOMENTS TO ENJOY OUR LIVES IS MORE ESSENTIAL THAN WE OFTEN GIVE IT CREDIT FOR.
SAVING THE WORLD IS INDEED IMPORTANT, BUT SO IS BEING A PART OF IT.
YOU WANT ME TO GET YOU AN AUTOGRAPH, DON'T YOU?
...YES, PLEASE.
MAYBE HE'S RIGHT. I HAVE BEEN WORKING PRETTY HARD LATELY.
(EVEN IF WE DON'T HAVE MUCH TO SHOW FOR IT...)

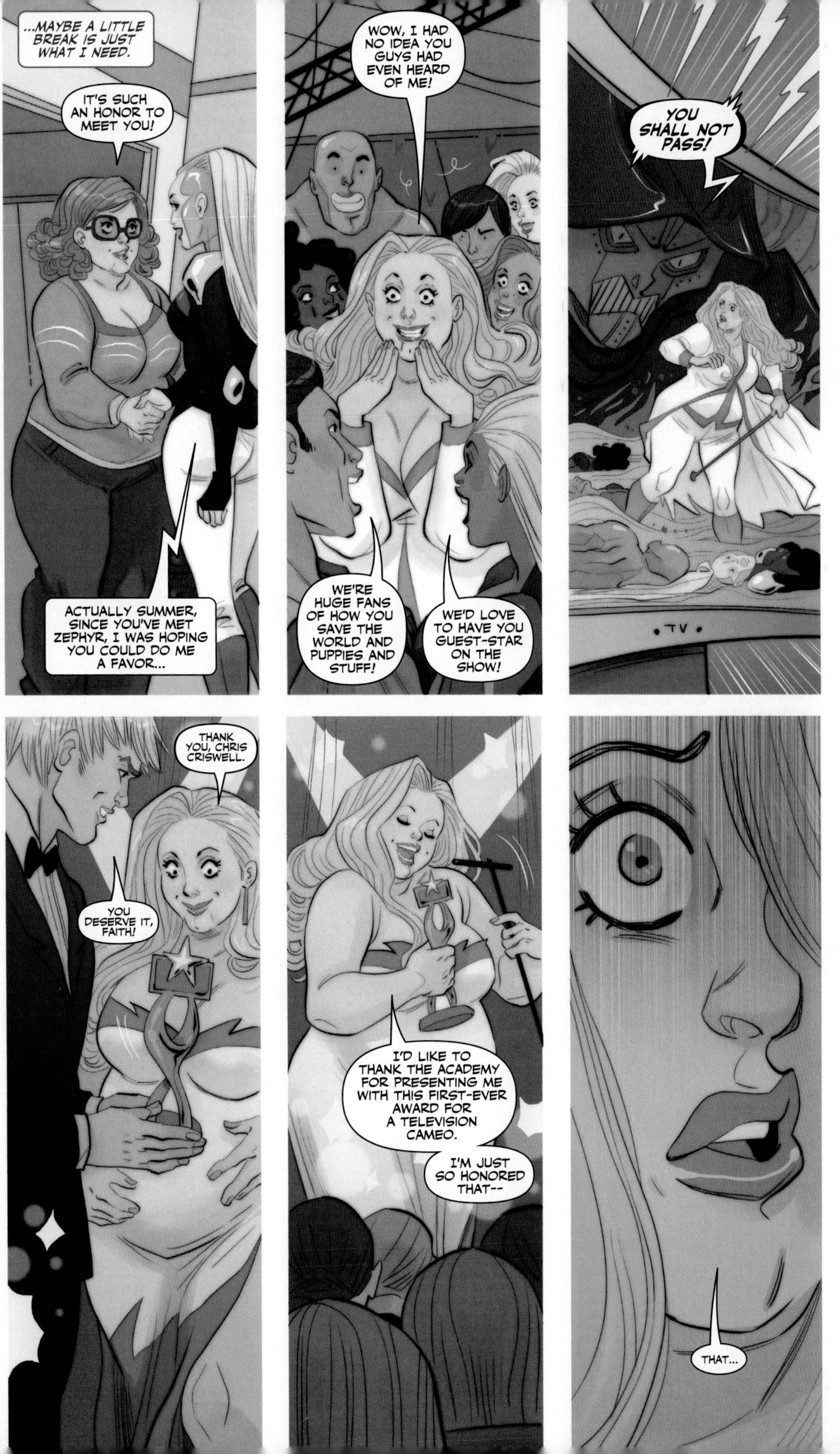
...MAYBE A LITTLE BREAK IS JUST WHAT I NEED.
IT'S SUCH AN HONOR TO MEET YOU!
ACTUALLY SUMMER, SINCE YOU'VE MET ZEPHYR, I WAS HOPING YOU COULD DO ME A FAVOR...
WOW, I HAD NO IDEA YOU GUYS HAD EVEN HEARD OF ME!
WE'RE HUGE FANS OF HOW YOU SAVE THE WORLD AND PUPPIES AND STUFF!
WE'D LOVE TO HAVE YOU GUEST-STAR ON THE SHOW!
YOU SHALL NOT PASS!
TV
THANK YOU, CHRIS CRISWELL.
YOU DESERVE IT, FAITH!
I'D LIKE TO THANK THE ACADEMY FOR PRESENTING ME WITH THIS FIRST-EVER AWARD FOR A TELEVISION CAMEO.
I'M JUST SO HONORED THAT--
THAT...

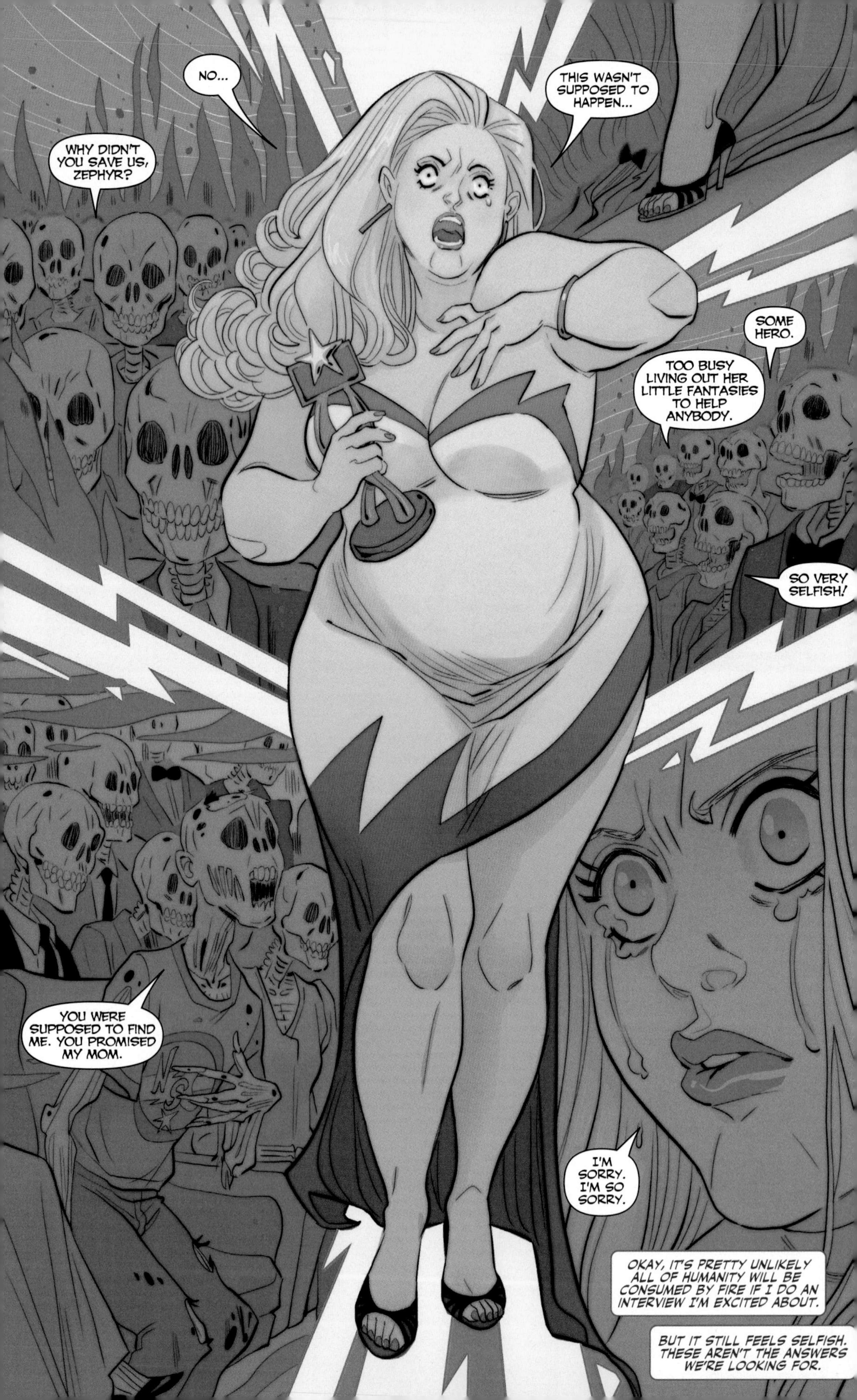
NO...
WHY DIDN'T YOU SAVE US, ZEPHYR?
THIS WASN'T SUPPOSED TO HAPPEN...
SOME HERO.
TOO BUSY LIVING OUT HER LITTLE FANTASIES TO HELP ANYBODY.
SO VERY SELFISH!
YOU WERE SUPPOSED TO FIND ME. YOU PROMISED MY MOM.
I'M SORRY. I'M SO SORRY.
OKAY, IT'S PRETTY UNLIKELY ALL OF HUMANITY WILL BE CONSUMED BY FIRE IF I DO AN INTERVIEW I'M EXCITED ABOUT.
BUT IT STILL FEELS SELFISH. THESE AREN'T THE ANSWERS WE'RE LOOKING FOR.

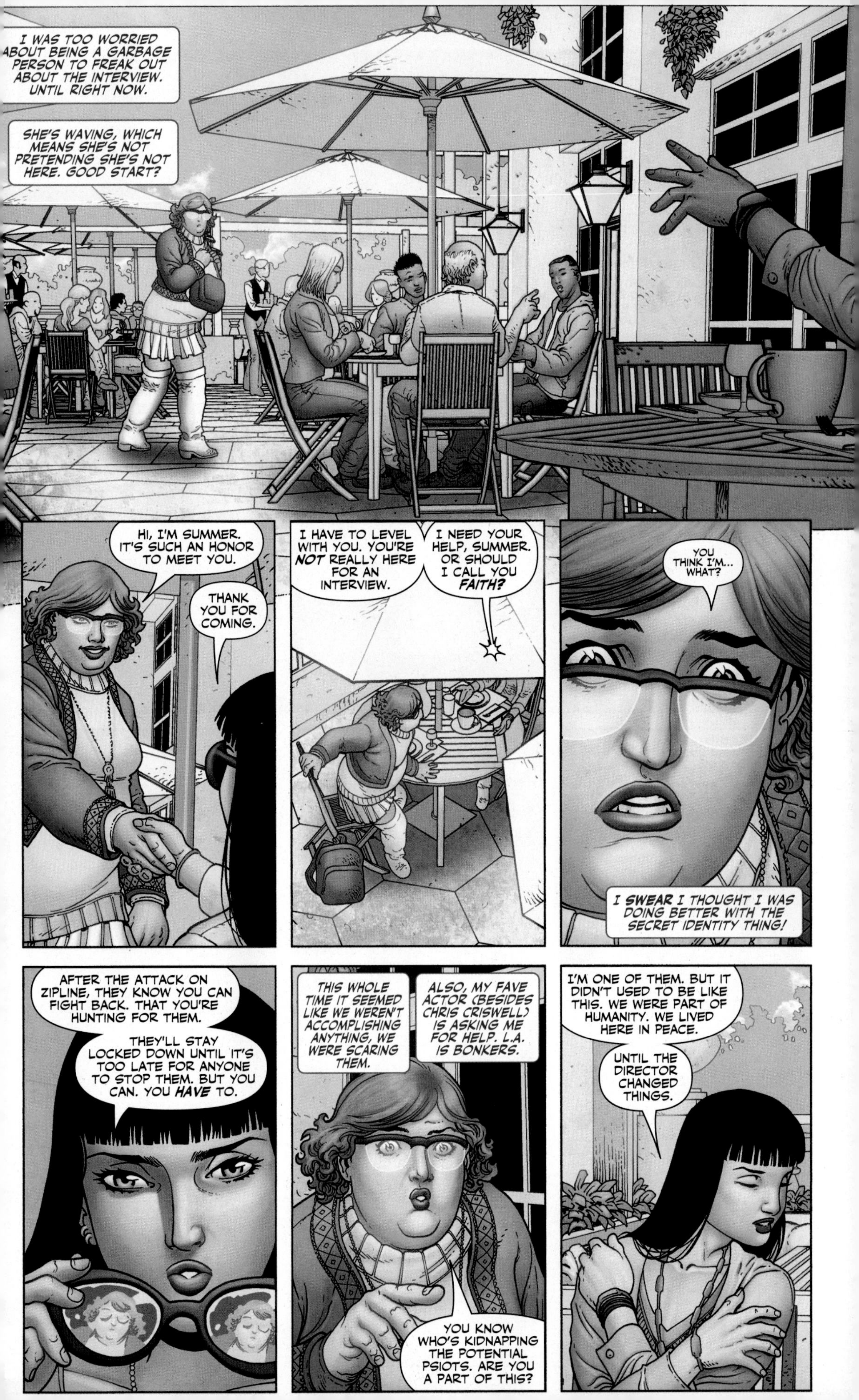
I WAS TOO WORRIED ABOUT BEING A GARBAGE PERSON TO FREAK OUT ABOUT THE INTERVIEW. UNTIL RIGHT NOW.
SHE'S WAVING, WHICH MEANS SHE'S NOT PRETENDING SHE'S NOT HERE. GOOD START?
HI, I'M SUMMER. IT'S SUCH AN HONOR TO MEET YOU.
THANK YOU FOR COMING.
I HAVE TO LEVEL WITH YOU. YOU'RE NOT REALLY HERE FOR AN INTERVIEW.
I NEED YOUR HELP, SUMMER. OR SHOULD I CALL YOU FAITH?
YOU THINK I'M... WHAT?
I SWEAR I THOUGHT I WAS DOING BETTER WITH THE SECRET IDENTITY THING!
AFTER THE ATTACK ON ZIPLINE, THEY KNOW YOU CAN FIGHT BACK. THAT YOU'RE HUNTING FOR THEM.
THEY'LL STAY LOCKED DOWN UNTIL IT'S TOO LATE FOR ANYONE TO STOP THEM. BUT YOU CAN. YOU HAVE TO.
THIS WHOLE TIME IT SEEMED LIKE WE WEREN'T ACCOMPLISHING ANYTHING, WE WERE SCARING THEM.
ALSO, MY FAVE ACTOR (BESIDES CHRIS CRISWELL) IS ASKING ME FOR HELP. L.A. IS BONKERS.
YOU KNOW WHO'S KIDNAPPING THE POTENTIAL PSIOTS. ARE YOU A PART OF THIS?
I'M ONE OF THEM. BUT IT DIDN'T USED TO BE LIKE THIS. WE WERE PART OF HUMANITY. WE LIVED HERE IN PEACE.
UNTIL THE DIRECTOR CHANGED THINGS.

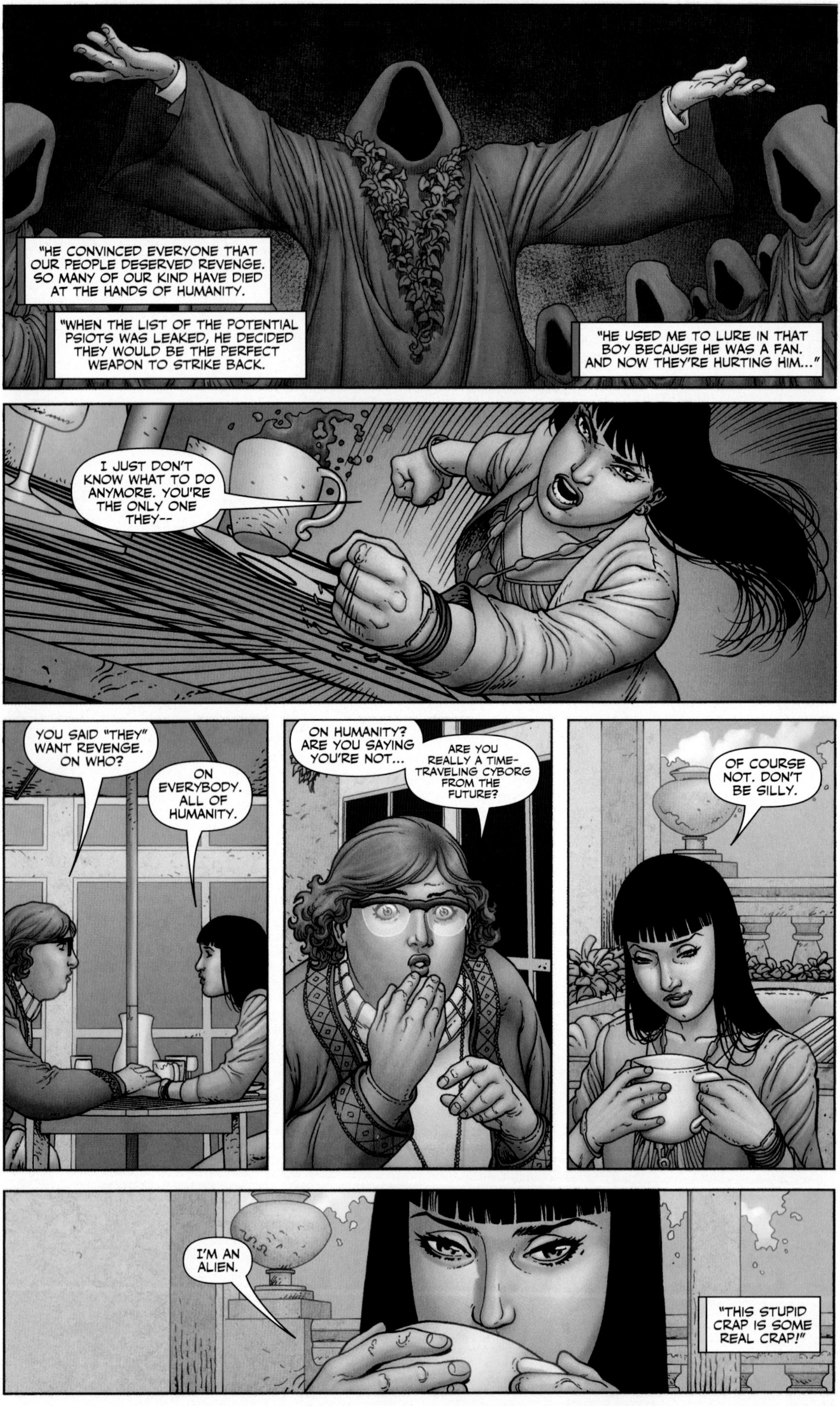
"HE CONVINCED EVERYONE THAT OUR PEOPLE DESERVED REVENGE. SO MANY OF OUR KIND HAVE DIED AT THE HANDS OF HUMANITY.
"WHEN THE LIST OF THE POTENTIAL PSIOTS WAS LEAKED, HE DECIDED THEY WOULD BE THE PERFECT WEAPON TO STRIKE BACK.
"HE USED ME TO LURE IN THAT BOY BECAUSE HE WAS A FAN. AND NOW THEY'RE HURTING HIM..."
I JUST DON'T KNOW WHAT TO DO ANYMORE. YOU'RE THE ONLY ONE THEY--
YOU SAID "THEY" WANT REVENGE. ON WHO?
ON EVERYBODY. ALL OF HUMANITY.
ON HUMANITY? ARE YOU SAYING YOU'RE NOT...
ARE YOU REALLY A TIME-TRAVELING CYBORG FROM THE FUTURE?
OF COURSE NOT. DON'T BE SILLY.
I'M AN ALIEN.
"THIS STUPID CRAP IS SOME REAL CRAP!"

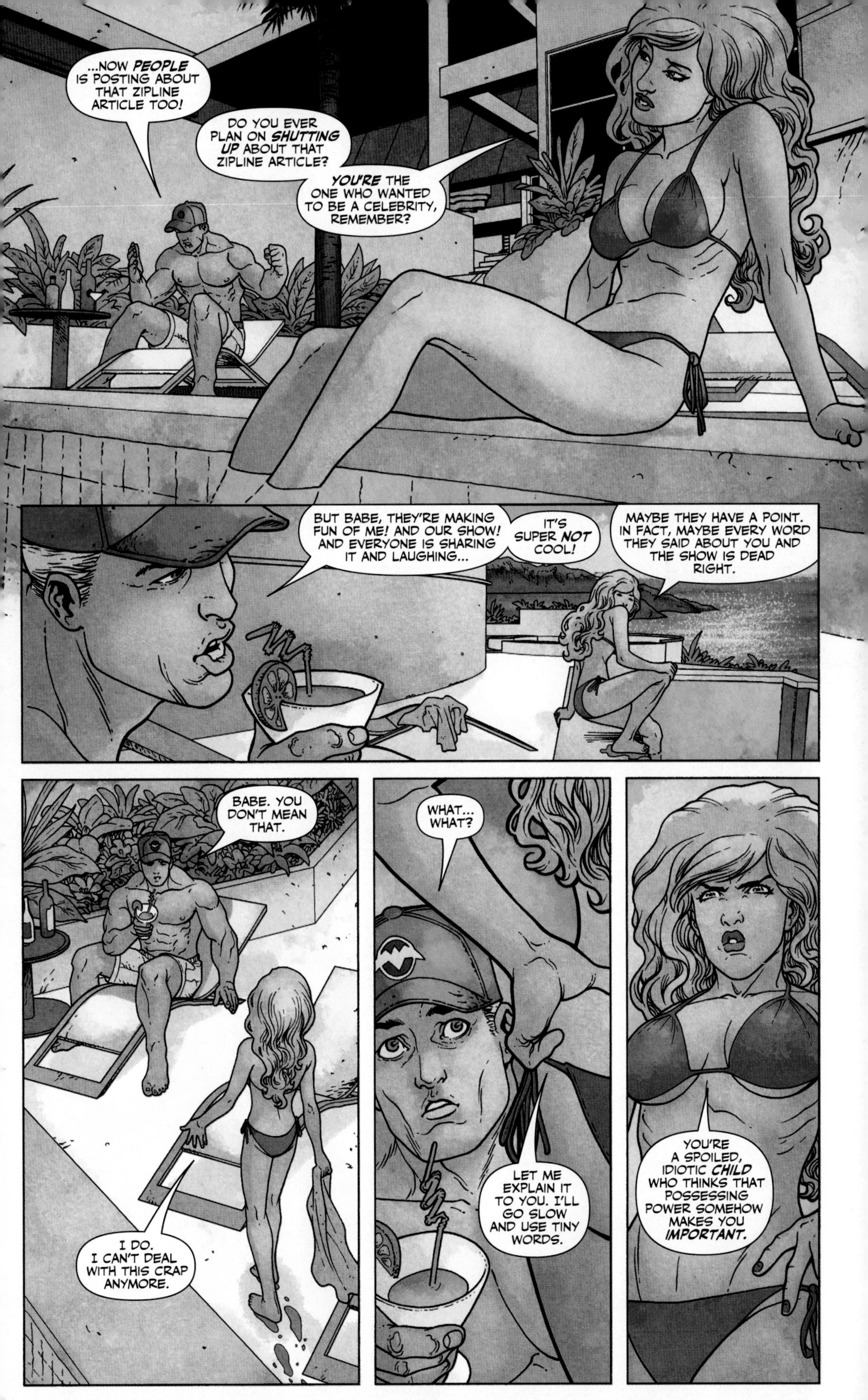
...NOW PEOPLE IS POSTING ABOUT THAT ZIPLINE ARTICLE TOO!
DO YOU EVER PLAN ON SHUTTING UP ABOUT THAT ZIPLINE ARTICLE?
YOU'RE THE ONE WHO WANTED TO BE A CELEBRITY, REMEMBER?
BUT BABE, THEY'RE MAKING FUN OF ME! AND OUR SHOW! AND EVERYONE IS SHARING IT AND LAUGHING...
IT'S SUPER NOT COOL!
MAYBE THEY HAVE A POINT. IN FACT, MAYBE EVERY WORD THEY SAID ABOUT YOU AND THE SHOW IS DEAD RIGHT.
BABE. YOU DON'T MEAN THAT.
I DO. I CAN'T DEAL WITH THIS CRAP ANYMORE.
WHAT... WHAT?
LET ME EXPLAIN IT TO YOU. I'LL GO SLOW AND USE TINY WORDS.
YOU'RE A SPOILED, IDIOTIC CHILD WHO THINKS THAT POSSESSING POWER SOMEHOW MAKES YOU IMPORTANT.

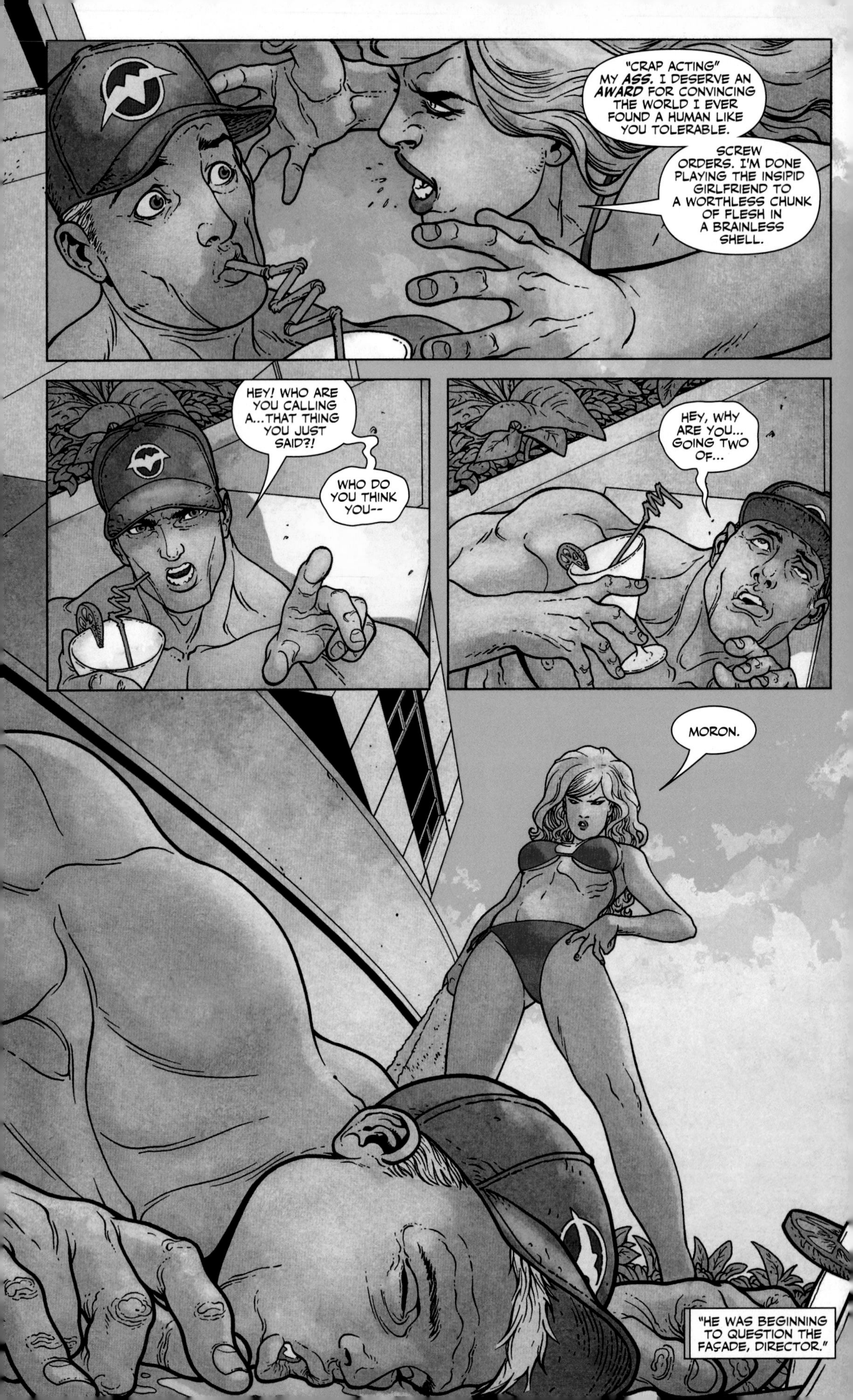
"CRAP ACTING" MY ASS. I DESERVE AN AWARD FOR CONVINCING THE WORLD I EVER FOUND A HUMAN LIKE YOU TOLERABLE.
SCREW ORDERS. I'M DONE PLAYING THE INSIPID GIRLFRIEND TO A WORTHLESS CHUNK OF FLESH IN A BRAINLESS SHELL.
HEY! WHO ARE YOU CALLING A...THAT THING YOU JUST SAID?!
WHO DO YOU THINK YOU--
HEY, WHY ARE YOU... GOING TWO OF...
MORON.
"HE WAS BEGINNING TO QUESTION THE FAÇADE, DIRECTOR."

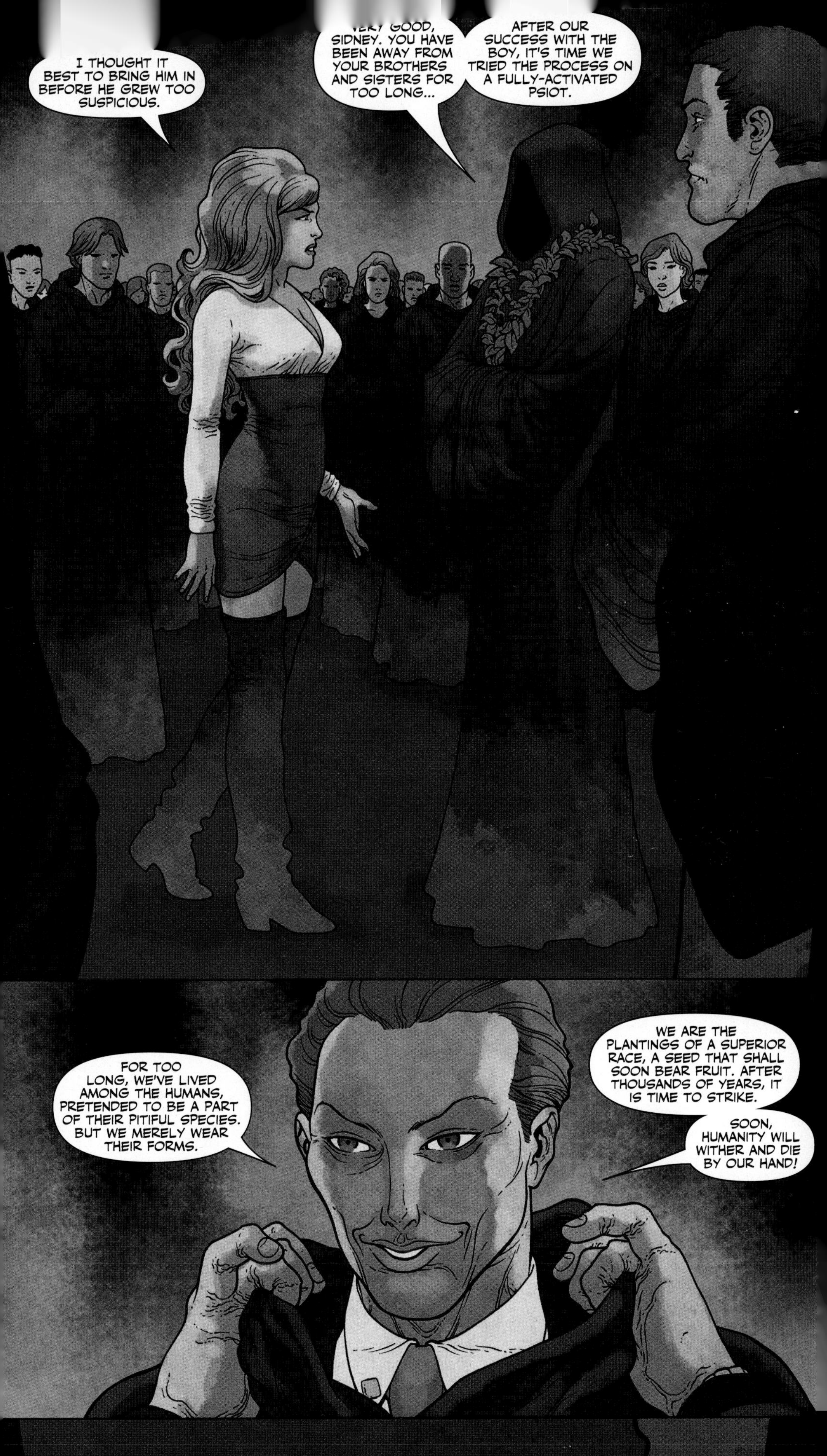
I THOUGHT IT BEST TO BRING HIM IN BEFORE HE GREW TOO SUSPICIOUS.
VERY GOOD, SIDNEY. YOU HAVE BEEN AWAY FROM YOUR BROTHERS AND SISTERS FOR TOO LONG...
AFTER OUR SUCCESS WITH THE BOY, IT'S TIME WE TRIED THE PROCESS ON A FULLY-ACTIVATED PSIOT.
FOR TOO LONG, WE'VE LIVED AMONG THE HUMANS, PRETENDED TO BE A PART OF THEIR PITIFUL SPECIES. BUT WE MERELY WEAR THEIR FORMS.
WE ARE THE PLANTINGS OF A SUPERIOR RACE, A SEED THAT SHALL SOON BEAR FRUIT. AFTER THOUSANDS OF YEARS, IT IS TIME TO STRIKE.
SOON, HUMANITY WILL WITHER AND DIE BY OUR HAND!

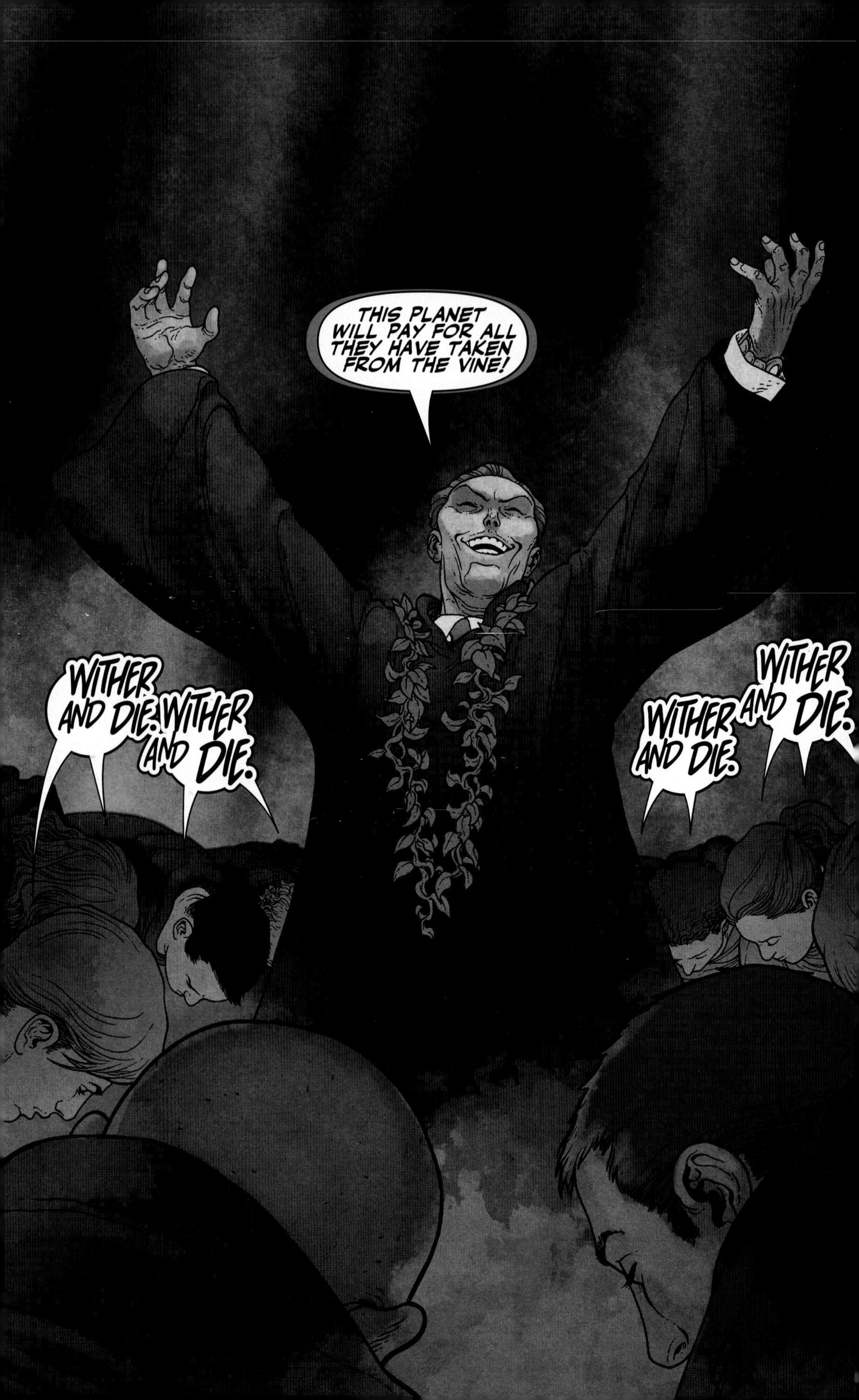
THIS PLANET WILL PAY FOR ALL THEY HAVE TAKEN FROM THE VINE!
WITHER AND DIE.
WITHER AND DIE.
WITHER AND DIE.
WITHER AND DIE.

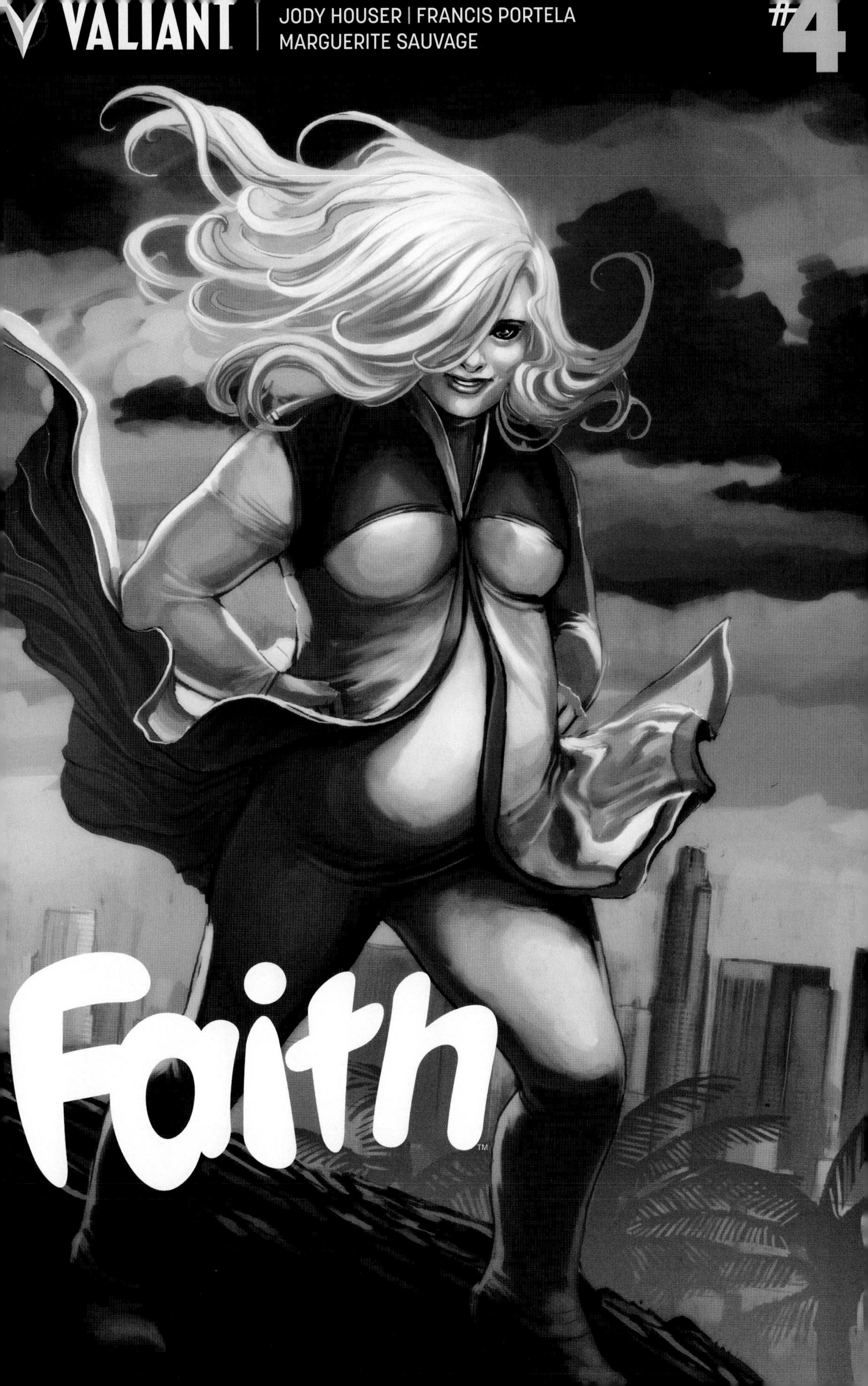
VALIANT
JODY HOUSER | FRANCIS PORTELA
MARGUERITE SAUVAGE
#4
Faith™

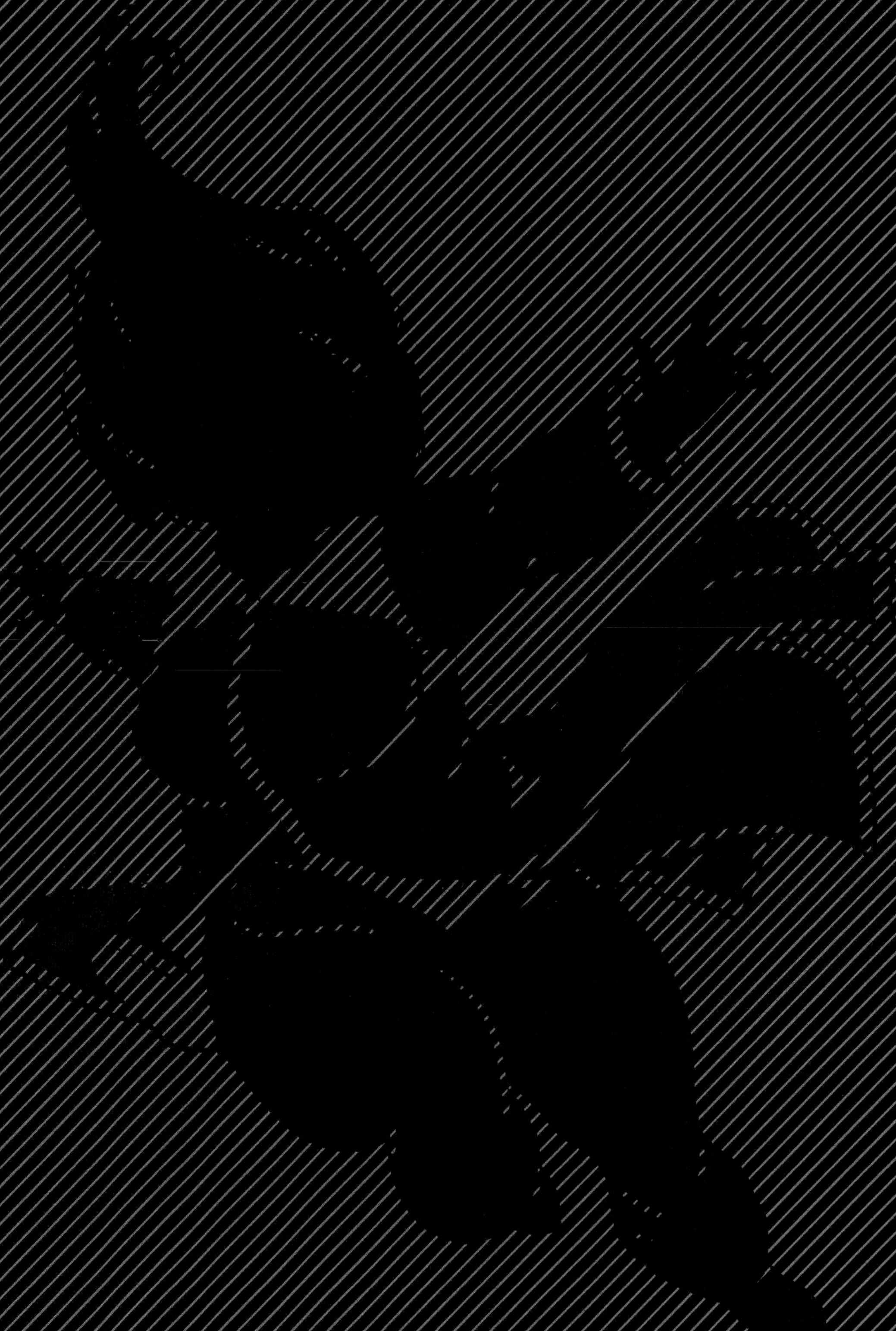

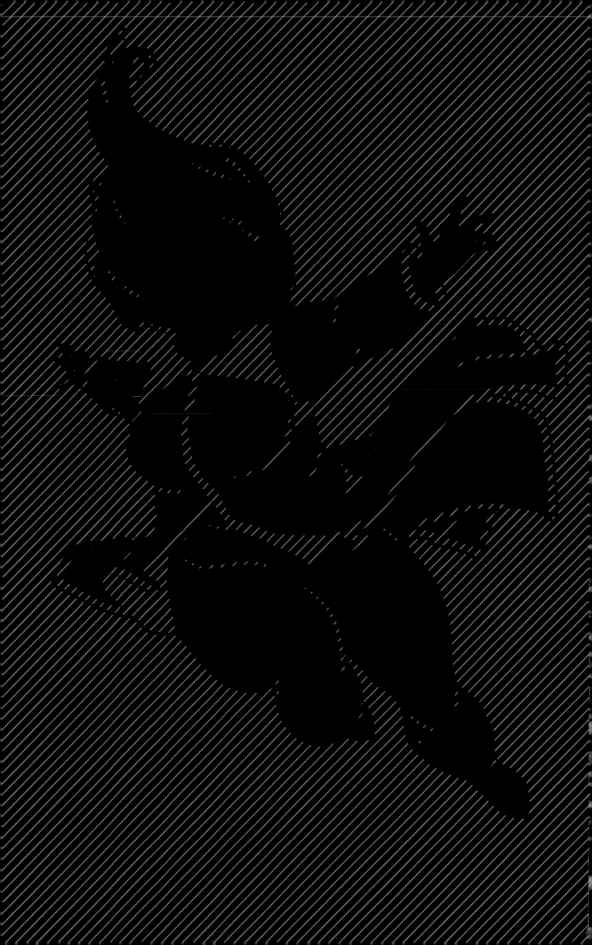

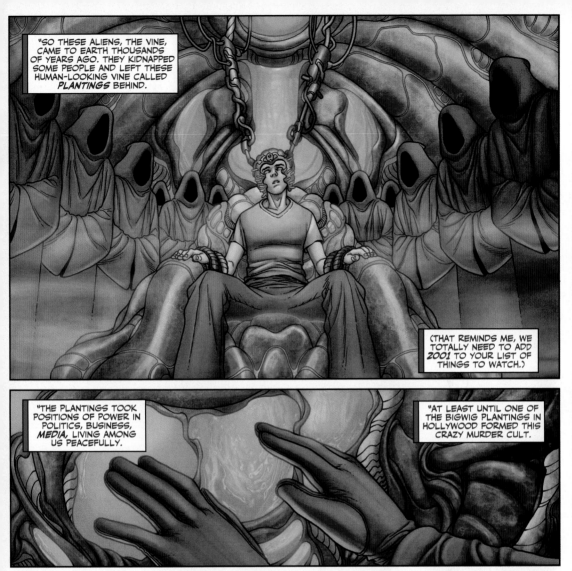

"SO THESE ALIENS, THE VINE, CAME TO EARTH THOUSANDS OF YEARS AGO. THEY KIDNAPPED SOME PEOPLE AND LEFT THESE HUMAN-LOOKING VINE CALLED *PLANTINGS* BEHIND.

(THAT REMINDS ME, WE TOTALLY NEED TO ADD *2001* TO YOUR LIST OF THINGS TO WATCH.)

"THE PLANTINGS TOOK POSITIONS OF POWER IN POLITICS, BUSINESS, *MEDIA*, LIVING AMONG US PEACEFULLY.

"AT LEAST UNTIL ONE OF THE BIGWIG PLANTINGS IN HOLLYWOOD FORMED THIS CRAZY MURDER CULT.

"I GUESS THEY'RE MAD ABOUT THE REGULAR ALIEN VINE WHO CAME TO EARTH AND GOT THEIR BUTTS KICKED?

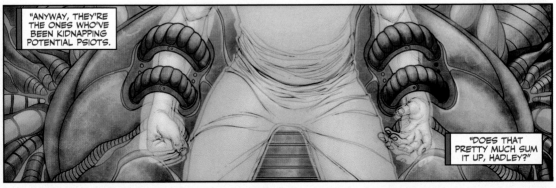

"ANYWAY, THEY'RE THE ONES WHO'VE BEEN KIDNAPPING POTENTIAL PSIOTS.

"DOES THAT PRETTY MUCH SUM IT UP, HADLEY?"

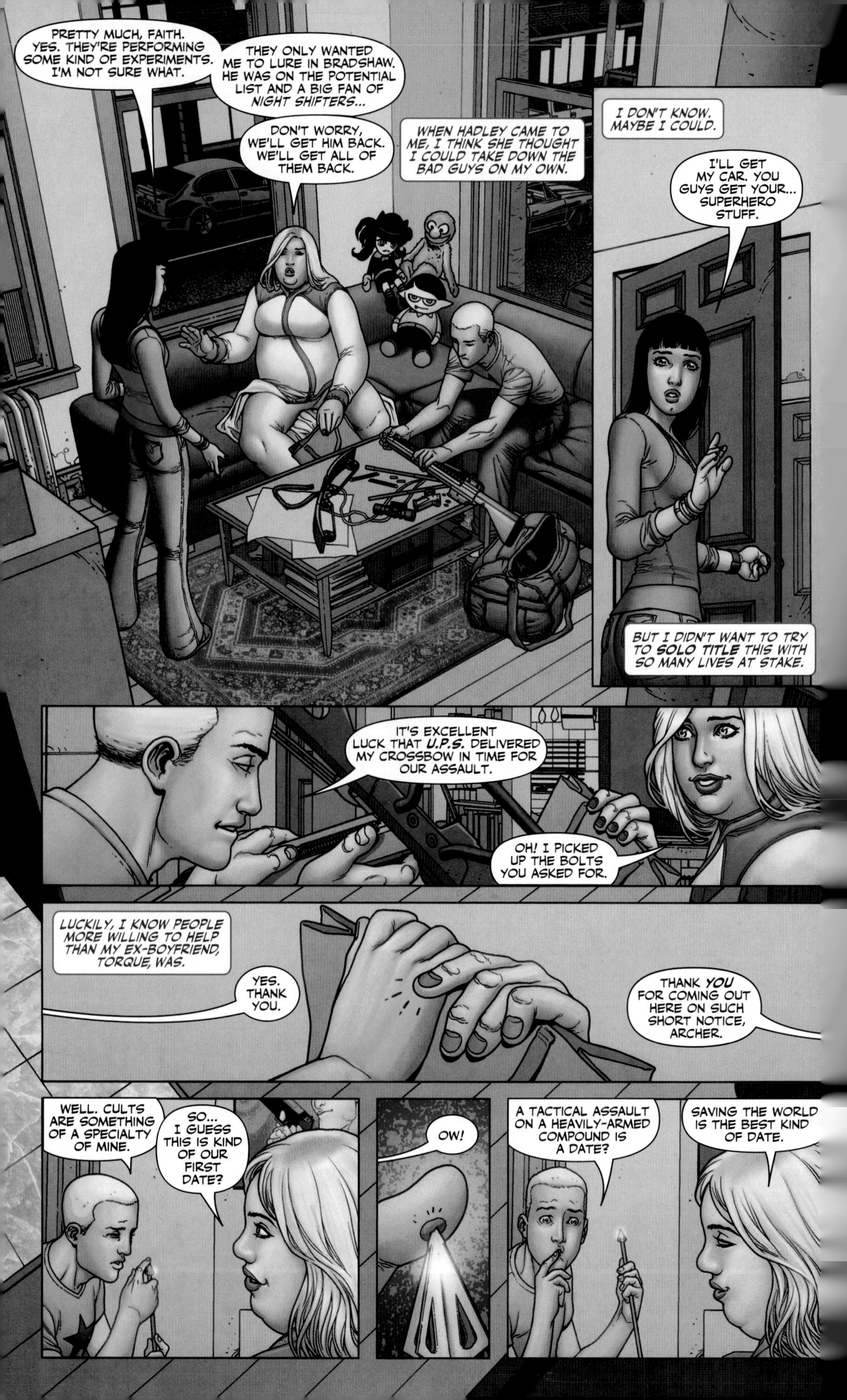
PRETTY MUCH, FAITH. YES. THEY'RE PERFORMING SOME KIND OF EXPERIMENTS. I'M NOT SURE WHAT.
THEY ONLY WANTED ME TO LURE IN BRADSHAW. HE WAS ON THE POTENTIAL LIST AND A BIG FAN OF NIGHT SHIFTERS...
DON'T WORRY, WE'LL GET HIM BACK. WE'LL GET ALL OF THEM BACK.
WHEN HADLEY CAME TO ME, I THINK SHE THOUGHT I COULD TAKE DOWN THE BAD GUYS ON MY OWN.
I DON'T KNOW. MAYBE I COULD.
I'LL GET MY CAR. YOU GUYS GET YOUR... SUPERHERO STUFF.
BUT I DIDN'T WANT TO TRY TO SOLO TITLE THIS WITH SO MANY LIVES AT STAKE.
IT'S EXCELLENT LUCK THAT U.P.S. DELIVERED MY CROSSBOW IN TIME FOR OUR ASSAULT.
OH! I PICKED UP THE BOLTS YOU ASKED FOR.
LUCKILY, I KNOW PEOPLE MORE WILLING TO HELP THAN MY EX-BOYFRIEND, TORQUE, WAS.
YES. THANK YOU.
THANK YOU FOR COMING OUT HERE ON SUCH SHORT NOTICE, ARCHER.
WELL. CULTS ARE SOMETHING OF A SPECIALTY OF MINE.
SO... I GUESS THIS IS KIND OF OUR FIRST DATE?
OW!
A TACTICAL ASSAULT ON A HEAVILY-ARMED COMPOUND IS A DATE?
SAVING THE WORLD IS THE BEST KIND OF DATE.

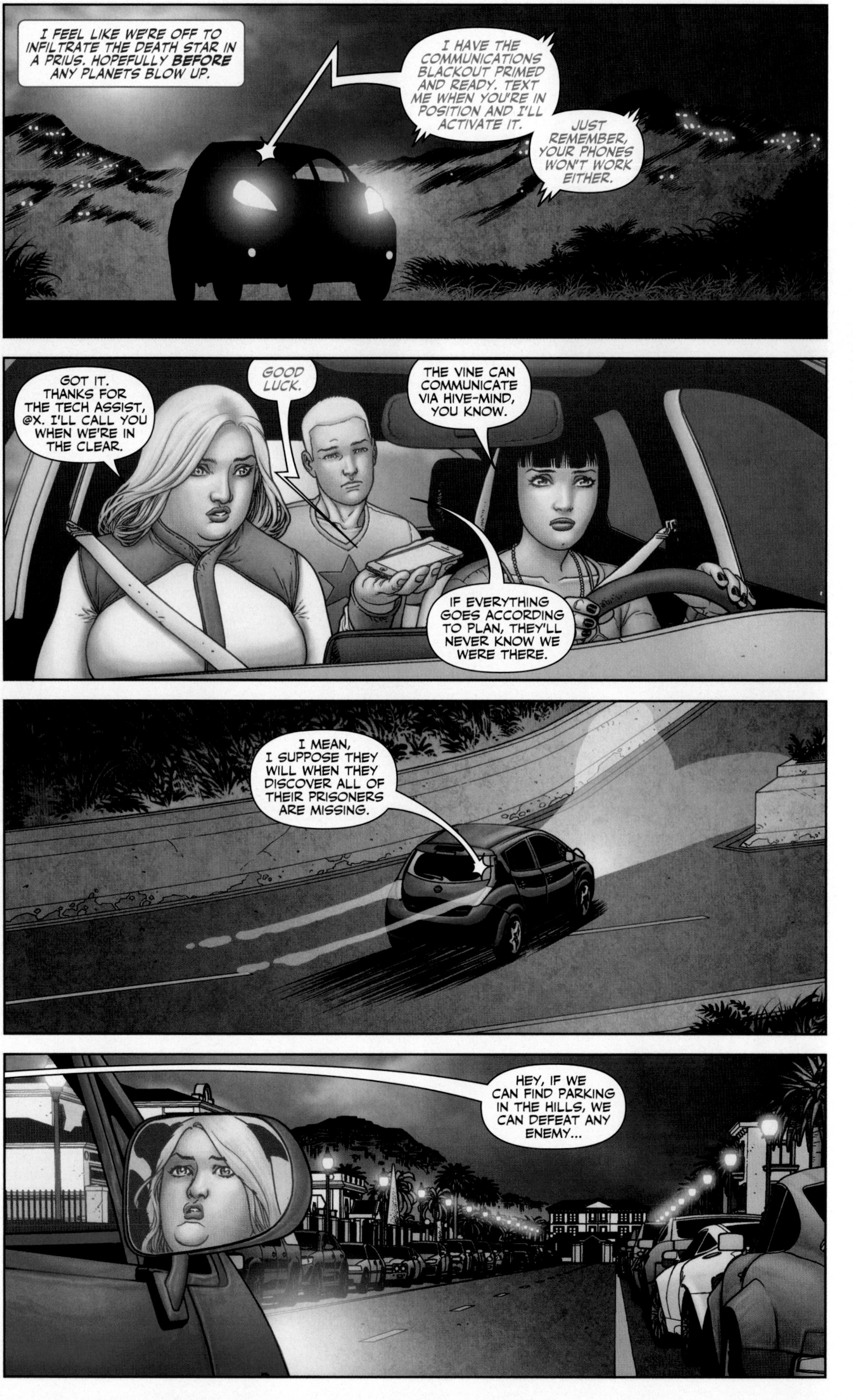
I FEEL LIKE WE'RE OFF TO INFILTRATE THE DEATH STAR IN A PRIUS. HOPEFULLY BEFORE ANY PLANETS BLOW UP.
I HAVE THE COMMUNICATIONS BLACKOUT PRIMED AND READY. TEXT ME WHEN YOU'RE IN POSITION AND I'LL ACTIVATE IT.
JUST REMEMBER, YOUR PHONES WON'T WORK EITHER.
GOT IT. THANKS FOR THE TECH ASSIST, @X. I'LL CALL YOU WHEN WE'RE IN THE CLEAR.
GOOD LUCK.
THE VINE CAN COMMUNICATE VIA HIVE-MIND, YOU KNOW.
IF EVERYTHING GOES ACCORDING TO PLAN, THEY'LL NEVER KNOW WE WERE THERE.
I MEAN, I SUPPOSE THEY WILL WHEN THEY DISCOVER ALL OF THEIR PRISONERS ARE MISSING.
HEY, IF WE CAN FIND PARKING IN THE HILLS, WE CAN DEFEAT ANY ENEMY...

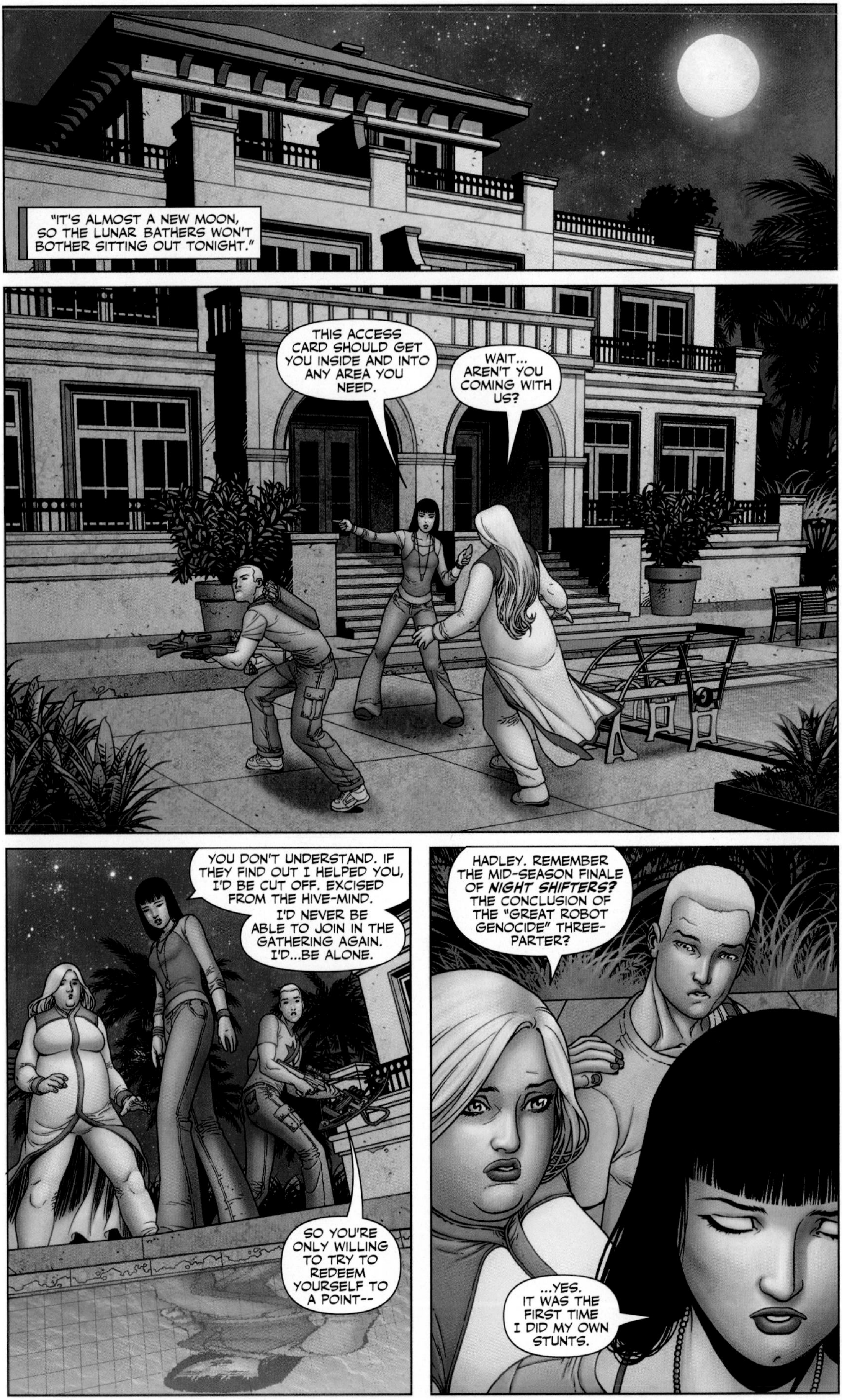
"IT'S ALMOST A NEW MOON, SO THE LUNAR BATHERS WON'T BOTHER SITTING OUT TONIGHT."
THIS ACCESS CARD SHOULD GET YOU INSIDE AND INTO ANY AREA YOU NEED.
WAIT... AREN'T YOU COMING WITH US?
YOU DON'T UNDERSTAND. IF THEY FIND OUT I HELPED YOU, I'D BE CUT OFF. EXCISED FROM THE HIVE-MIND.
I'D NEVER BE ABLE TO JOIN IN THE GATHERING AGAIN. I'D...BE ALONE.
SO YOU'RE ONLY WILLING TO TRY TO REDEEM YOURSELF TO A POINT--
HADLEY. REMEMBER THE MID-SEASON FINALE OF *NIGHT SHIFTERS?* THE CONCLUSION OF THE "GREAT ROBOT GENOCIDE" THREE-PARTER?
...YES. IT WAS THE FIRST TIME I DID MY OWN STUNTS.

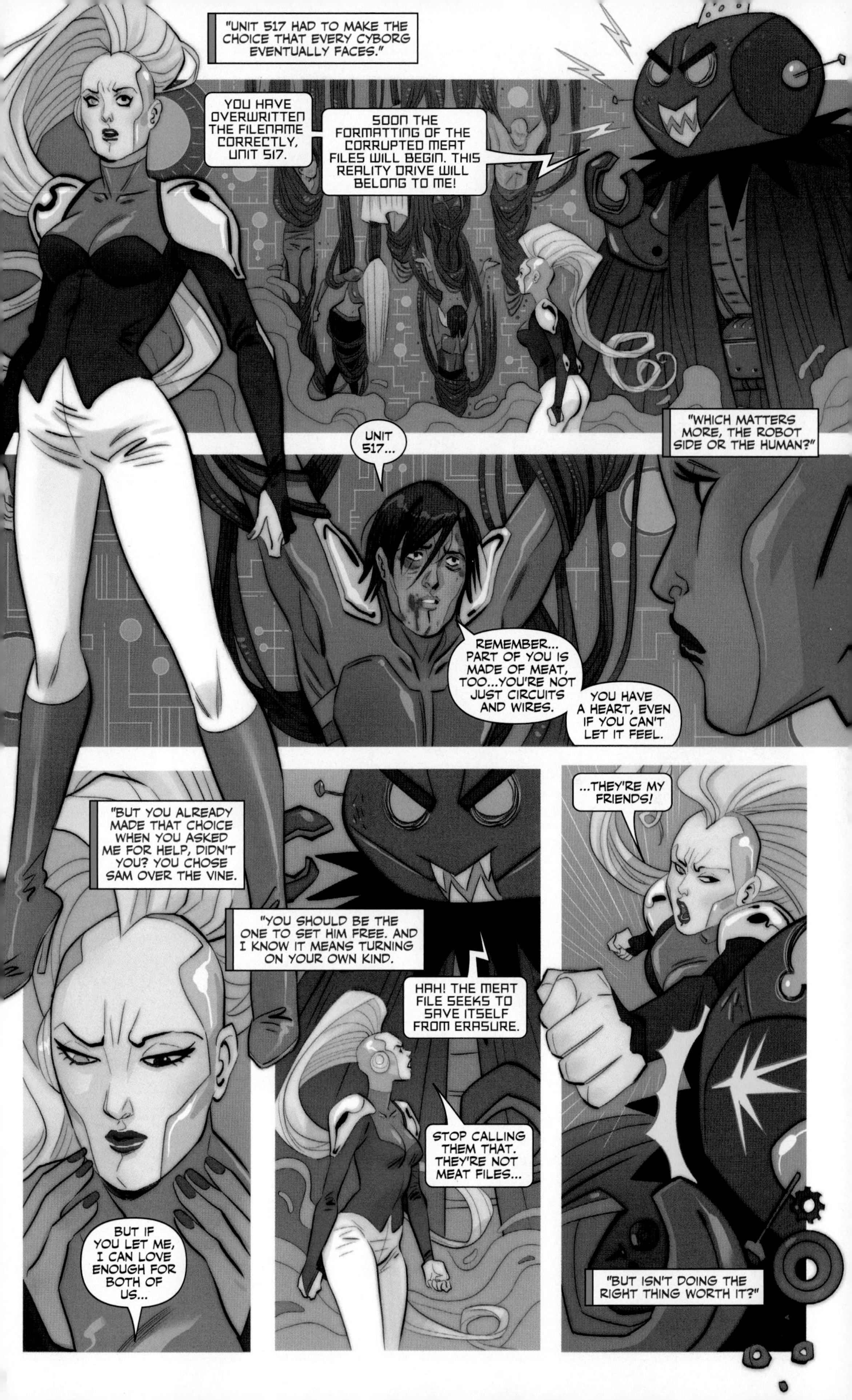
"UNIT 517 HAD TO MAKE THE CHOICE THAT EVERY CYBORG EVENTUALLY FACES."
YOU HAVE OVERWRITTEN THE FILENAME CORRECTLY, UNIT 517.
SOON THE FORMATTING OF THE CORRUPTED MEAT FILES WILL BEGIN. THIS REALITY DRIVE WILL BELONG TO ME!
"WHICH MATTERS MORE, THE ROBOT SIDE OR THE HUMAN?"
UNIT 517...
REMEMBER... PART OF YOU IS MADE OF MEAT, TOO...YOU'RE NOT JUST CIRCUITS AND WIRES.
YOU HAVE A HEART, EVEN IF YOU CAN'T LET IT FEEL.
"BUT YOU ALREADY MADE THAT CHOICE WHEN YOU ASKED ME FOR HELP, DIDN'T YOU? YOU CHOSE SAM OVER THE VINE.
BUT IF YOU LET ME, I CAN LOVE ENOUGH FOR BOTH OF US...
"YOU SHOULD BE THE ONE TO SET HIM FREE. AND I KNOW IT MEANS TURNING ON YOUR OWN KIND.
HAH! THE MEAT FILE SEEKS TO SAVE ITSELF FROM ERASURE.
STOP CALLING THEM THAT. THEY'RE NOT MEAT FILES...
...THEY'RE MY FRIENDS!
"BUT ISN'T DOING THE RIGHT THING WORTH IT?"

CLICK!

COME ON. LET'S GO.

I THINK I JUST LEVELED UP IN INSPIRATIONAL SPEECHIFYING.

MOST PEOPLE WILL BE ASLEEP. EARLY CALL TIMES TOMORROW.

THERE ARE GUARDS, THOUGH...

DON'T WORRY...

I SHALL GET THIS.

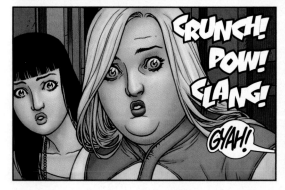

CRUNCH! POW! CLANG!

GYAH!

CRASSH! SCRUNCH!

HE'S PRETTY GOOD, HUH?

YEAH.

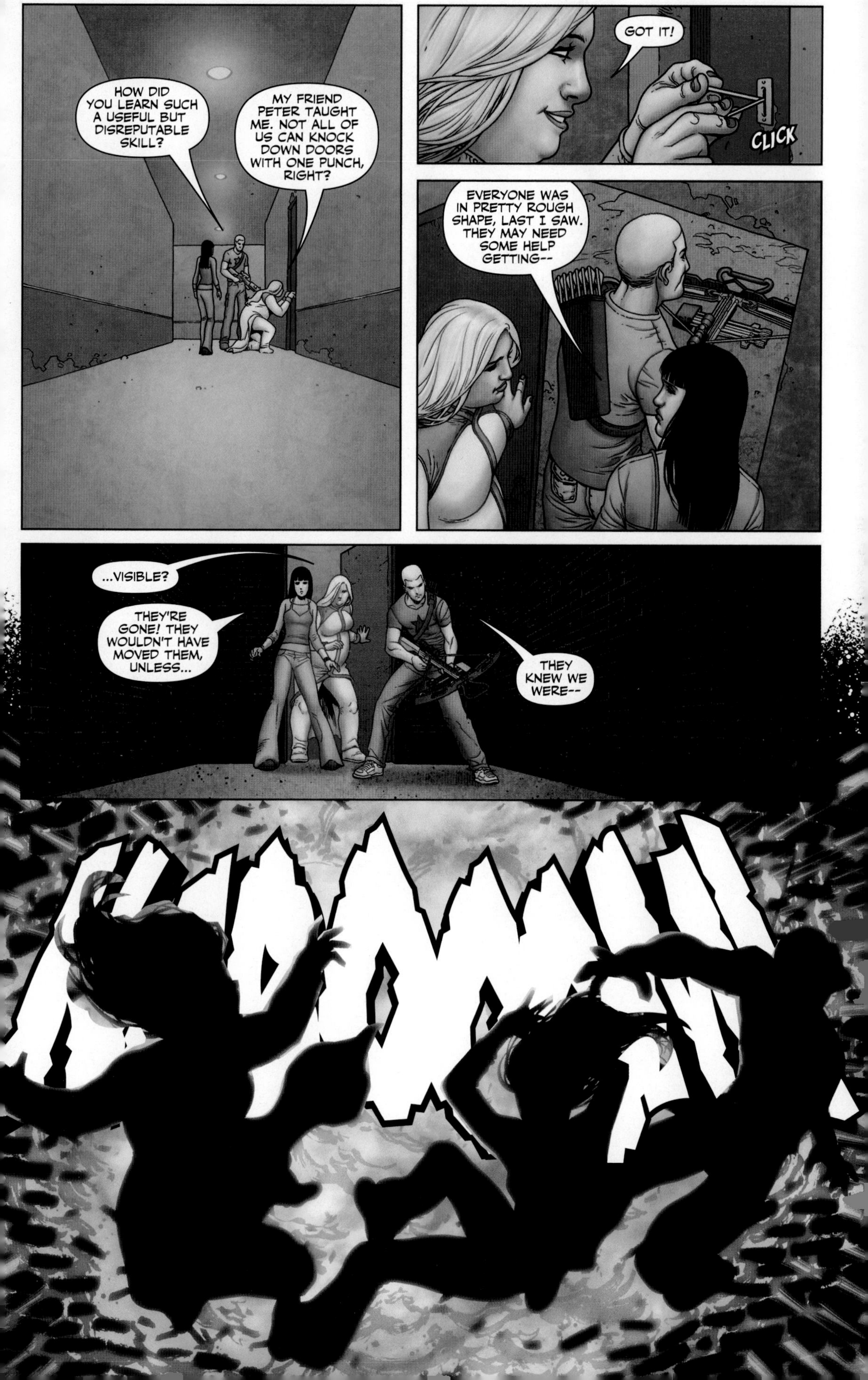
HOW DID YOU LEARN SUCH A USEFUL BUT DISREPUTABLE SKILL?
MY FRIEND PETER TAUGHT ME. NOT ALL OF US CAN KNOCK DOWN DOORS WITH ONE PUNCH, RIGHT?
GOT IT!
CLICK
EVERYONE WAS IN PRETTY ROUGH SHAPE, LAST I SAW. THEY MAY NEED SOME HELP GETTING--
...VISIBLE?
THEY'RE GONE! THEY WOULDN'T HAVE MOVED THEM, UNLESS...
THEY KNEW WE WERE--

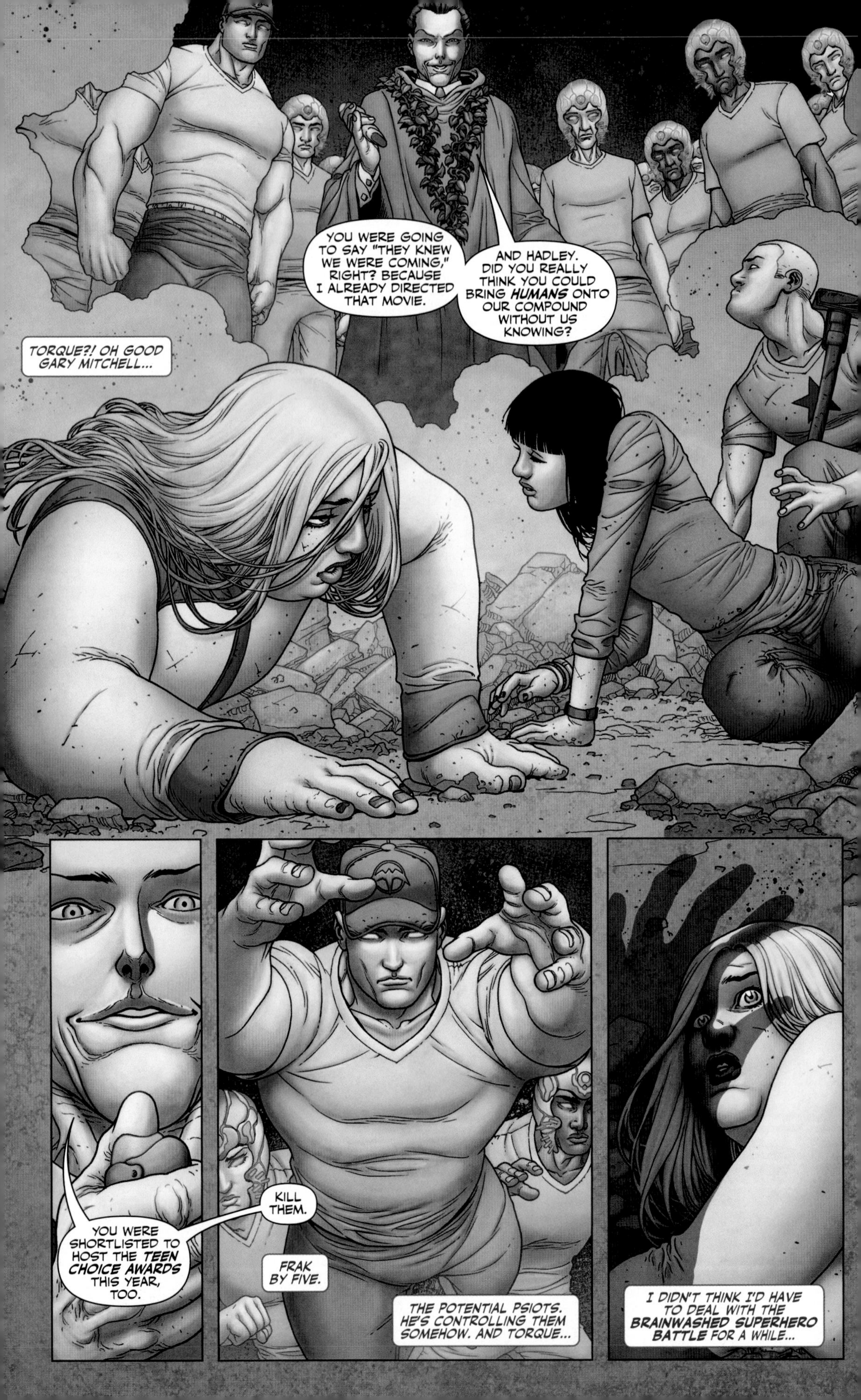
YOU WERE GOING TO SAY "THEY KNEW WE WERE COMING," RIGHT? BECAUSE I ALREADY DIRECTED THAT MOVIE.
AND HADLEY. DID YOU REALLY THINK YOU COULD BRING HUMANS ONTO OUR COMPOUND WITHOUT US KNOWING?
TORQUE?! OH GOOD GARY MITCHELL...
YOU WERE SHORTLISTED TO HOST THE TEEN CHOICE AWARDS THIS YEAR, TOO.
KILL THEM.
FRAK BY FIVE.
THE POTENTIAL PSIOTS. HE'S CONTROLLING THEM SOMEHOW. AND TORQUE...
I DIDN'T THINK I'D HAVE TO DEAL WITH THE BRAINWASHED SUPERHERO BATTLE FOR A WHILE...

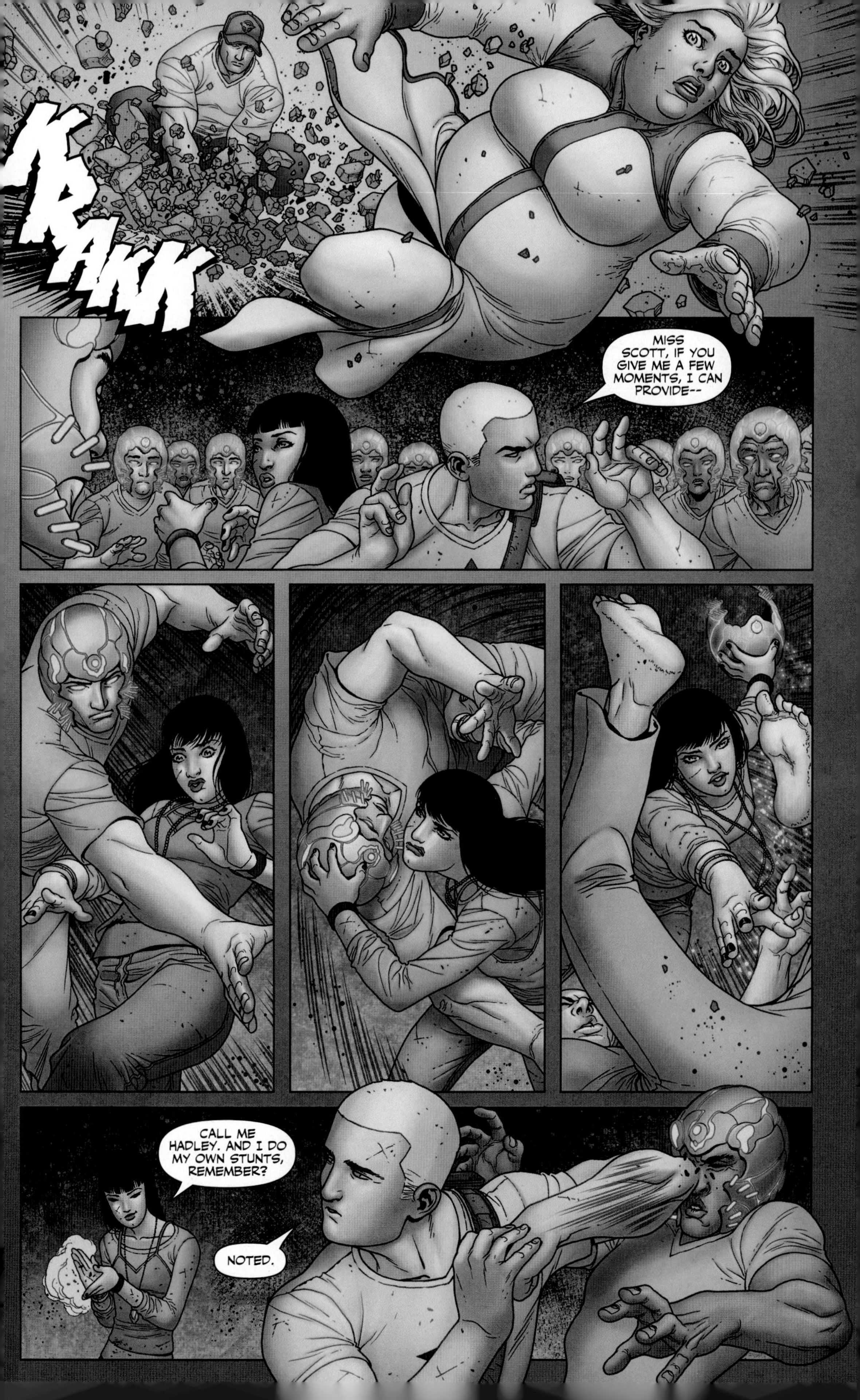
KRAKK
MISS SCOTT, IF YOU GIVE ME A FEW MOMENTS, I CAN PROVIDE--
CALL ME HADLEY. AND I DO MY OWN STUNTS, REMEMBER?
NOTED.

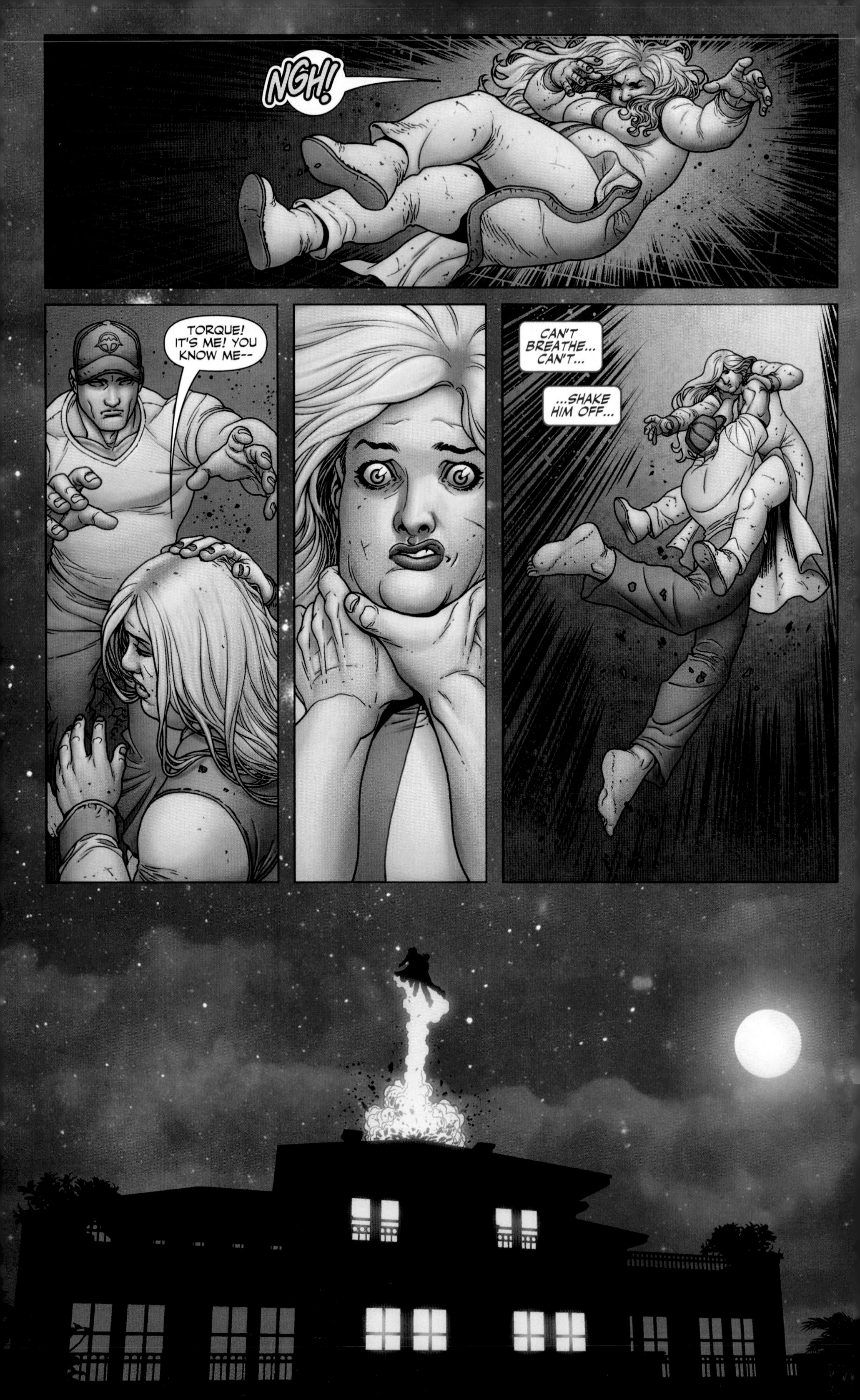
NGH!
TORQUE! IT'S ME! YOU KNOW ME--
CAN'T BREATHE... CAN'T...
...SHAKE HIM OFF...

GOTTA... SNAP OUT OF IT...

MIND CONTROL DEVICE. IF I CAN JUST...

SAW THE REAL HIM WHEN...WE WERE TOGETHER...

NOT JUST... THE SHELL... EVERYONE ELSE SEES...

...REACH INSIDE HIS PSIOT PROJECTION...

...FIND THE REAL JOHN TORKELSON... IN THE ILLUSION...

...FIND THE REAL HIM...

LLY WO

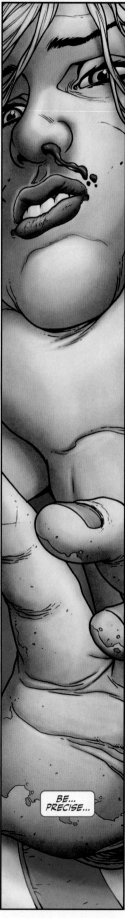

BE... PRECISE...

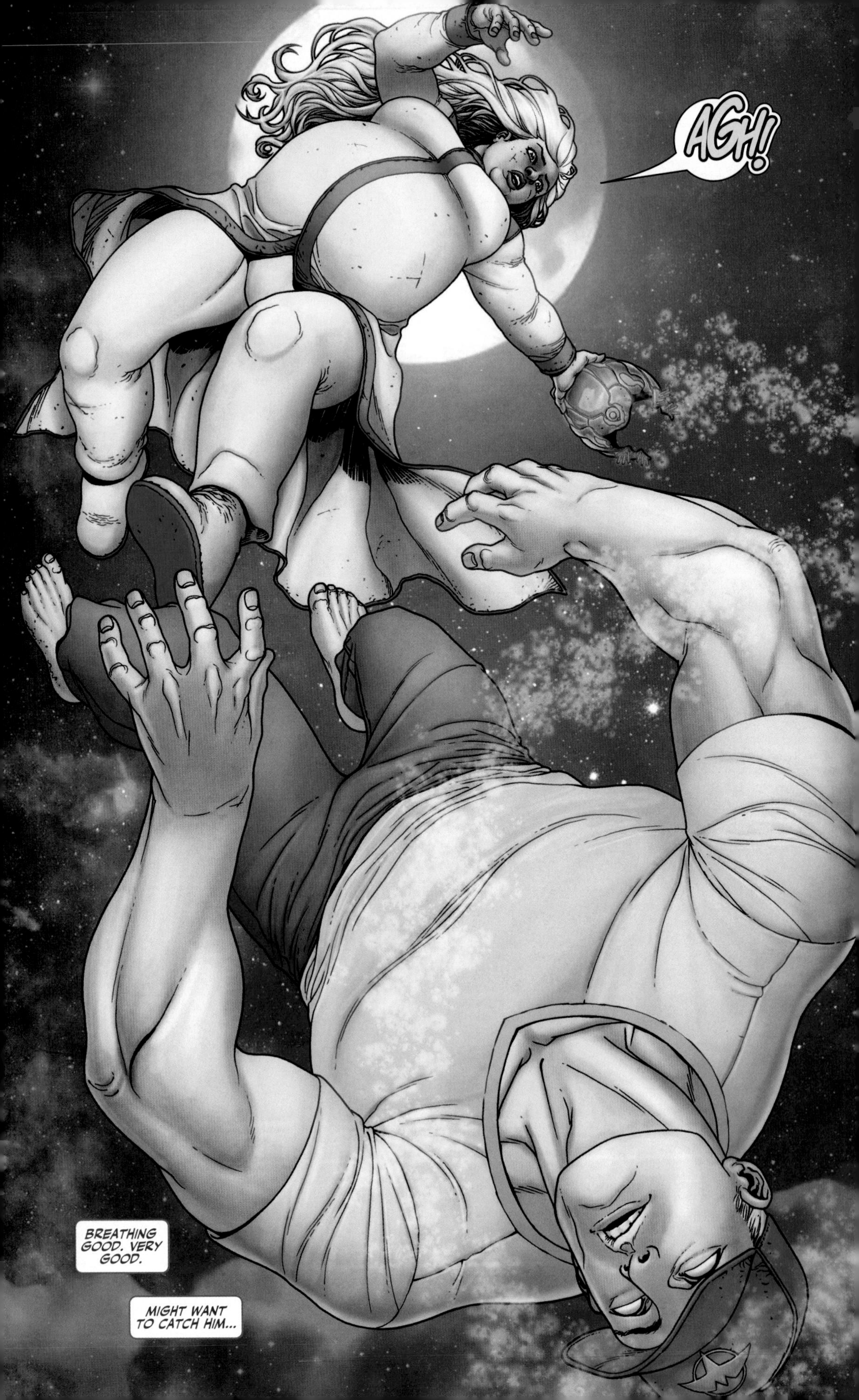
AGH!
BREATHING GOOD. VERY GOOD.
MIGHT WANT TO CATCH HIM...

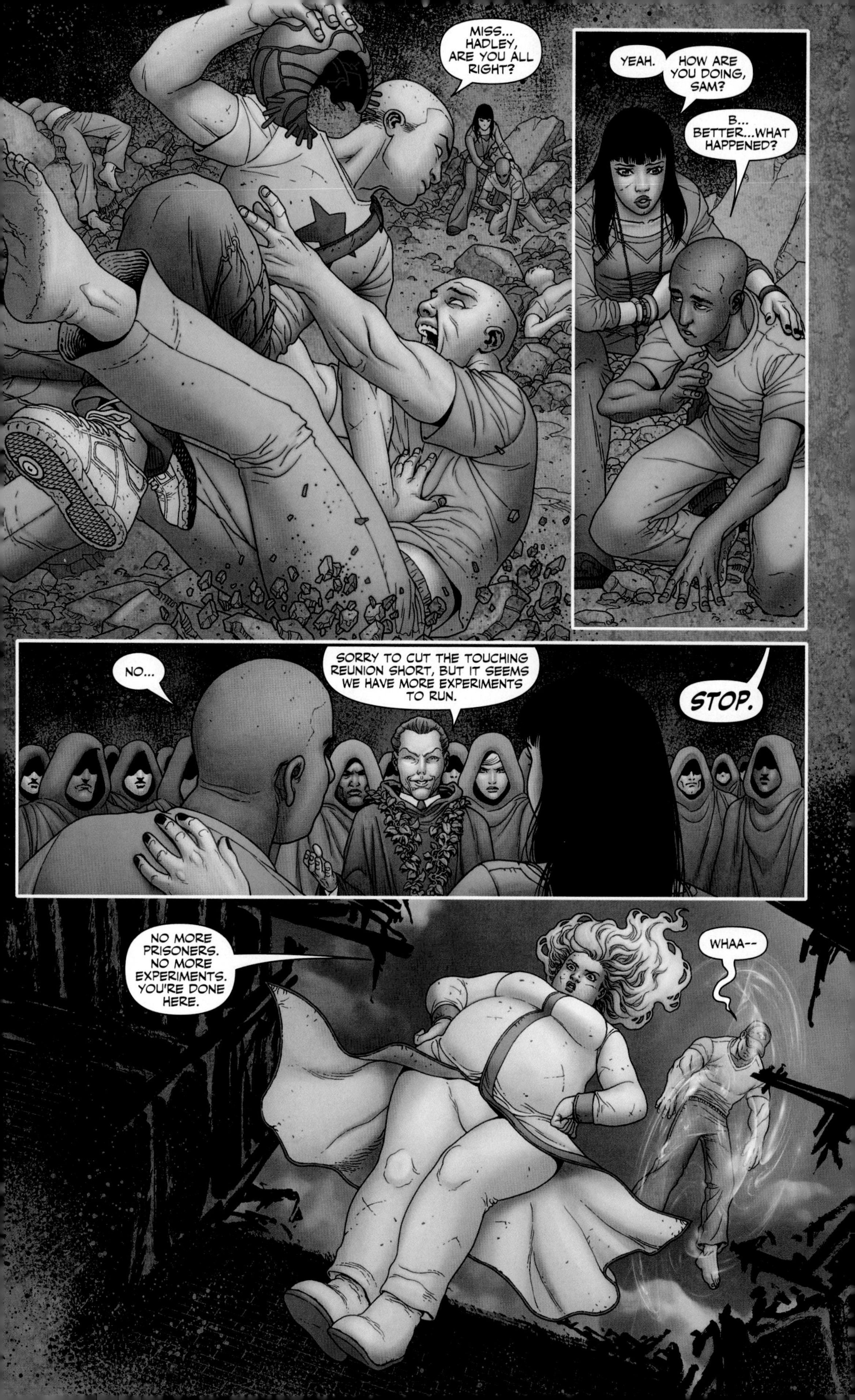
MISS... HADLEY, ARE YOU ALL RIGHT?
YEAH.
HOW ARE YOU DOING, SAM?
B... BETTER...WHAT HAPPENED?
NO...
SORRY TO CUT THE TOUCHING REUNION SHORT, BUT IT SEEMS WE HAVE MORE EXPERIMENTS TO RUN.
STOP.
NO MORE PRISONERS. NO MORE EXPERIMENTS. YOU'RE DONE HERE.
WHAA--

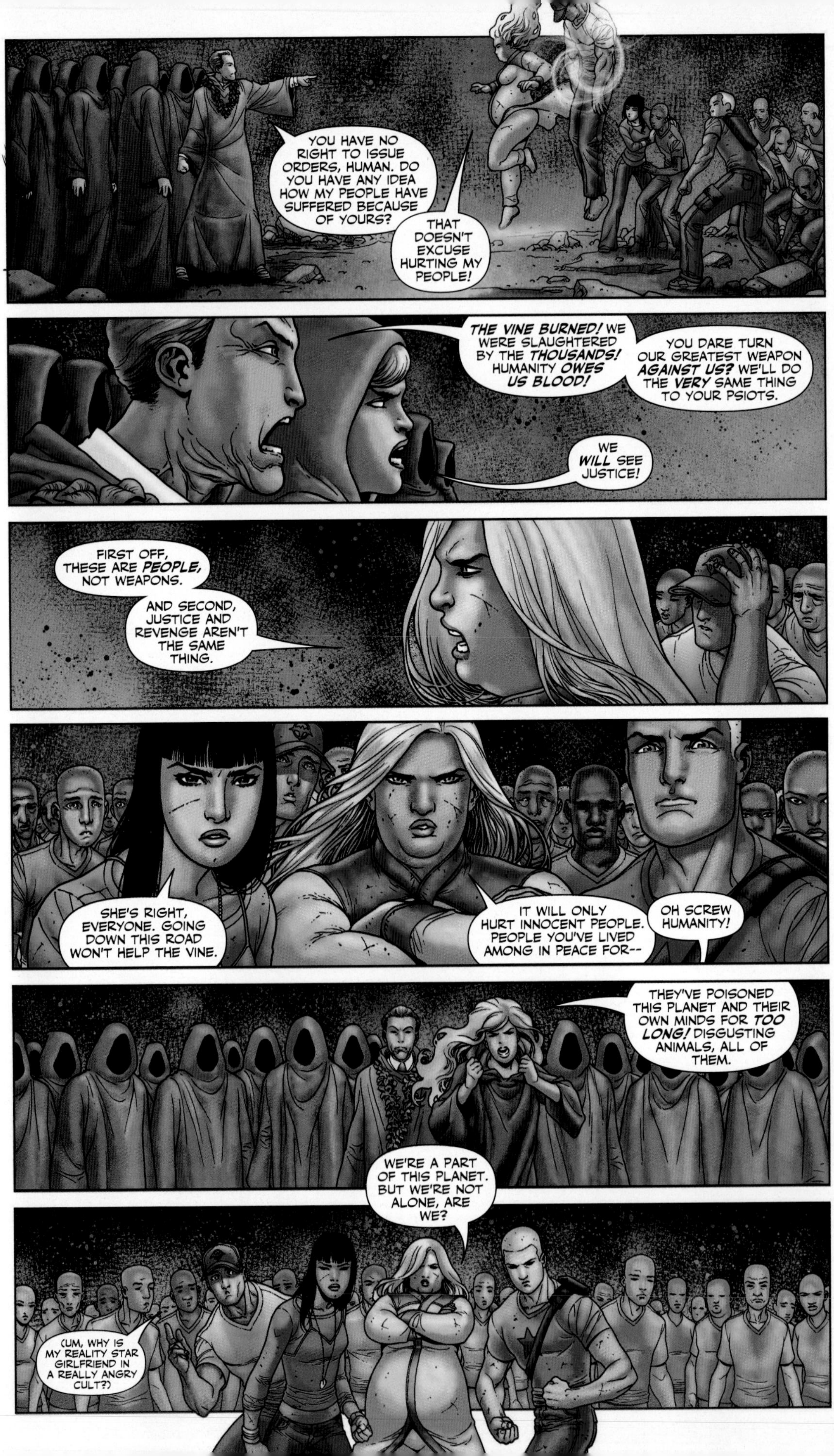

YOU HAVE NO RIGHT TO ISSUE ORDERS, HUMAN. DO YOU HAVE ANY IDEA HOW MY PEOPLE HAVE SUFFERED BECAUSE OF YOURS?
THAT DOESN'T EXCUSE HURTING MY PEOPLE!
THE VINE BURNED! WE WERE SLAUGHTERED BY THE THOUSANDS! HUMANITY OWES US BLOOD!
YOU DARE TURN OUR GREATEST WEAPON AGAINST US? WE'LL DO THE VERY SAME THING TO YOUR PSIOTS.
WE WILL SEE JUSTICE!
FIRST OFF, THESE ARE PEOPLE, NOT WEAPONS.
AND SECOND, JUSTICE AND REVENGE AREN'T THE SAME THING.
SHE'S RIGHT, EVERYONE. GOING DOWN THIS ROAD WON'T HELP THE VINE.
IT WILL ONLY HURT INNOCENT PEOPLE. PEOPLE YOU'VE LIVED AMONG IN PEACE FOR--
OH SCREW HUMANITY!
THEY'VE POISONED THIS PLANET AND THEIR OWN MINDS FOR TOO LONG! DISGUSTING ANIMALS, ALL OF THEM.
WE'RE A PART OF THIS PLANET. BUT WE'RE NOT ALONE, ARE WE?
(UM, WHY IS MY REALITY STAR GIRLFRIEND IN A REALLY ANGRY CULT?)

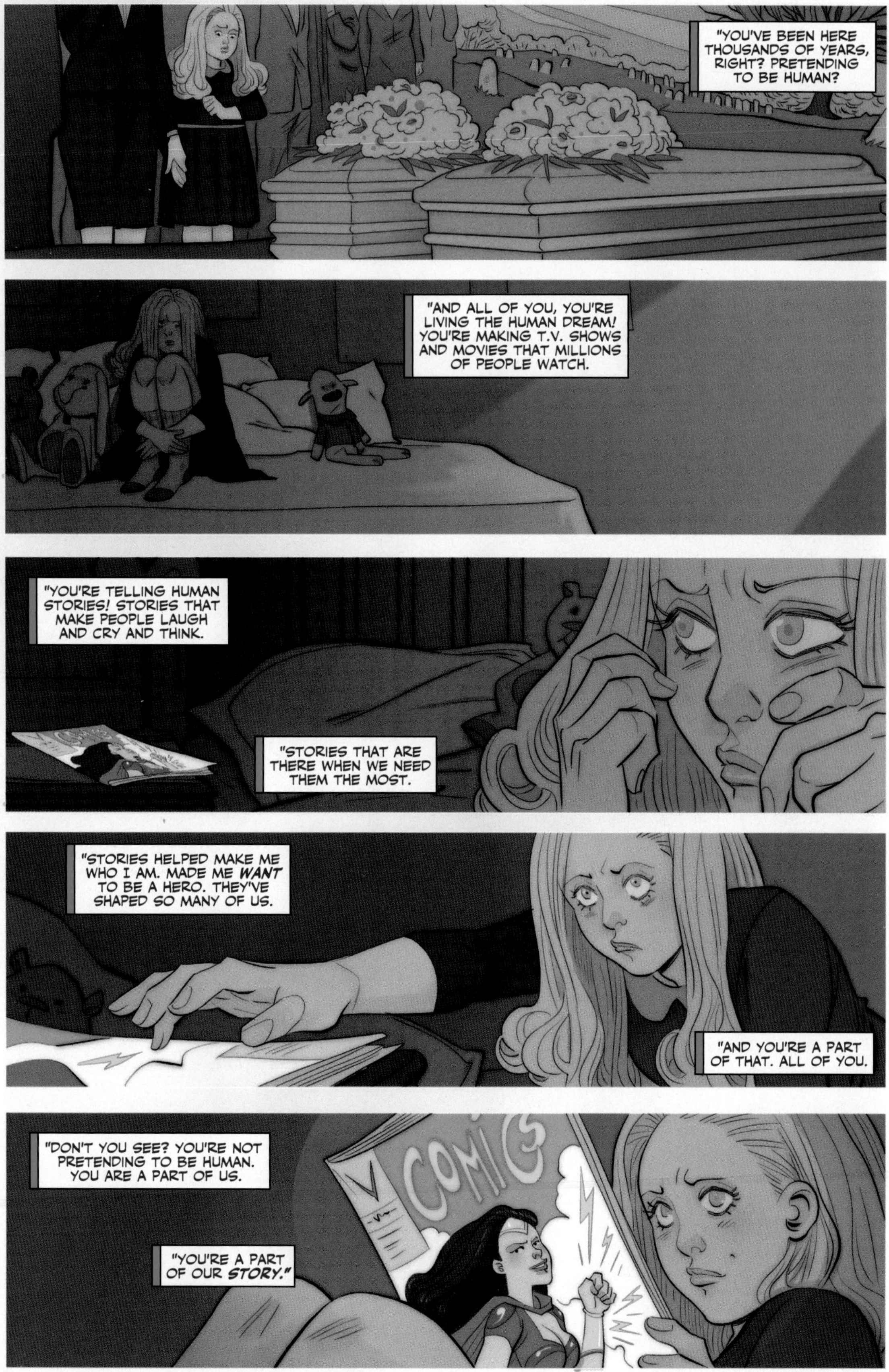
"YOU'VE BEEN HERE THOUSANDS OF YEARS, RIGHT? PRETENDING TO BE HUMAN?
"AND ALL OF YOU, YOU'RE LIVING THE HUMAN DREAM! YOU'RE MAKING T.V. SHOWS AND MOVIES THAT MILLIONS OF PEOPLE WATCH.
"YOU'RE TELLING HUMAN STORIES! STORIES THAT MAKE PEOPLE LAUGH AND CRY AND THINK.
"STORIES THAT ARE THERE WHEN WE NEED THEM THE MOST.
"STORIES HELPED MAKE ME WHO I AM. MADE ME *WANT* TO BE A HERO. THEY'VE SHAPED SO MANY OF US.
"AND YOU'RE A PART OF THAT. ALL OF YOU.
"DON'T YOU SEE? YOU'RE NOT PRETENDING TO BE HUMAN. YOU ARE A PART OF US.
COMICS
"YOU'RE A PART OF OUR ***STORY.***"

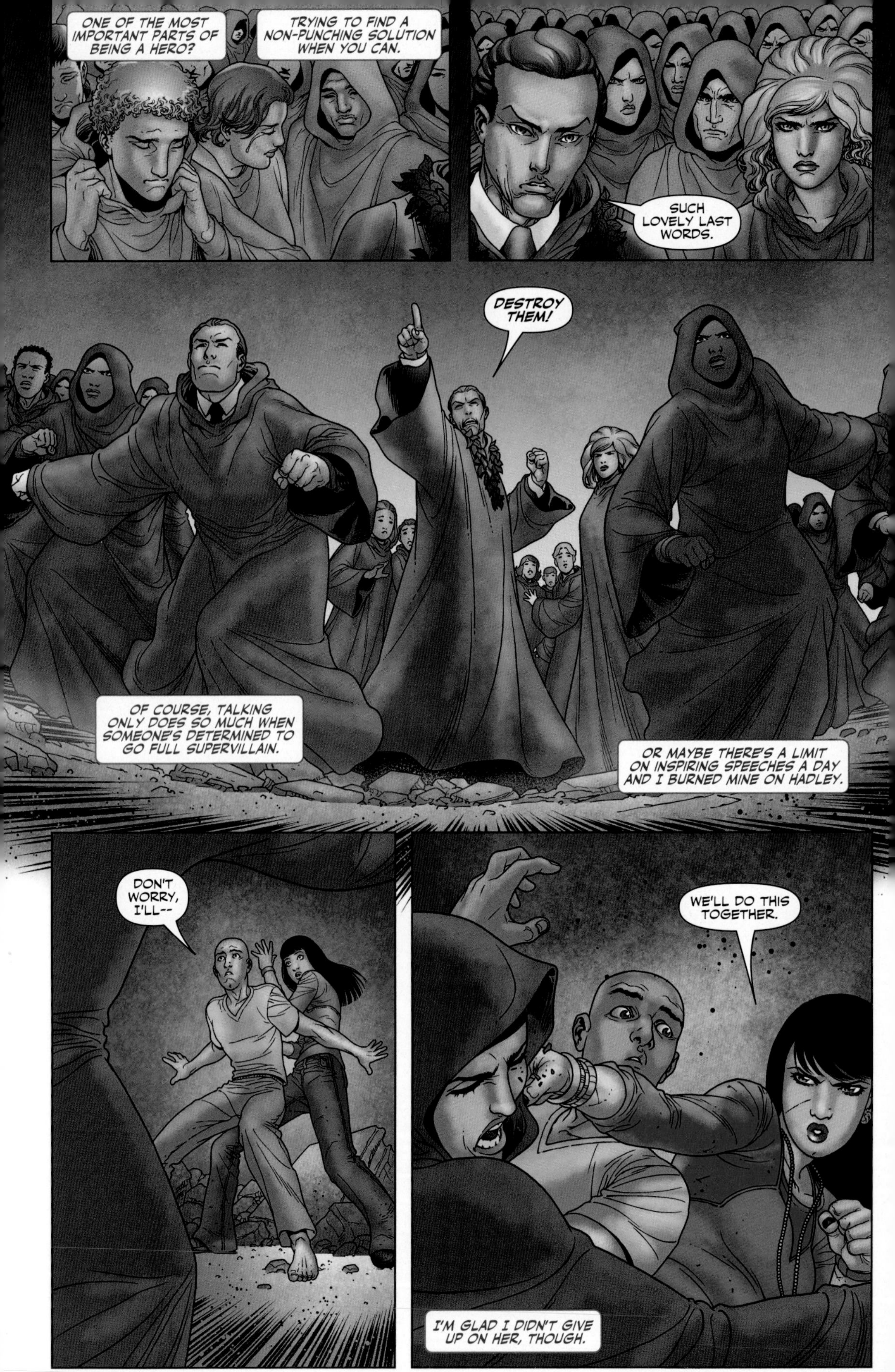
ONE OF THE MOST IMPORTANT PARTS OF BEING A HERO?
TRYING TO FIND A NON-PUNCHING SOLUTION WHEN YOU CAN.
SUCH LOVELY LAST WORDS.
DESTROY THEM!
OF COURSE, TALKING ONLY DOES SO MUCH WHEN SOMEONE'S DETERMINED TO GO FULL SUPERVILLAIN.
OR MAYBE THERE'S A LIMIT ON INSPIRING SPEECHES A DAY AND I BURNED MINE ON HADLEY.
DON'T WORRY, I'LL--
WE'LL DO THIS TOGETHER.
I'M GLAD I DIDN'T GIVE UP ON HER, THOUGH.

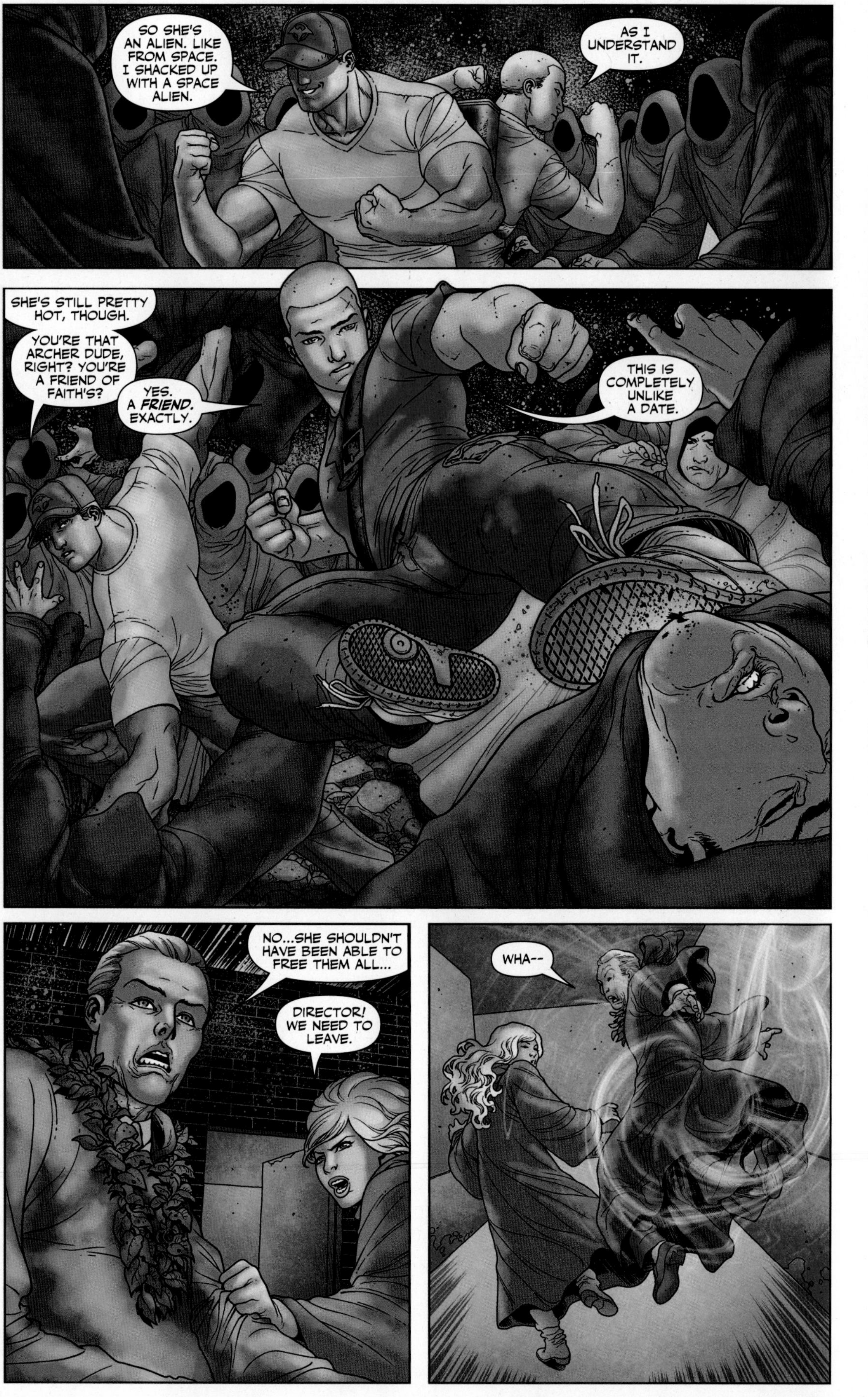
SO SHE'S AN ALIEN. LIKE FROM SPACE. I SHACKED UP WITH A SPACE ALIEN.
AS I UNDERSTAND IT.
SHE'S STILL PRETTY HOT, THOUGH.
YOU'RE THAT ARCHER DUDE, RIGHT? YOU'RE A FRIEND OF FAITH'S?
YES. A FRIEND. EXACTLY.
THIS IS COMPLETELY UNLIKE A DATE.
NO...SHE SHOULDN'T HAVE BEEN ABLE TO FREE THEM ALL...
DIRECTOR! WE NEED TO LEAVE.
WHA--

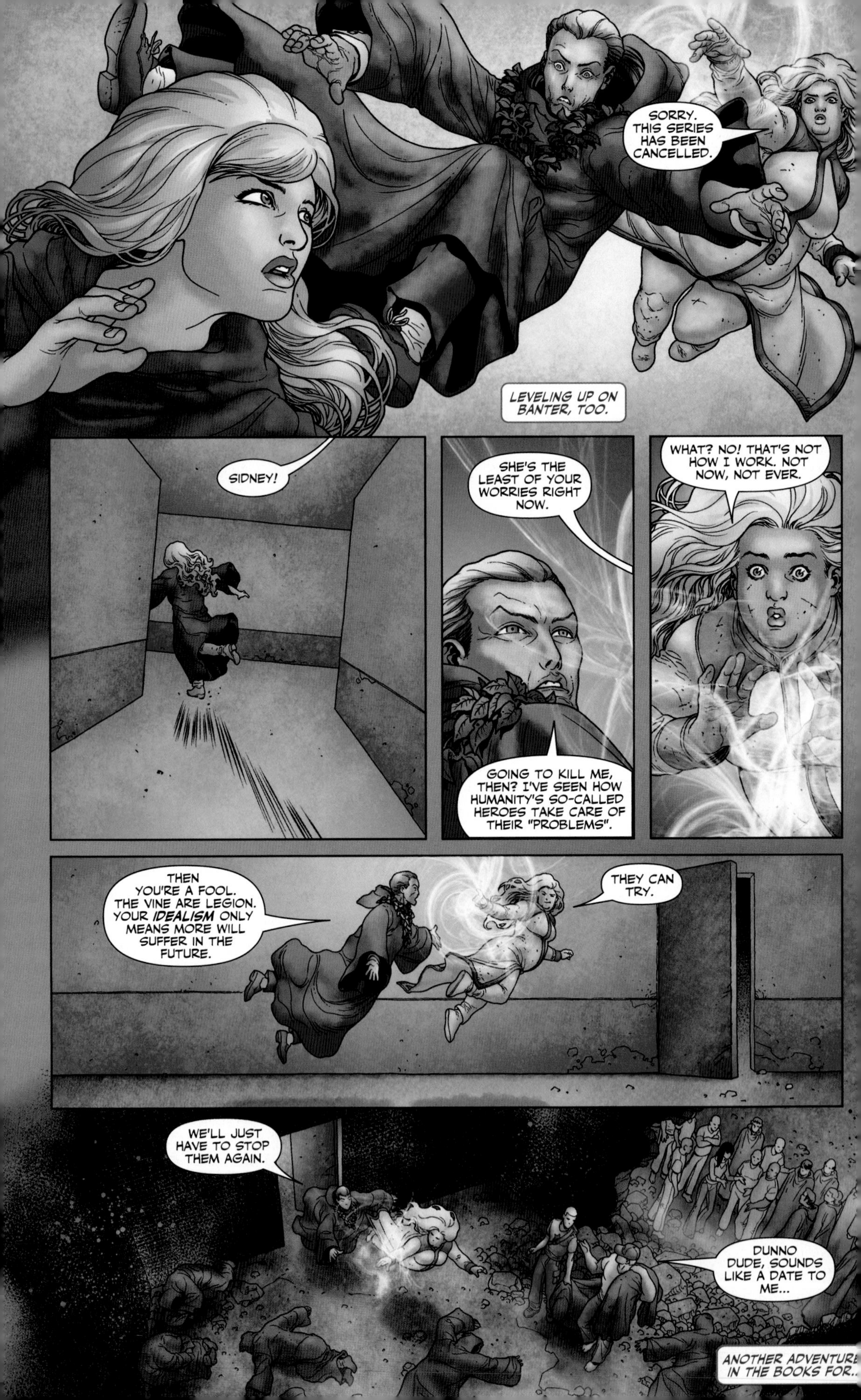
SORRY. THIS SERIES HAS BEEN CANCELLED.
LEVELING UP ON BANTER, TOO.
SIDNEY!
SHE'S THE LEAST OF YOUR WORRIES RIGHT NOW.
GOING TO KILL ME, THEN? I'VE SEEN HOW HUMANITY'S SO-CALLED HEROES TAKE CARE OF THEIR "PROBLEMS".
WHAT? NO! THAT'S NOT HOW I WORK. NOT NOW, NOT EVER.
THEN YOU'RE A FOOL. THE VINE ARE LEGION. YOUR IDEALISM ONLY MEANS MORE WILL SUFFER IN THE FUTURE.
THEY CAN TRY.
WE'LL JUST HAVE TO STOP THEM AGAIN.
DUNNO DUDE, SOUNDS LIKE A DATE TO ME...
ANOTHER ADVENTURE IN THE BOOKS FOR...

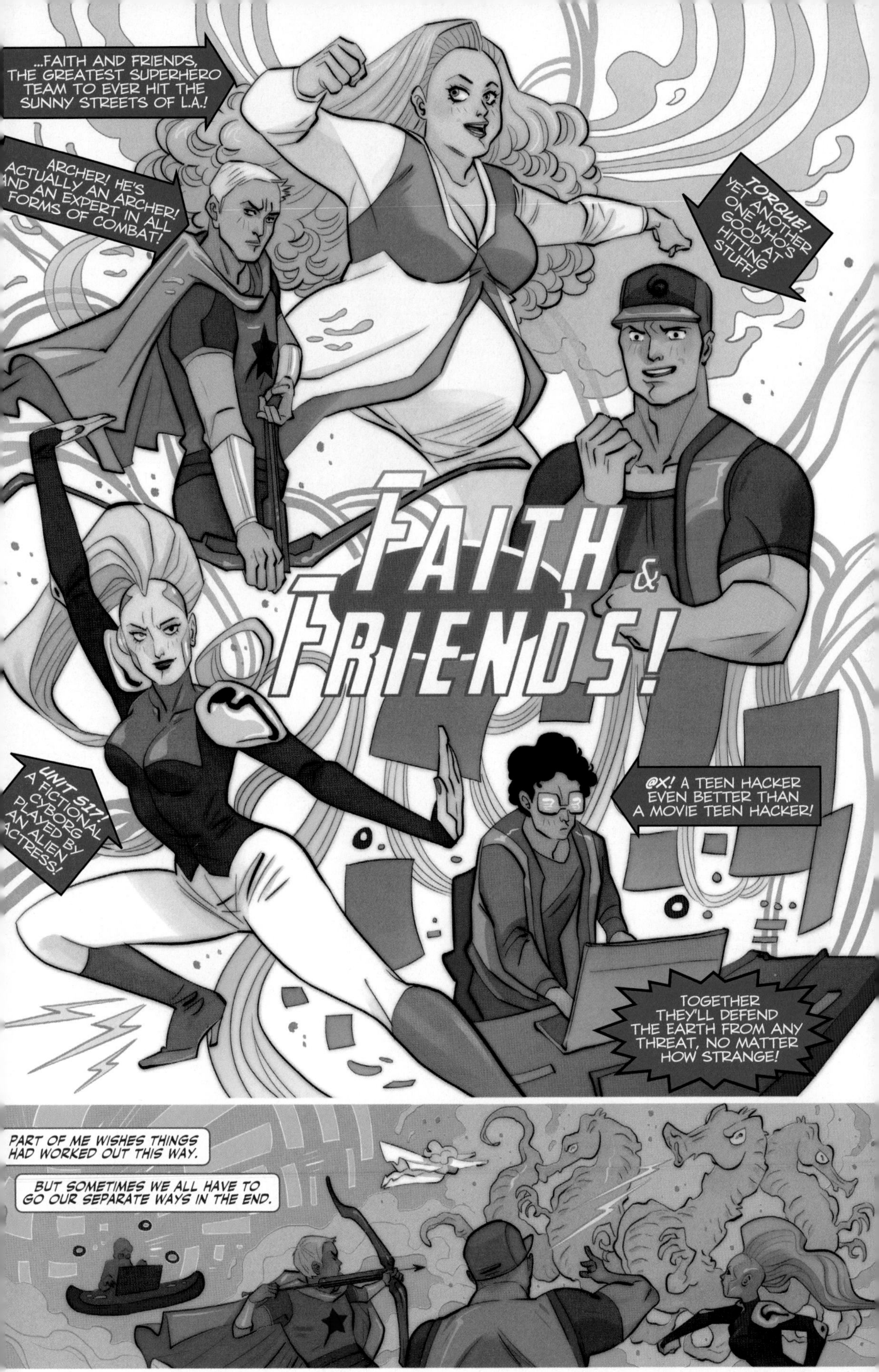
...FAITH AND FRIENDS, THE GREATEST SUPERHERO TEAM TO EVER HIT THE SUNNY STREETS OF L.A.!
ARCHER! HE'S ACTUALLY AN ARCHER! AND AN EXPERT IN ALL FORMS OF COMBAT!
TORQUE! YET ANOTHER ONE WHO'S GOOD AT HITTING STUFF!
FAITH & FRIENDS!
UNIT 517! A FICTIONAL CYBORG PLAYED BY AN ALIEN ACTRESS!
@X! A TEEN HACKER EVEN BETTER THAN A MOVIE TEEN HACKER!
TOGETHER THEY'LL DEFEND THE EARTH FROM ANY THREAT, NO MATTER HOW STRANGE!
PART OF ME WISHES THINGS HAD WORKED OUT THIS WAY.
BUT SOMETIMES WE ALL HAVE TO GO OUR SEPARATE WAYS IN THE END.

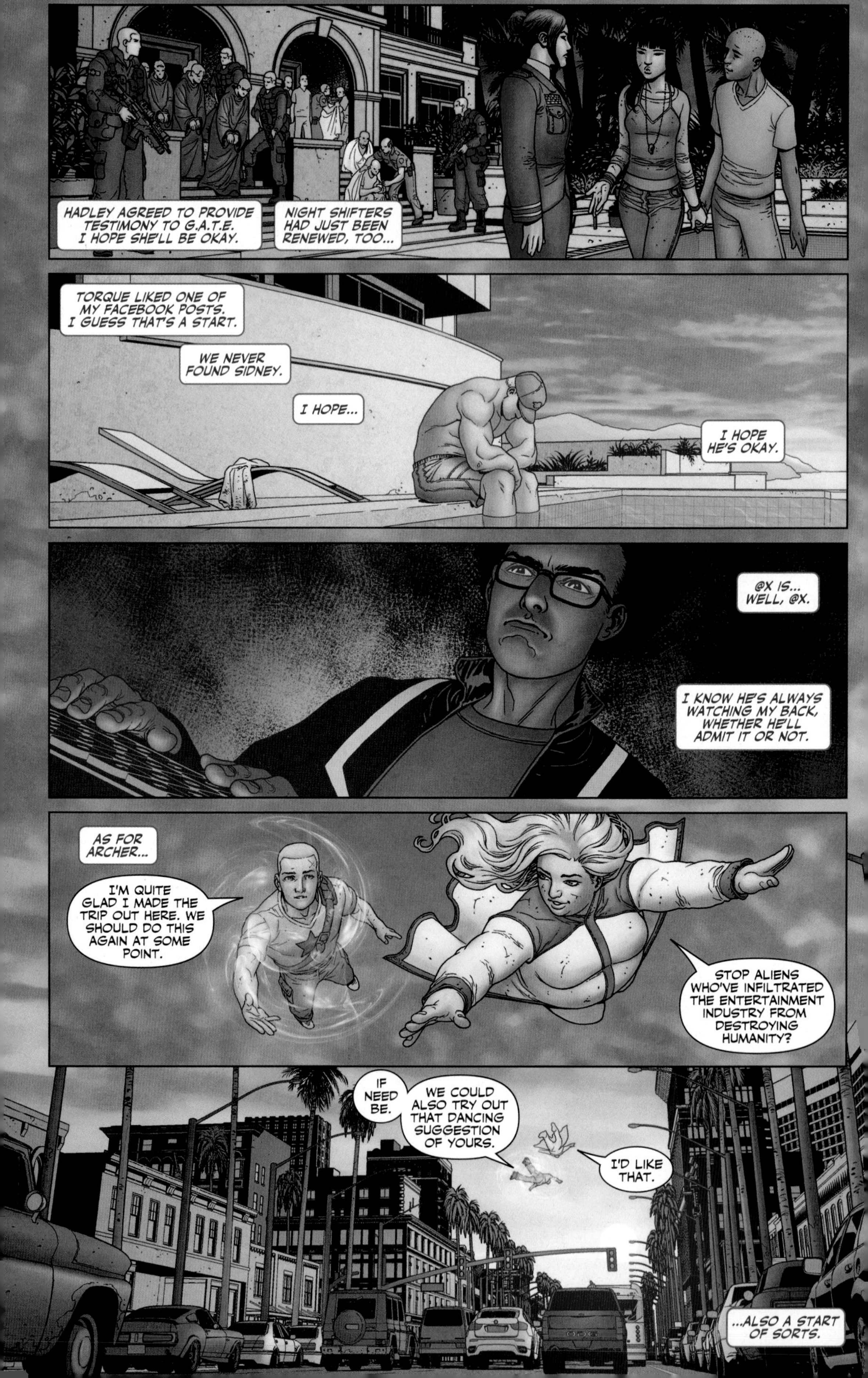
HADLEY AGREED TO PROVIDE TESTIMONY TO G.A.T.E. I HOPE SHE'LL BE OKAY.
NIGHT SHIFTERS HAD JUST BEEN RENEWED, TOO...
TORQUE LIKED ONE OF MY FACEBOOK POSTS. I GUESS THAT'S A START.
WE NEVER FOUND SIDNEY.
I HOPE...
I HOPE HE'S OKAY.
@X IS... WELL, @X.
I KNOW HE'S ALWAYS WATCHING MY BACK, WHETHER HE'LL ADMIT IT OR NOT.
AS FOR ARCHER...
I'M QUITE GLAD I MADE THE TRIP OUT HERE. WE SHOULD DO THIS AGAIN AT SOME POINT.
STOP ALIENS WHO'VE INFILTRATED THE ENTERTAINMENT INDUSTRY FROM DESTROYING HUMANITY?
IF NEED BE.
WE COULD ALSO TRY OUT THAT DANCING SUGGESTION OF YOURS.
I'D LIKE THAT.
...ALSO A START OF SORTS.

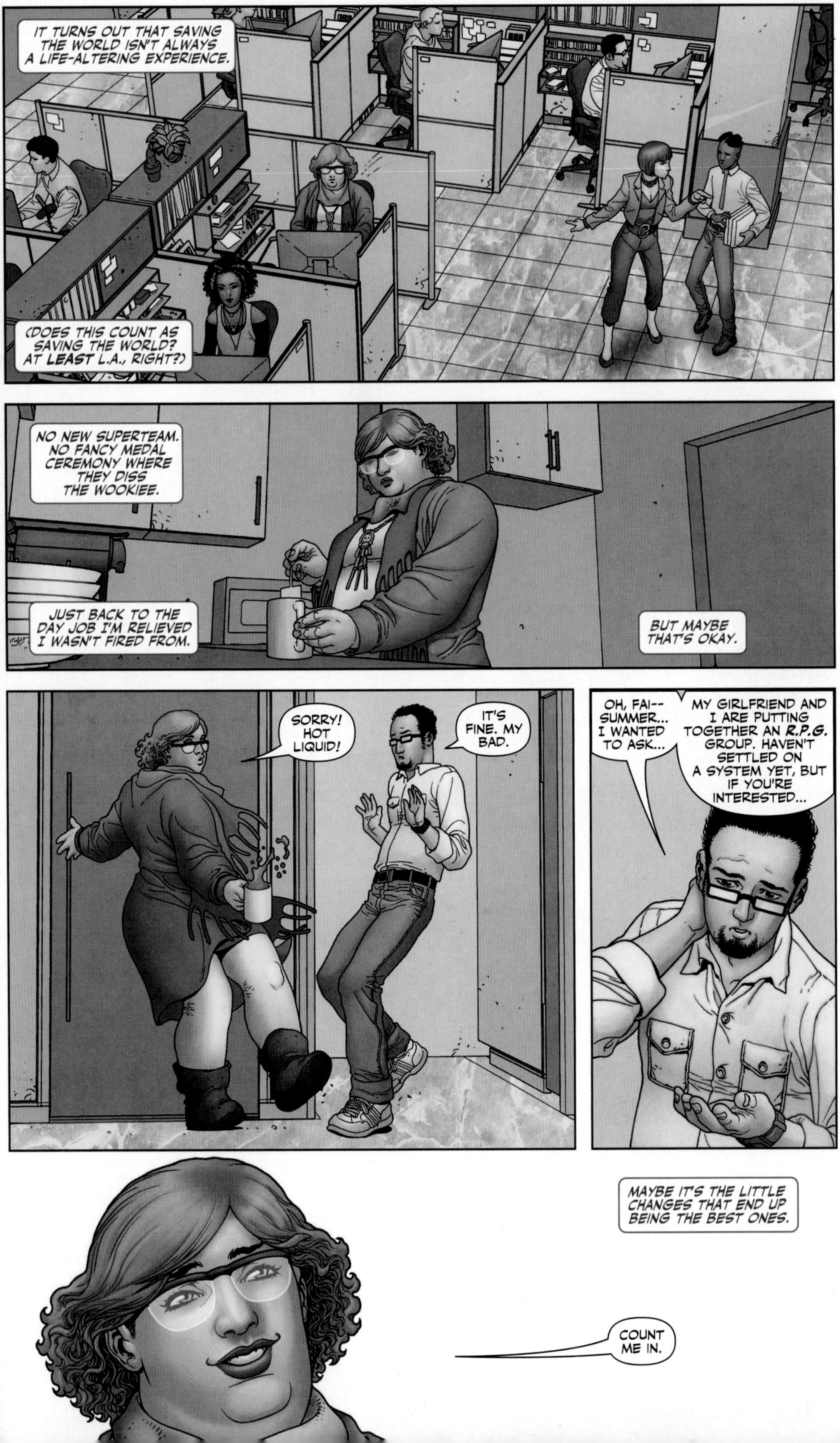
IT TURNS OUT THAT SAVING THE WORLD ISN'T ALWAYS A LIFE-ALTERING EXPERIENCE.
(DOES THIS COUNT AS SAVING THE WORLD? AT LEAST L.A., RIGHT?)
NO NEW SUPERTEAM. NO FANCY MEDAL CEREMONY WHERE THEY DISS THE WOOKIEE.
JUST BACK TO THE DAY JOB I'M RELIEVED I WASN'T FIRED FROM.
BUT MAYBE THAT'S OKAY.
SORRY! HOT LIQUID!
IT'S FINE. MY BAD.
OH, FAI-- SUMMER... I WANTED TO ASK...
MY GIRLFRIEND AND I ARE PUTTING TOGETHER AN R.P.G. GROUP. HAVEN'T SETTLED ON A SYSTEM YET, BUT IF YOU'RE INTERESTED...
MAYBE IT'S THE LITTLE CHANGES THAT END UP BEING THE BEST ONES.
COUNT ME IN.

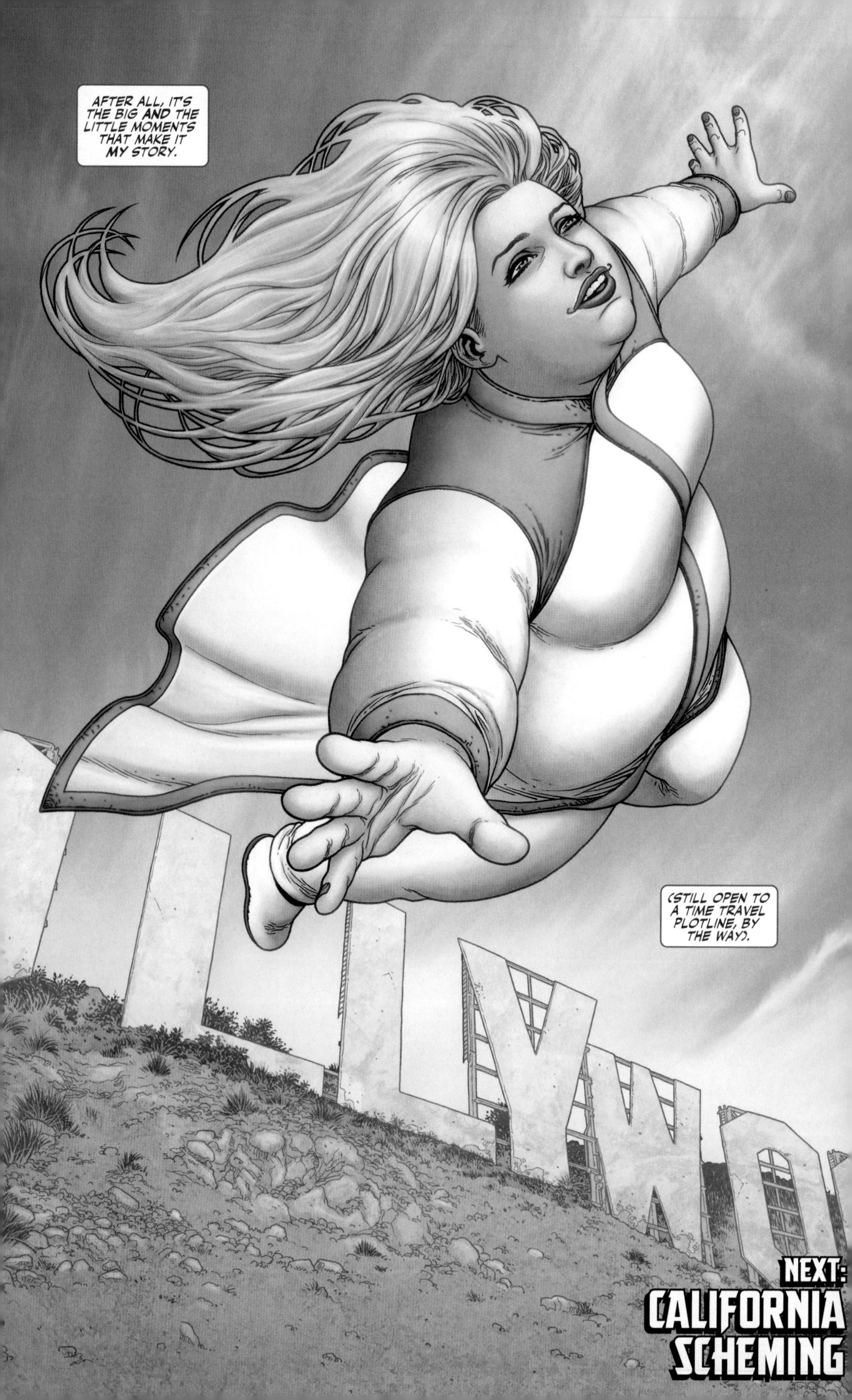
AFTER ALL, IT'S THE BIG AND THE LITTLE MOMENTS THAT MAKE IT MY STORY.
(STILL OPEN TO A TIME TRAVEL PLOTLINE, BY THE WAY).
NEXT:
CALIFORNIA SCHEMING

GALLERY

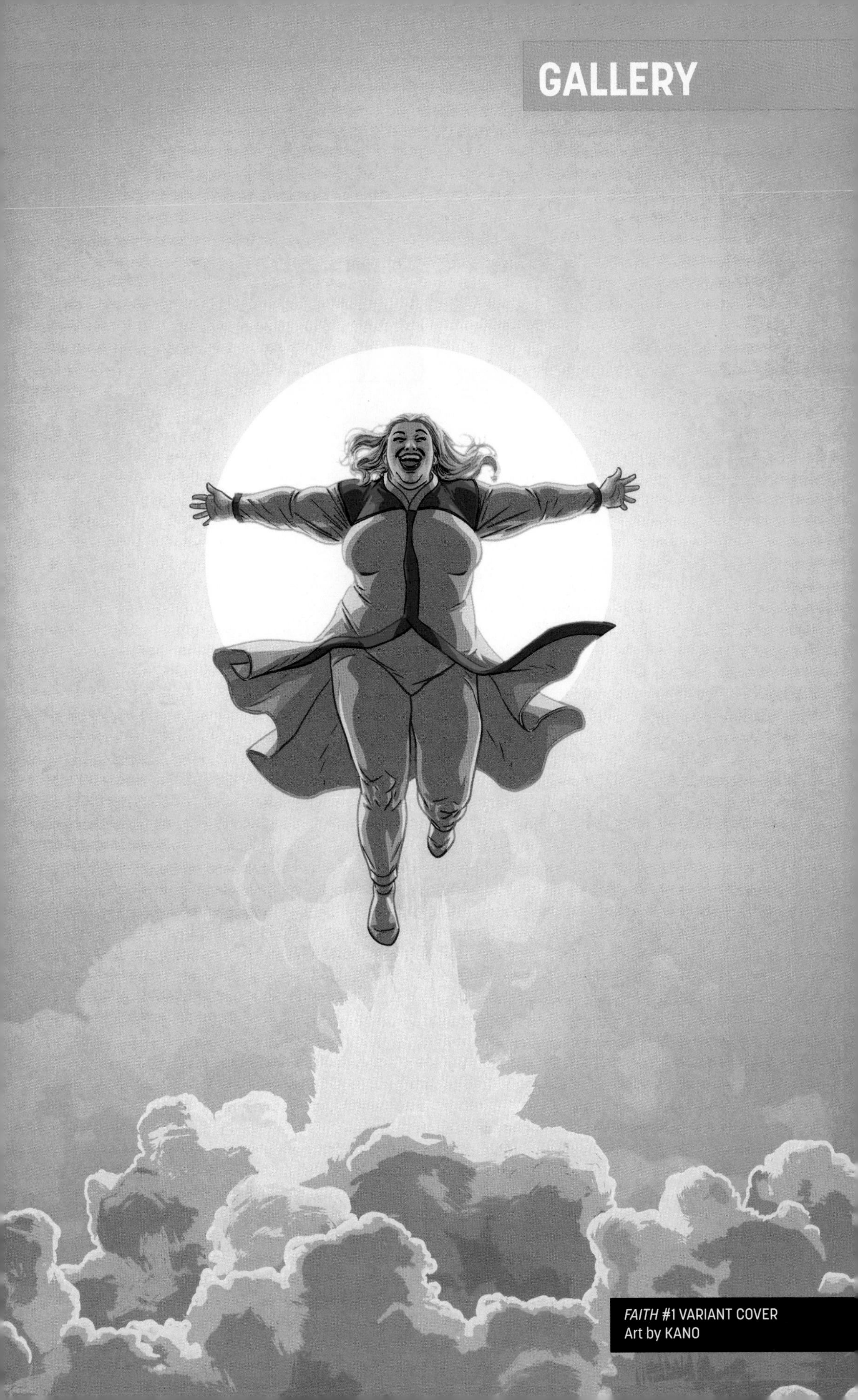

FAITH #1 VARIANT COVER
Art by KANO

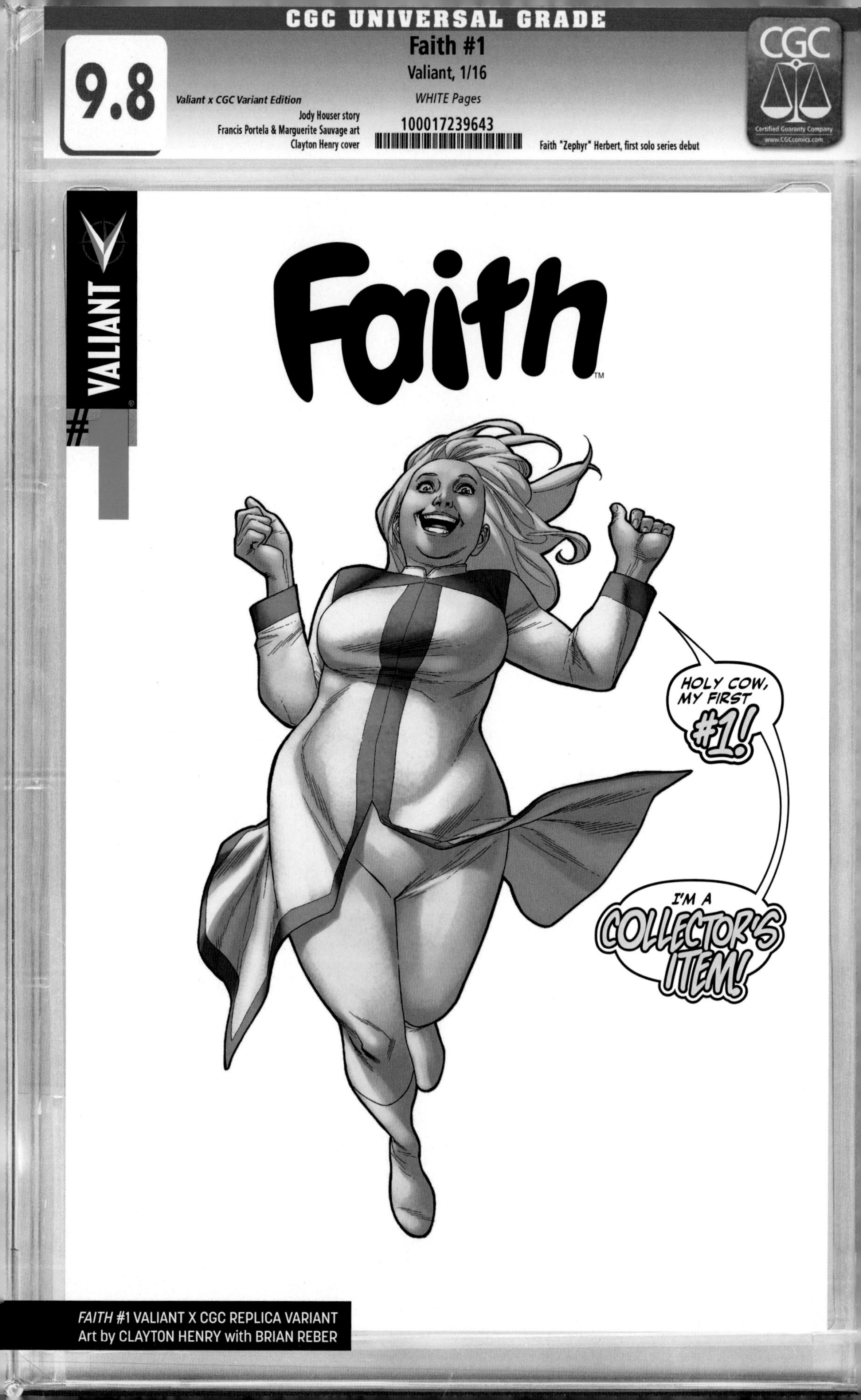
CGC UNIVERSAL GRADE
9.8
Faith #1
Valiant, 1/16
WHITE Pages
Valiant x CGC Variant Edition
Jody Houser story
Francis Portela & Marguerite Sauvage art
Clayton Henry cover
100017239643
Faith "Zephyr" Herbert, first solo series debut
CGC
Certified Guaranty Company
www.CGCcomics.com
VALIANT
#1
Faith™
HOLY COW, MY FIRST #1!
I'M A COLLECTOR'S ITEM!

FAITH #1 VALIANT X CGC REPLICA VARIANT
Art by CLAYTON HENRY with BRIAN REBER

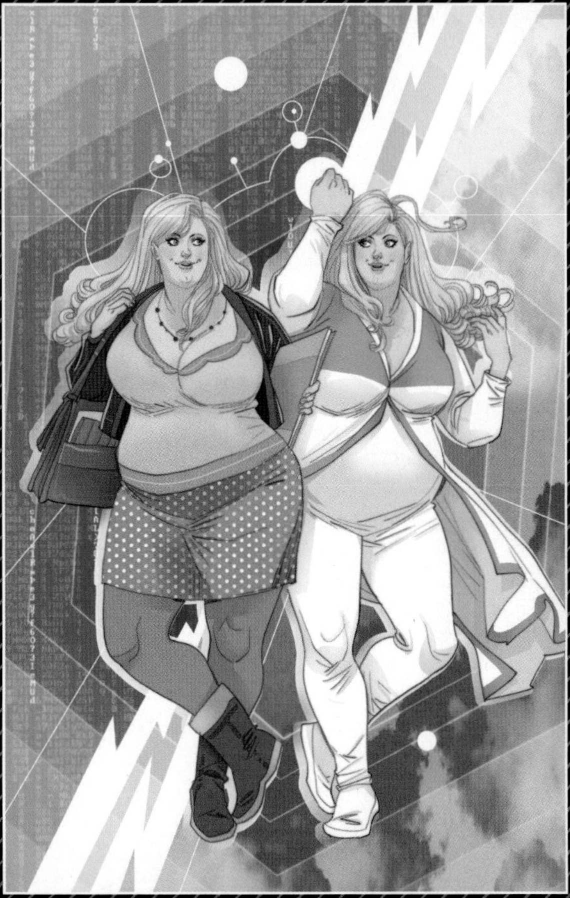

FAITH #1 COVER B
Art by MARGUERITE SAUVAGE

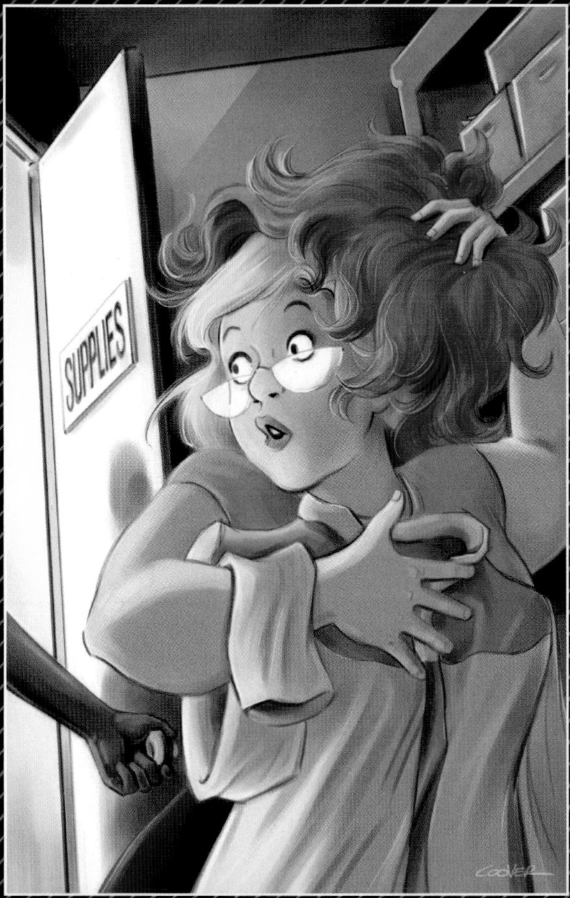
SUPPLIES
COOVER

FAITH #2 VARIANT COVER
Art by COLLEEN COOVER

FAITH #3 COVER B
Art by EMANUELA LUPACCHINO
with ULISES ARREOLA

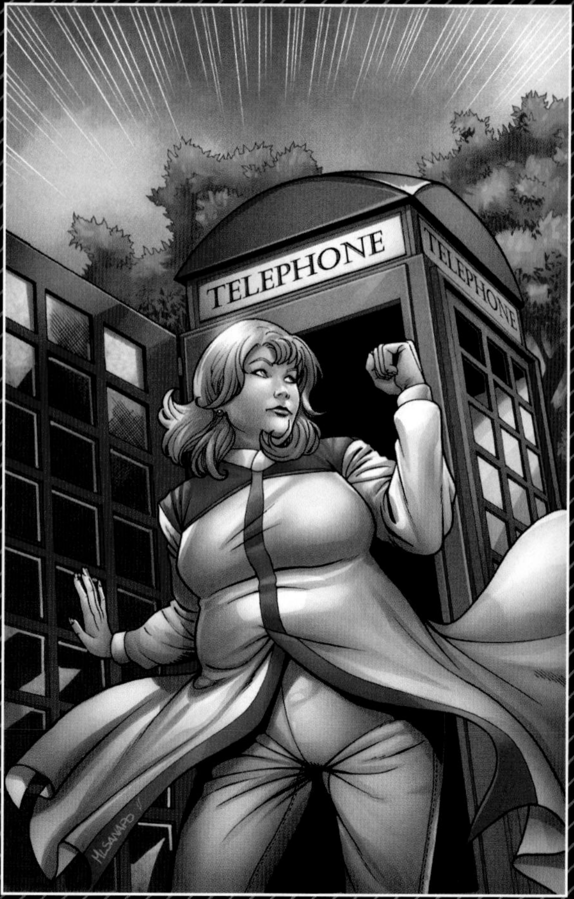
TELEPHONE
TELEPHONE

FAITH #4 COVER C
Art by CLAYTON HENRY with BRIAN REBER

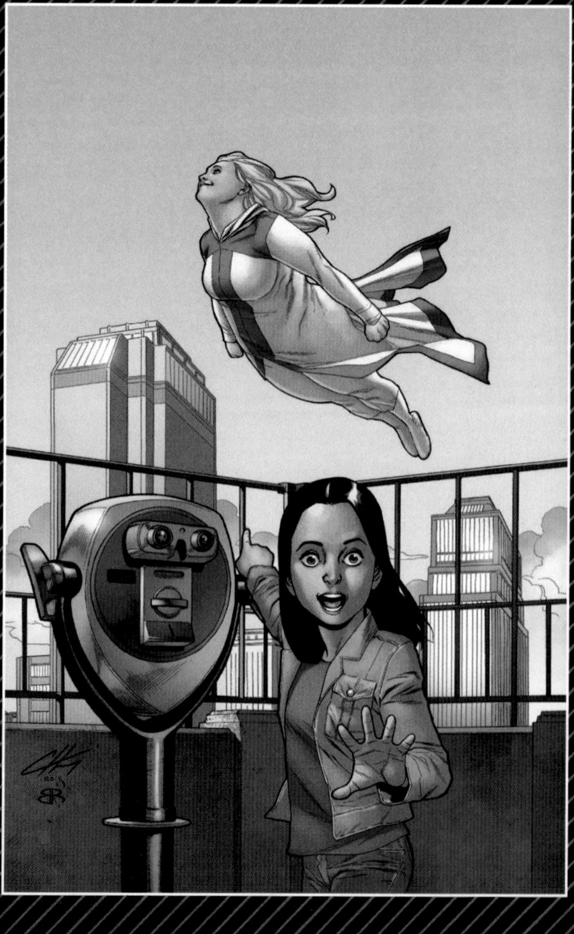

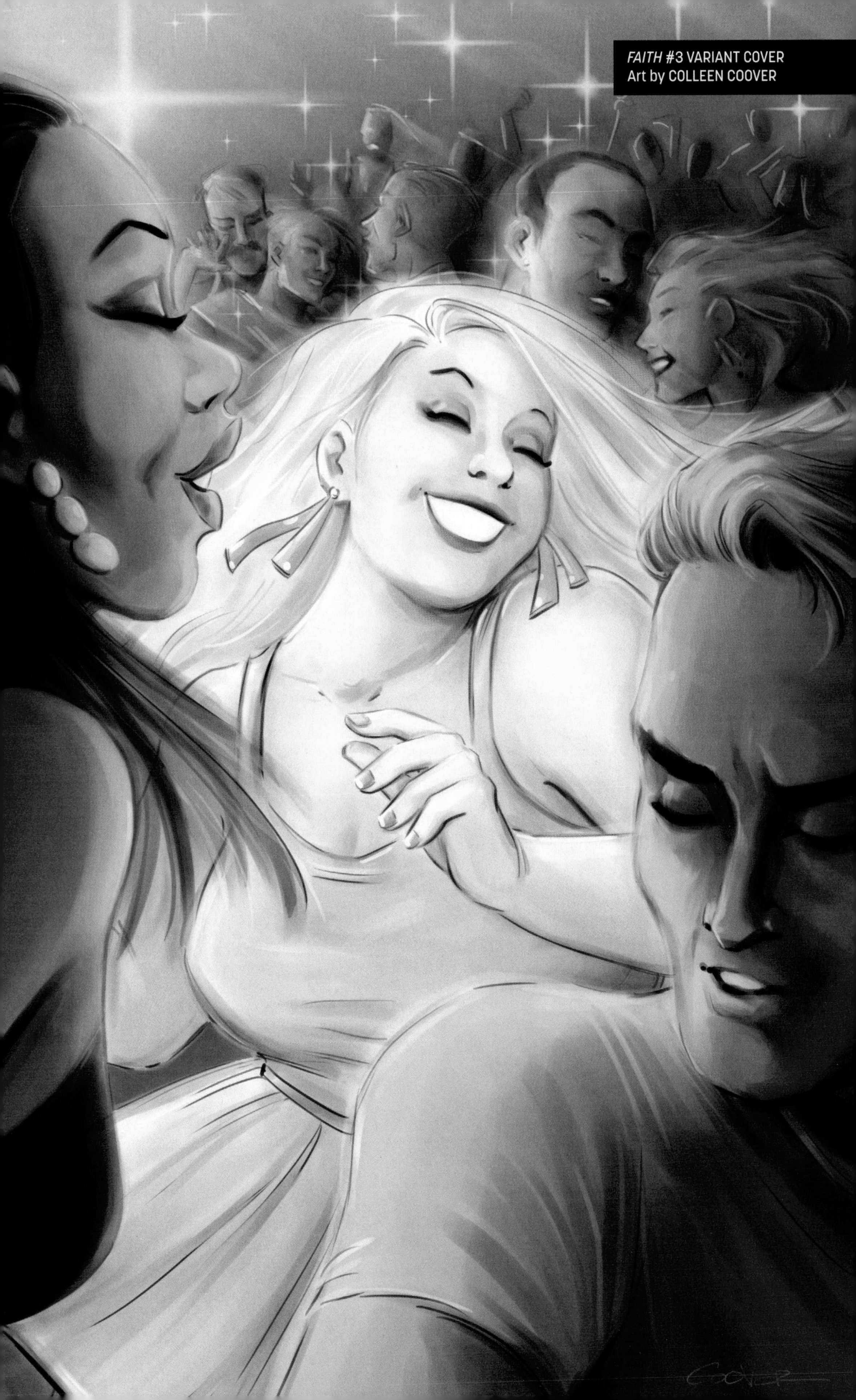

FAITH #3 VARIANT COVER
Art by COLLEEN COOVER

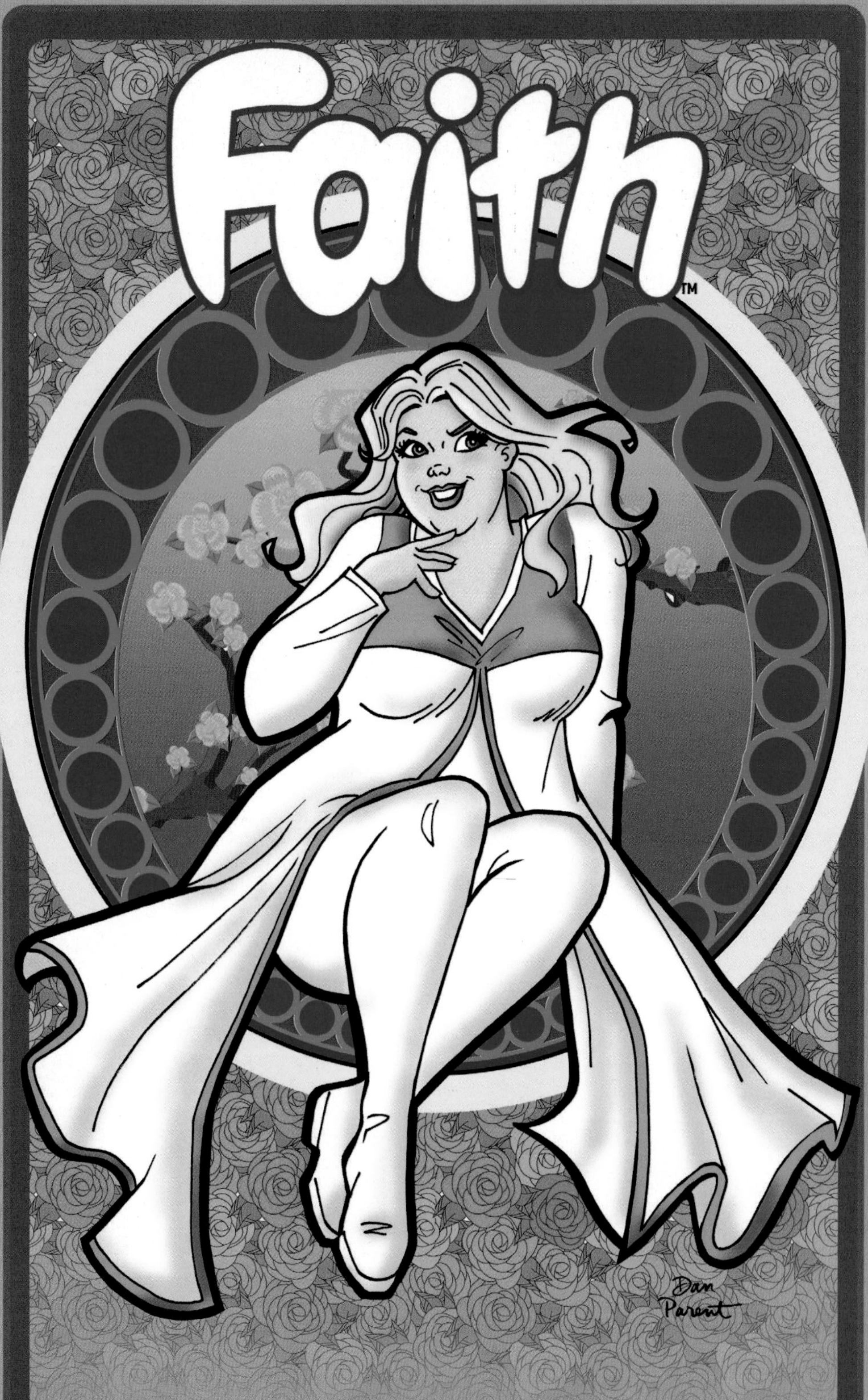
Faith
TM
Dan Parent

FAITH #4 COVER B
Art by DAN PARENT

FAITH #1, p. 12
Art by FRANCIS PORTELA

FAITH #1, p. 13
Art by FRANCIS PORTELA

FAITH #1, p. 15
Process art by FRANCIS PORTELA and MARGUERITE SAUVAGE

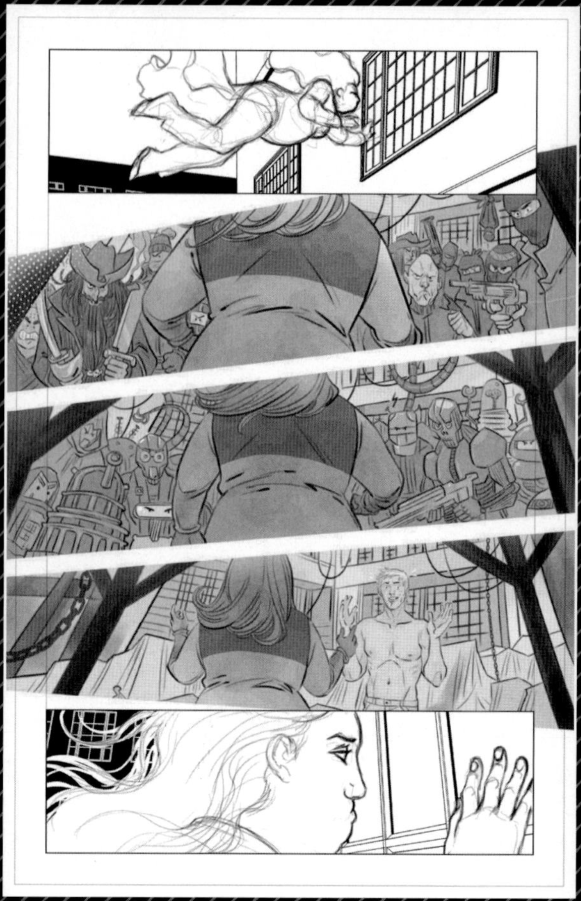

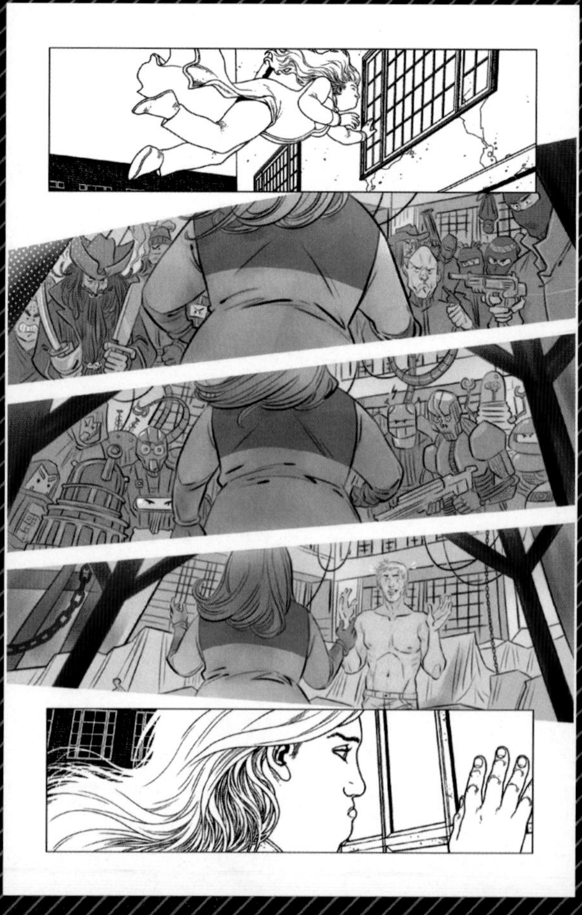

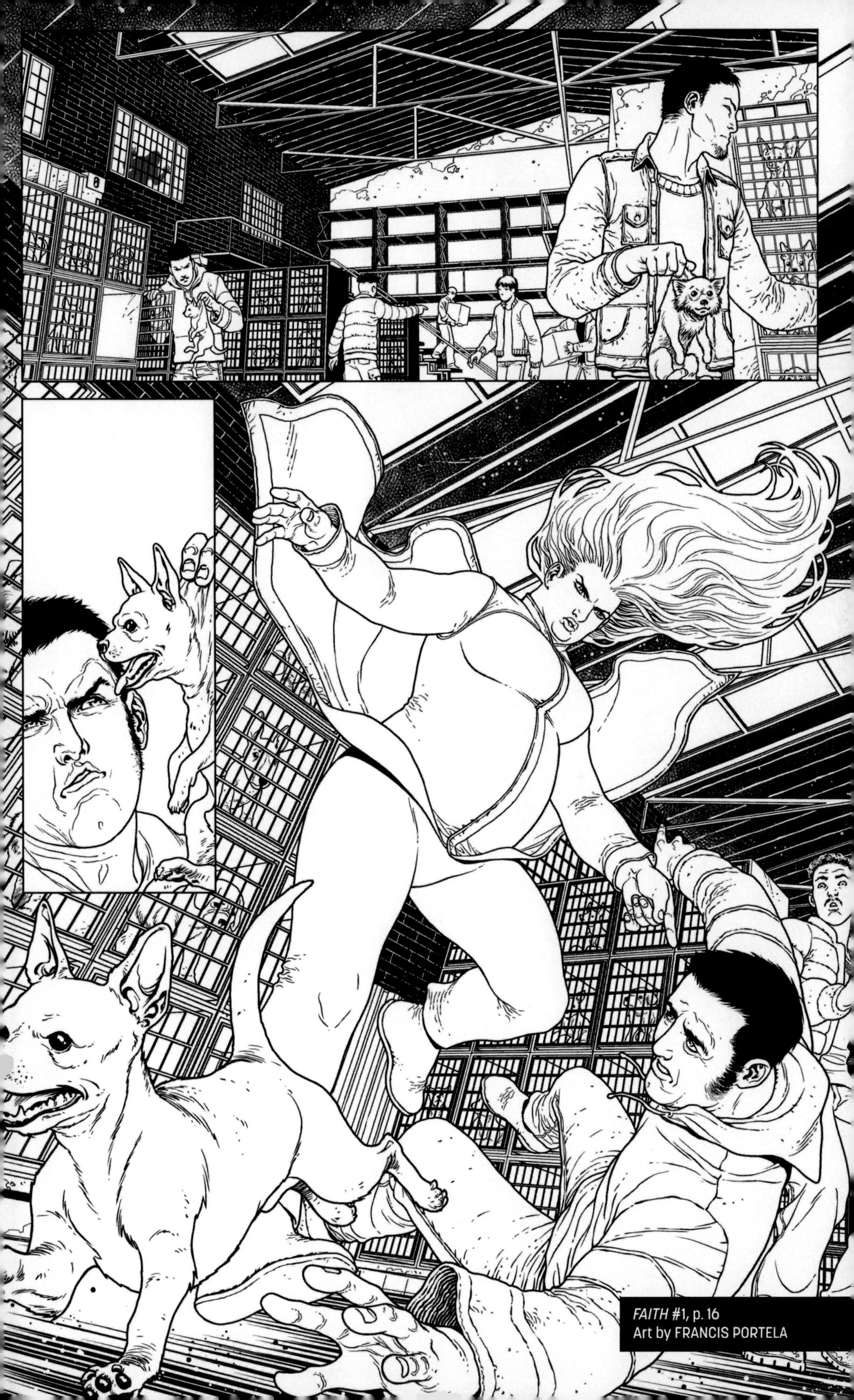

FAITH #1, p. 16
Art by FRANCIS PORTELA

FAITH #2, p. 2
Art by FRANCIS PORTELA

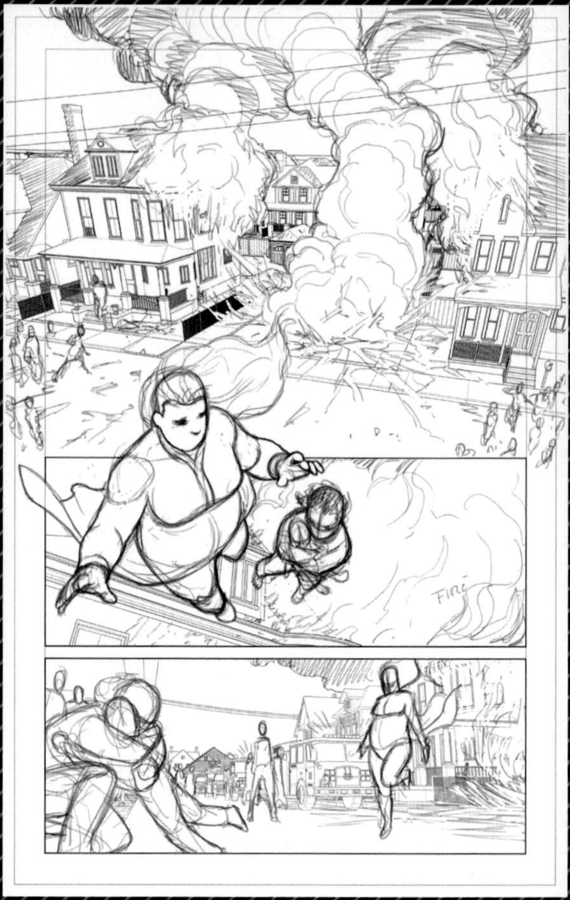

FAITH #2, p. 3
Process and final (facing) art
by FRANCIS PORTELA

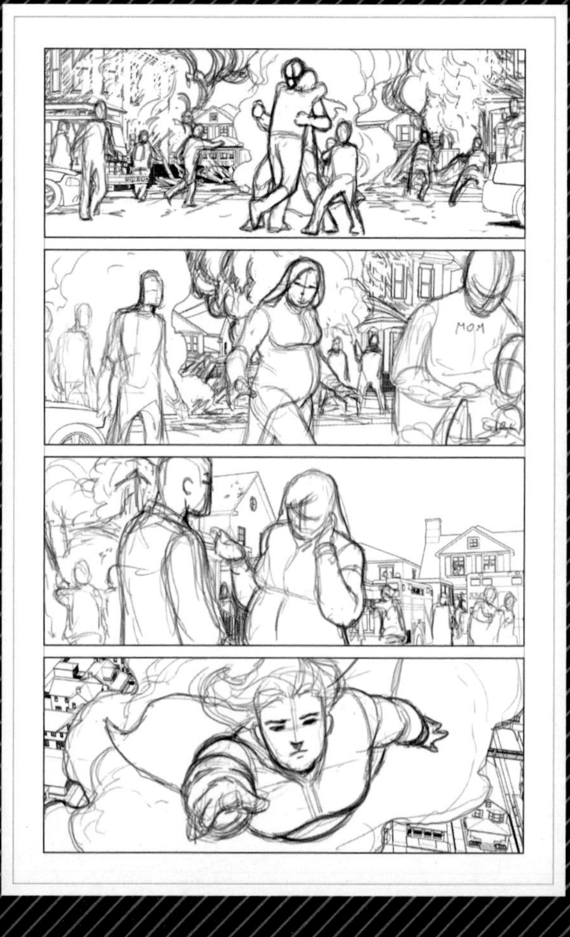
MOM

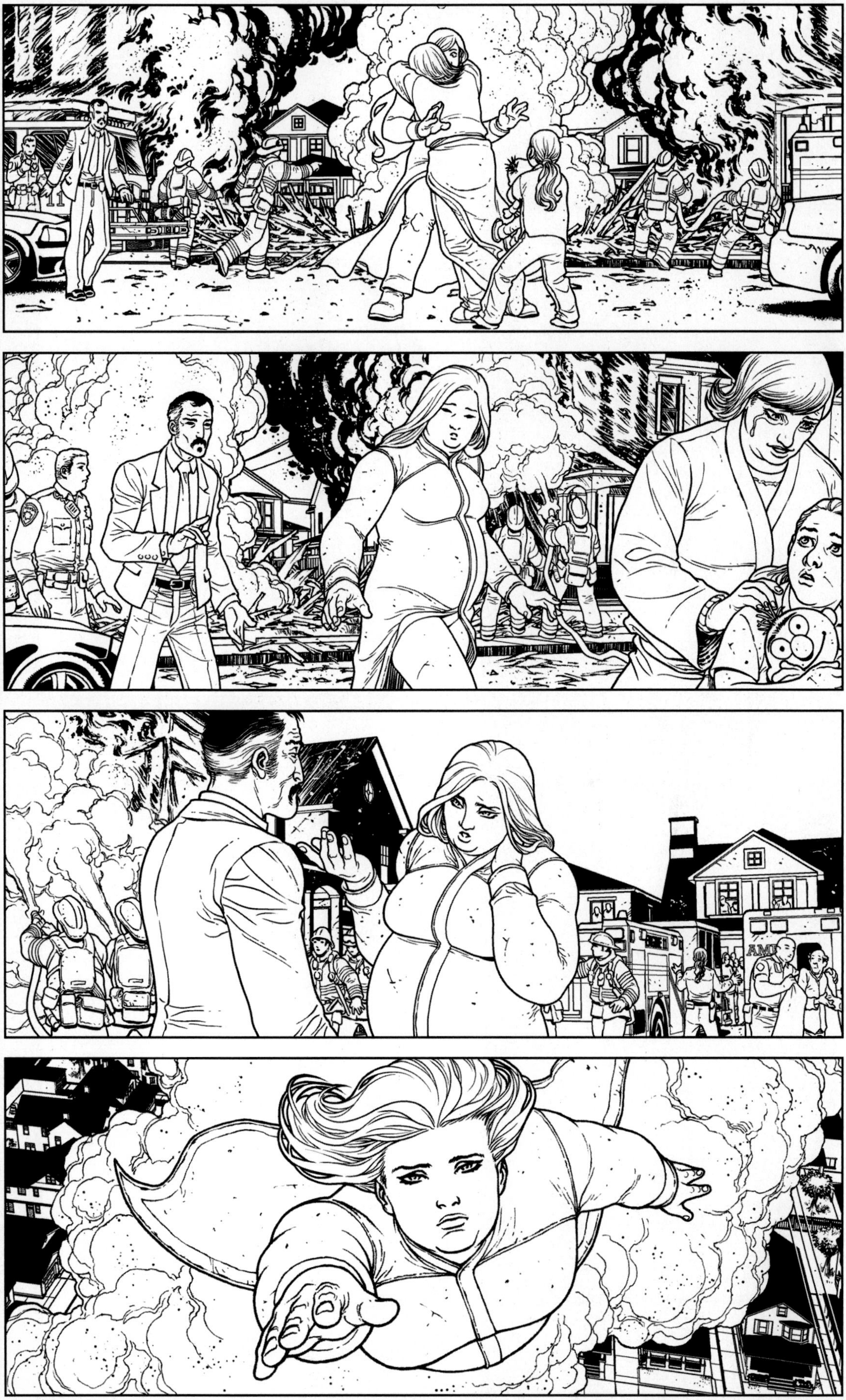

FAITH #2, p. 6
Art by FRANCIS PORTELA

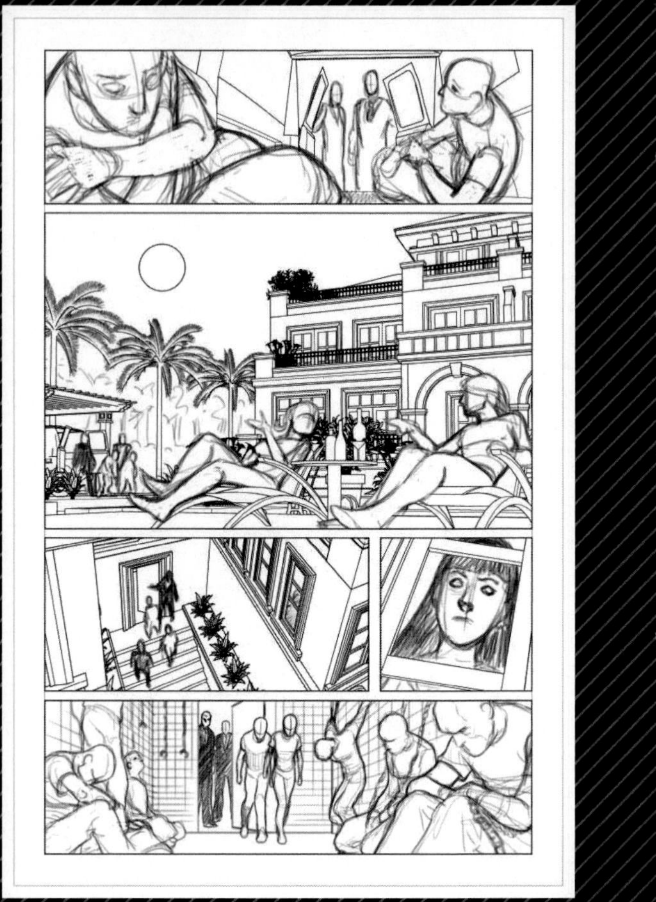

FAITH #2, p. 10
Process and final (facing) art
by FRANCIS PORTELA

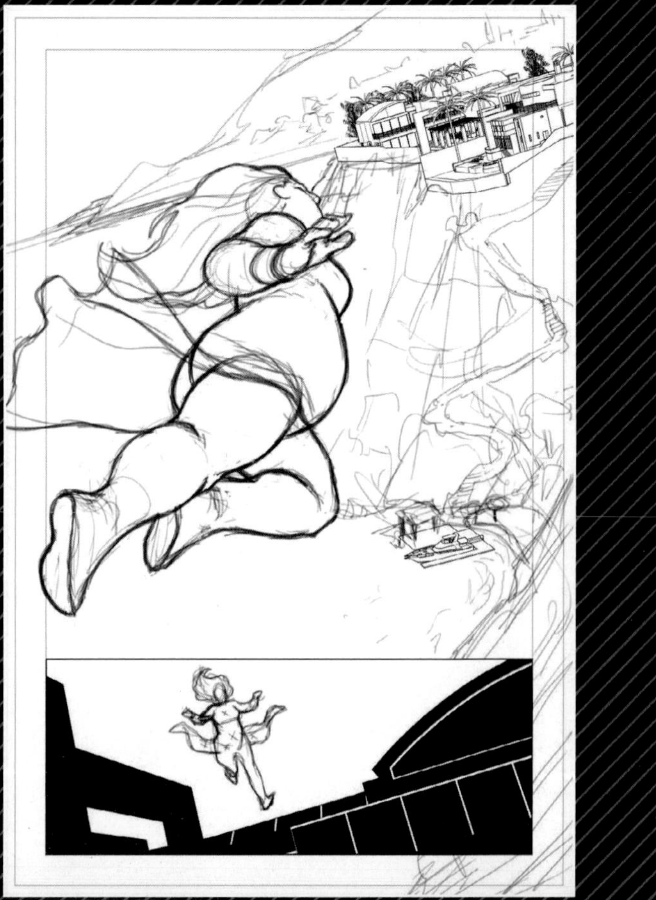

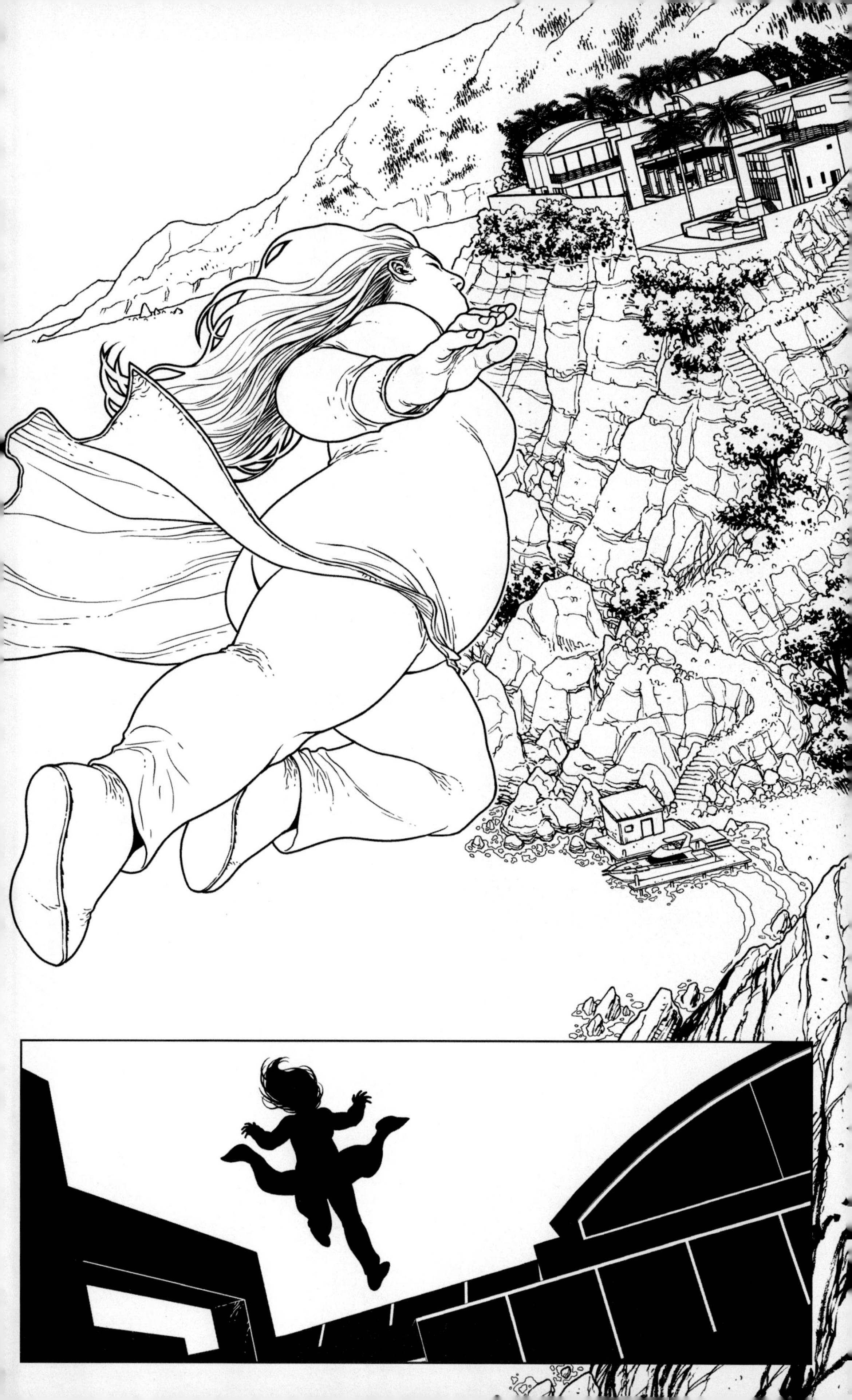

FAITH #3, p. 2
Art by FRANCIS PORTELA

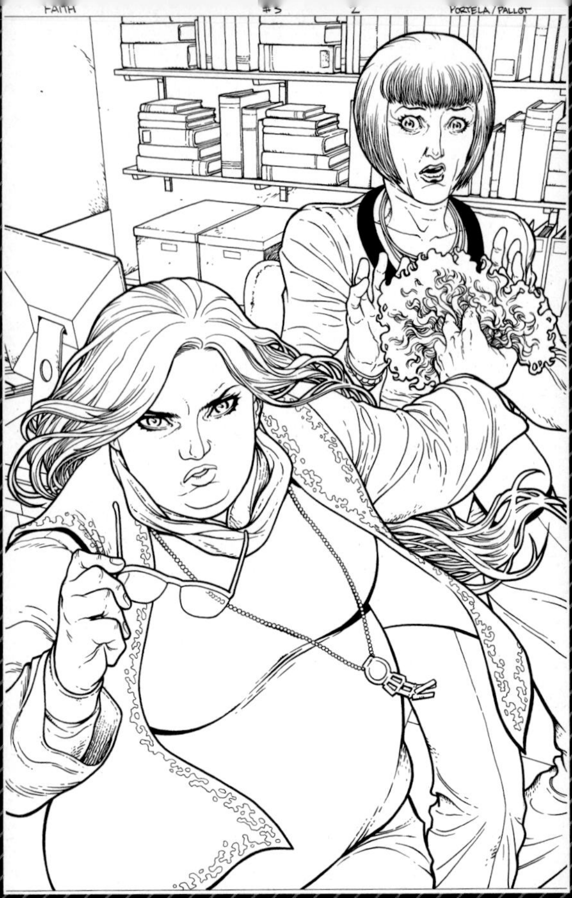
FAITH
PORTELA / PALLOT

FAITH #3, p. 3
Art by FRANCIS PORTELA

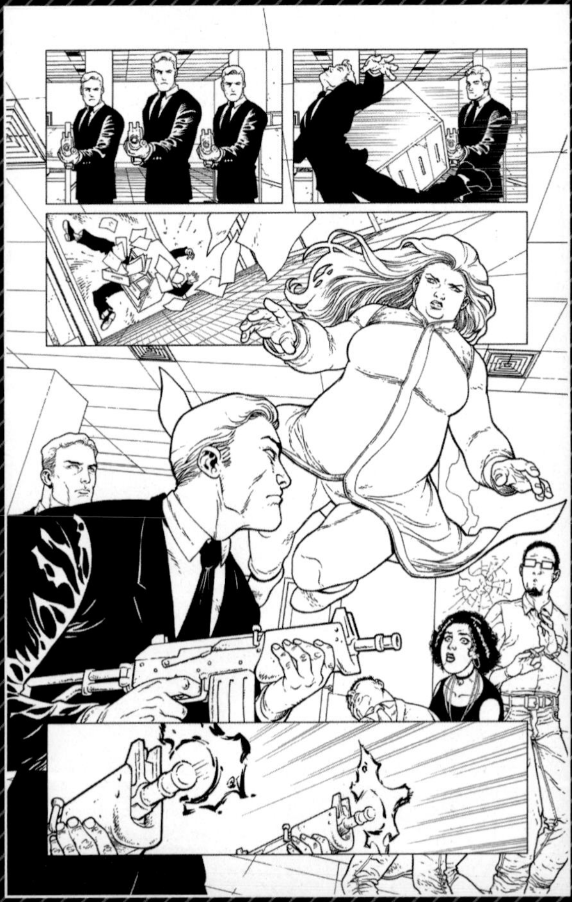

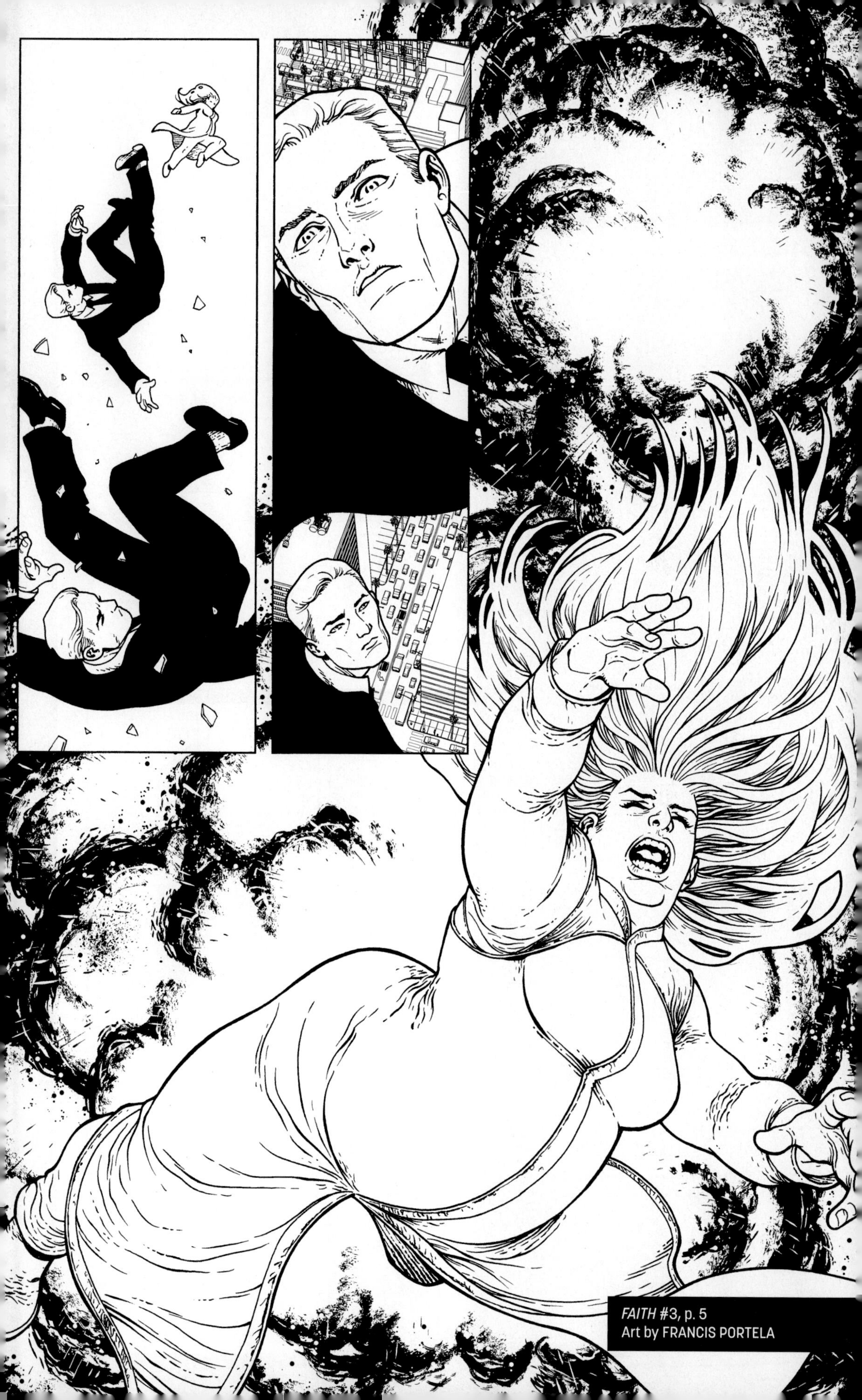

FAITH #3, p. 5
Art by FRANCIS PORTELA

FAITH #3, p. 15
Art by MARGUERITE SAUVAGE

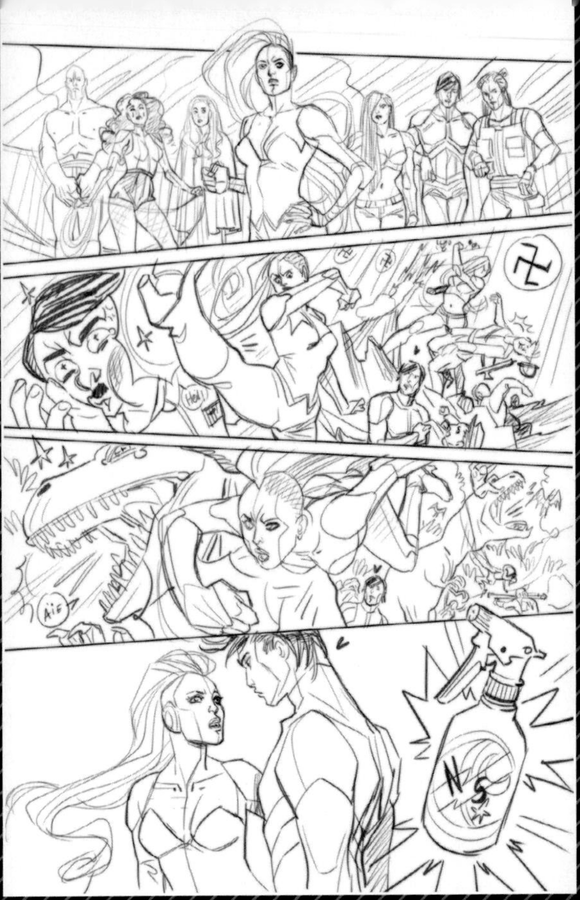

FAITH #3, p. 17
Art by MARGUERITE SAUVAGE

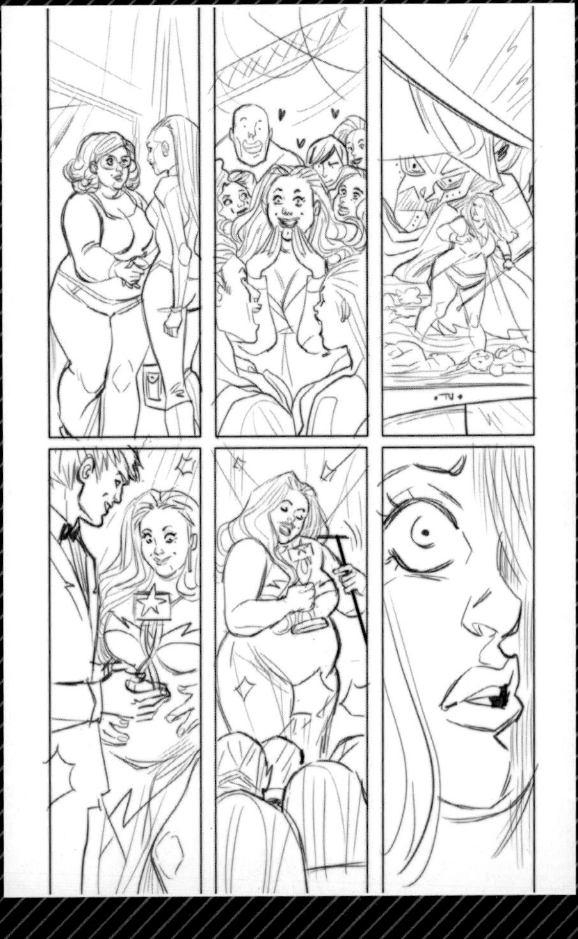

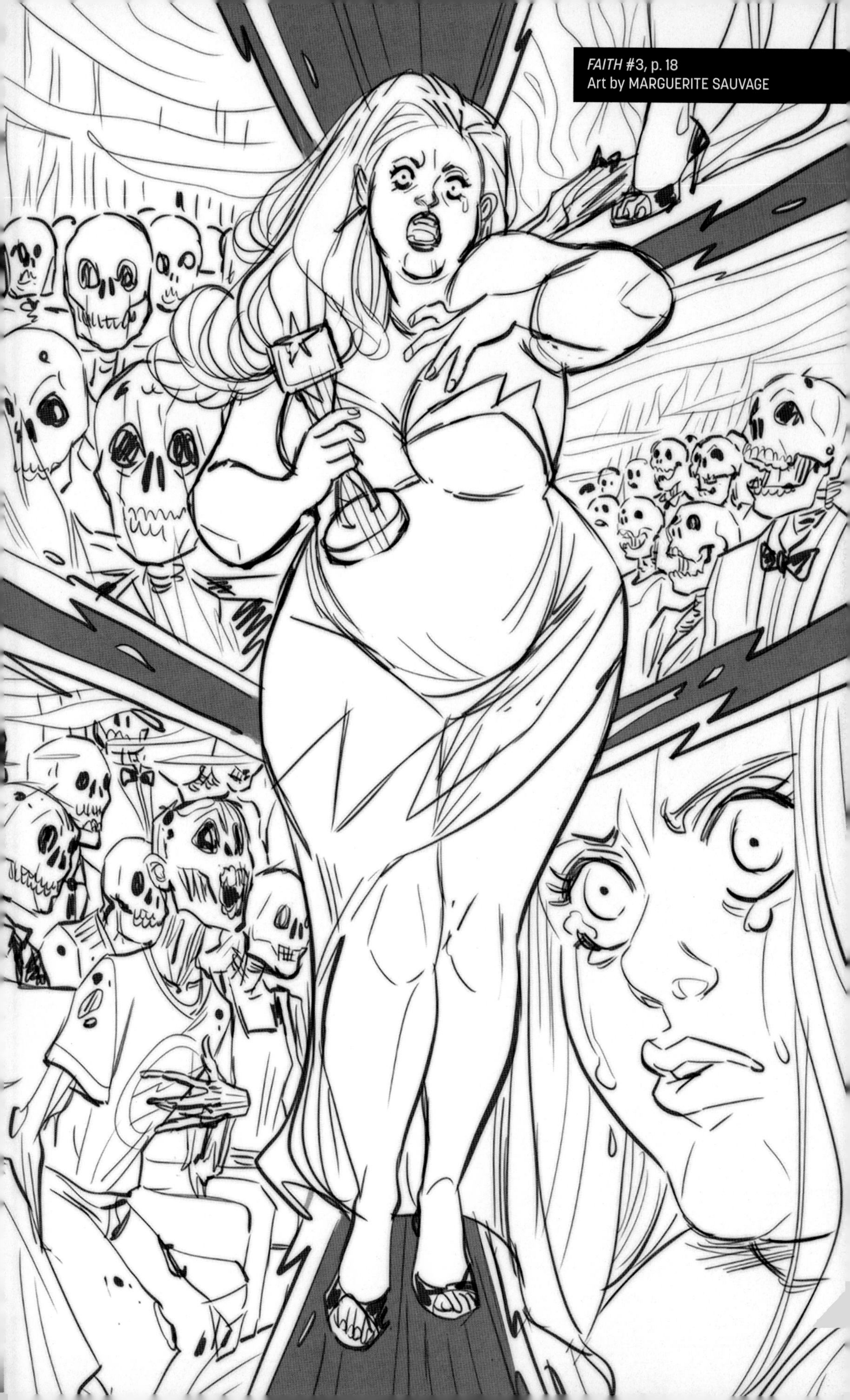

FAITH #3, p. 18
Art by MARGUERITE SAUVAGE

FAITH #4, p. 17
Art by FRANCIS PORTELA

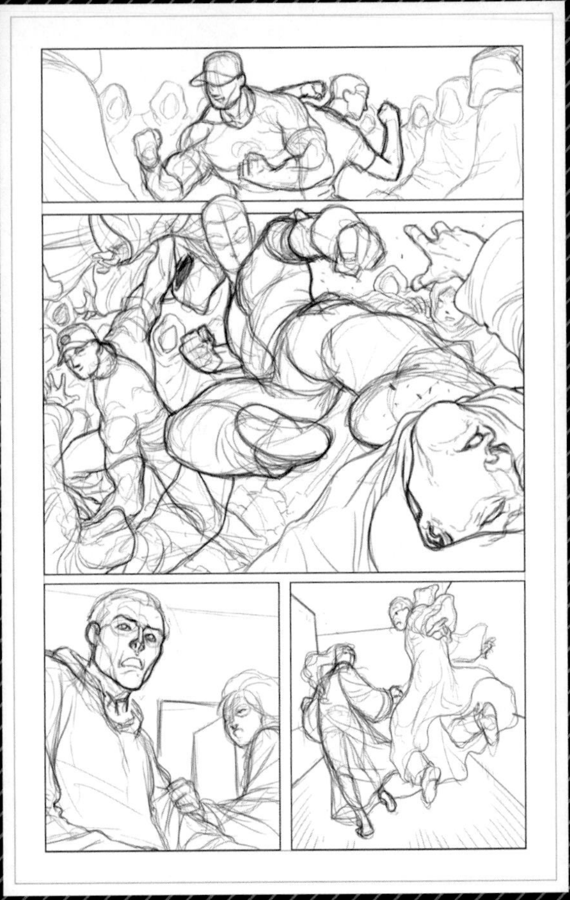

FAITH #4, p. 19
Art by MARGUERITE SAUVAGE

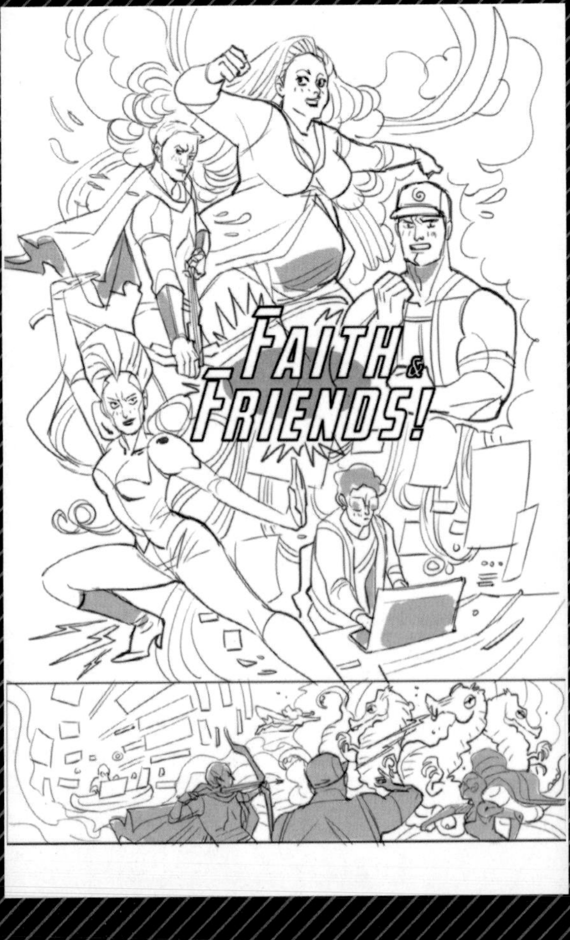
FAITH & FRIENDS!

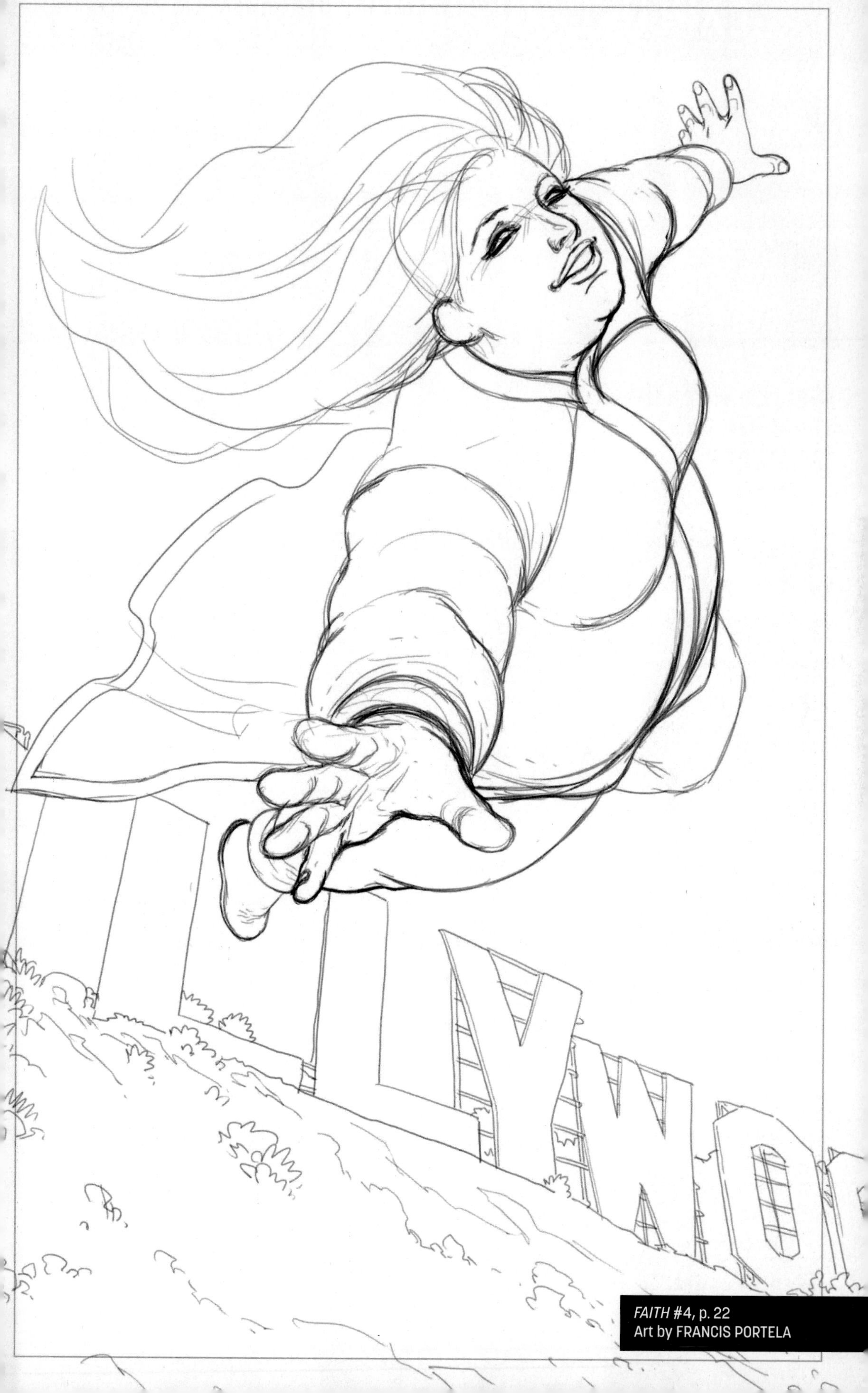

FAITH #4, p. 22
Art by FRANCIS PORTELA

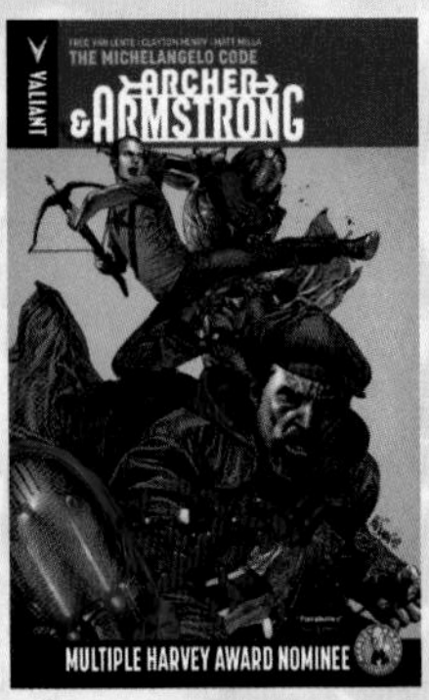
VALIANT
THE MICHELANGELO CODE
ARCHER & ARMSTRONG
MULTIPLE HARVEY AWARD NOMINEE

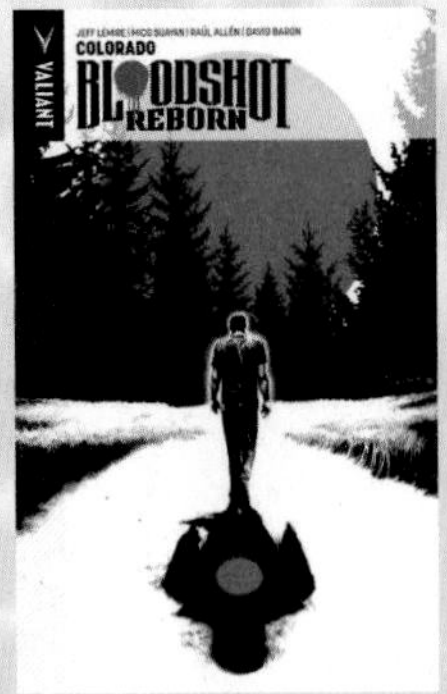
VALIANT
COLORADO
BLOODSHOT REBORN

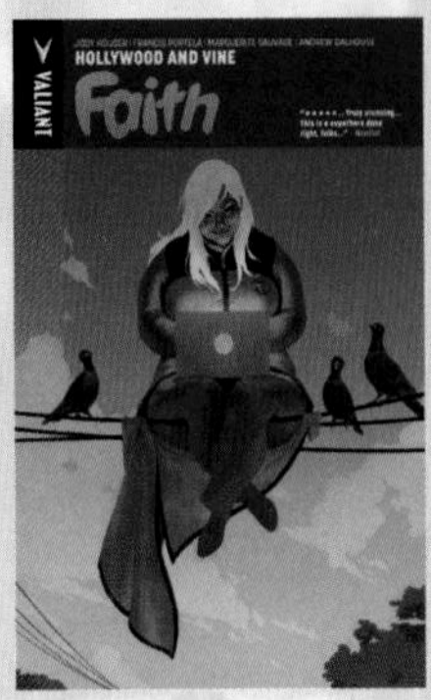
VALIANT
HOLLYWOOD AND VINE
Faith

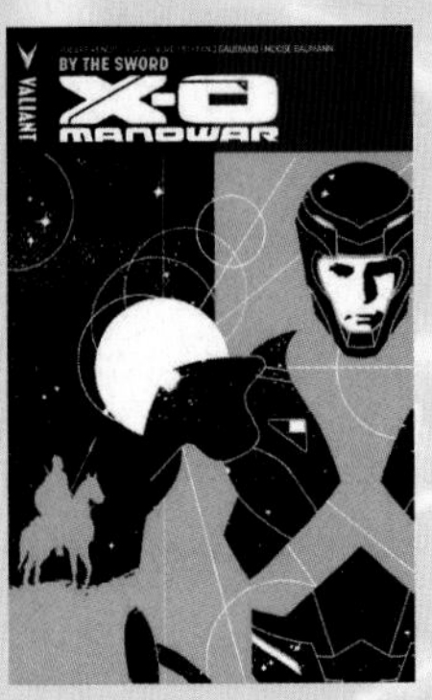
VALIANT
BY THE SWORD
X-O MANOWAR

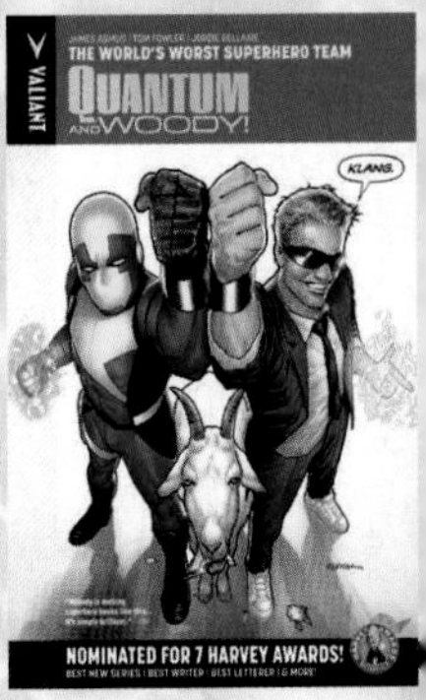
VALIANT
THE WORLD'S WORST SUPERHERO TEAM
QUANTUM AND WOODY!
KLANG
NOMINATED FOR 7 HARVEY AWARDS!

A&A: THE ADVENTURES OF ARCHER AND ARMSTRONG

Volume 1: In the Bag
ISBN: 9781682151495

ARCHER & ARMSTRONG

Volume 1: The Michelangelo Code
ISBN: 9780979640988

Volume 2: Wrath of the Eternal Warrior
ISBN: 9781939346049

Volume 3: Far Faraway
ISBN: 9781939346148

Volume 4: Sect Civil War
ISBN: 9781939346254

Volume 5: Mission: Improbable
ISBN: 9781939346353

Volume 6: American Wasteland
ISBN: 9781939346421

Volume 7: The One Percent and Other Tales
ISBN: 9781939346537

ARMOR HUNTERS

Armor Hunters
ISBN: 9781939346452

Armor Hunters: Bloodshot
ISBN: 9781939346469

Armor Hunters: Harbinger
ISBN: 9781939346506

Unity Vol. 3: Armor Hunters
ISBN: 9781939346445

X-O Manowar Vol. 7: Armor Hunters
ISBN: 9781939346476

BLOODSHOT

Volume 1: Setting the World on Fire
ISBN: 9780979640964

Volume 2: The Rise and the Fall
ISBN: 9781939346032

Volume 3: Harbinger Wars
ISBN: 9781939346124

Volume 4: H.A.R.D. Corps
ISBN: 9781939346193

Volume 5: Get Some!
ISBN: 9781939346315

Volume 6: The Glitch and Other Tales
ISBN: 9781939346711

BLOODSHOT REBORN

Volume 1: Colorado
ISBN: 9781939346674

Volume 2: The Hunt
ISBN: 9781939346827

Volume 3: The Analog Man
ISBN: 9781682151334

BOOK OF DEATH

Book of Death
ISBN: 9781939346971

Book of Death: The Fall of the Valiant Universe
ISBN: 9781939346988

DEAD DROP

ISBN: 9781939346858

THE DEATH-DEFYING DOCTOR MIRAGE

Volume 1
ISBN: 9781939346490

Volume 2: Second Lives
ISBN: 9781682151297

THE DELINQUENTS

ISBN: 9781939346513

DIVINITY

Volume 1
ISBN: 9781939346766

Volume 2
ISBN: 9781682151518

ETERNAL WARRIOR

Volume 1: Sword of the Wild
ISBN: 9781939346209

Volume 2: Eternal Emperor
ISBN: 9781939346292

Volume 3: Days of Steel
ISBN: 9781939346742

WRATH OF THE ETERNAL WARRIOR

Volume 1: Risen
ISBN: 9781682151235

HARBINGER

Volume 1: Omega Rising
ISBN: 9780979640957

Volume 2: Renegades
ISBN: 9781939346025

Volume 3: Harbinger Wars
ISBN: 9781939346117

Volume 4: Perfect Day
ISBN: 9781939346155

Volume 5: Death of a Renegade
ISBN: 9781939346339

Volume 6: Omegas
ISBN: 9781939346384

HARBINGER WARS

Harbinger Wars
ISBN: 9781939346094

Bloodshot Vol. 3: Harbinger Wars
ISBN: 9781939346124

Harbinger Vol. 3: Harbinger Wars
ISBN: 9781939346117

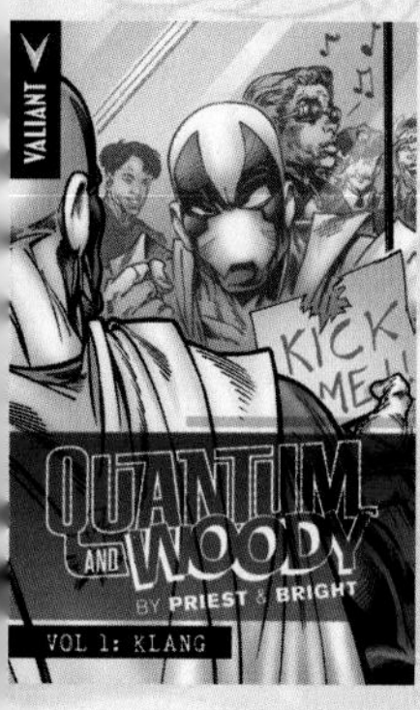
VALIANT
KICK ME
QUANTUM AND WOODY
BY PRIEST & BRIGHT
VOL 1: KLANG
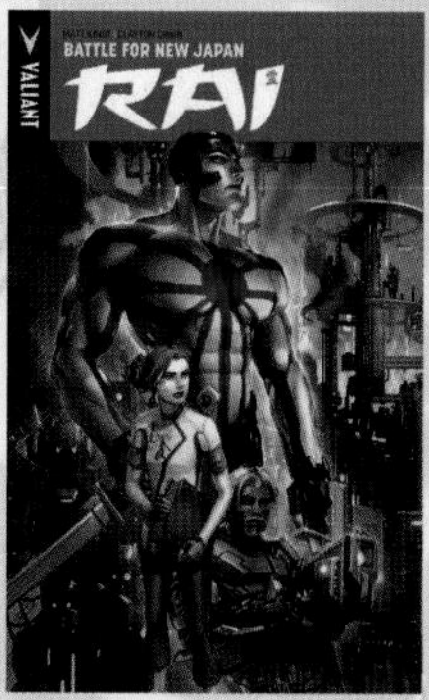
VALIANT
BATTLE FOR NEW JAPAN
RAI
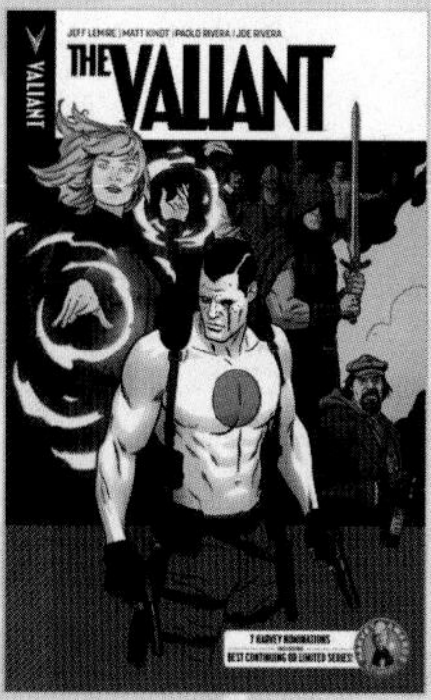
VALIANT
JEFF LEMIRE | MATT KINDT | PAOLO RIVERA | JOE RIVERA
THE VALIANT
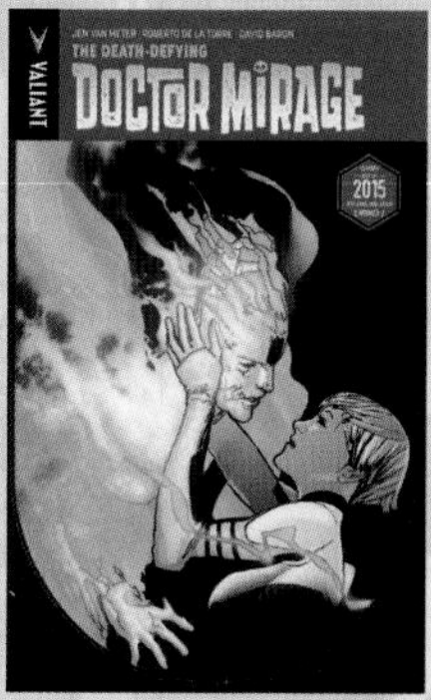
VALIANT
THE DEATH-DEFYING
DOCTOR MIRAGE
2015
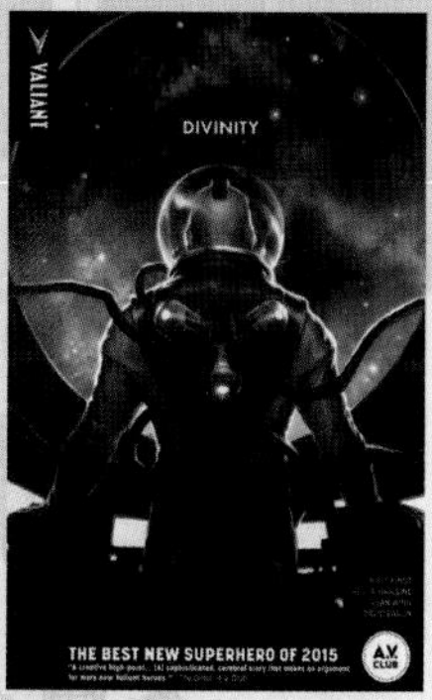
VALIANT
DIVINITY
THE BEST NEW SUPERHERO OF 2015
A.V. CLUB

IMPERIUM

Volume 1: Collecting Monsters
ISBN: 9781939346759

Volume 2: Broken Angels
ISBN: 9781939346896

Volume 3: The Vine Imperative
ISBN: 9781682151112

Volume 4: Stormbreak
ISBN: 9781682151372

NINJAK

Volume 1: Weaponeer
ISBN: 9781939346667

Volume 2: The Shadow Wars
ISBN: 9781939346940

Volume 3: Operation: Deadside
ISBN: 9781682151259

Volume 4: The Siege of King's Castle
ISBN: 9781682151617

QUANTUM AND WOODY

Volume 1: The World's Worst Superhero Team
ISBN: 9781939346186

Volume 2: In Security
ISBN: 9781939346230

Volume 3: Crooked Pasts, Present Tense
ISBN: 9781939346391

Volume 4: Quantum and Woody Must Die!
ISBN: 9781939346629

QUANTUM AND WOODY BY PRIEST & BRIGHT

Volume 1: Klang
ISBN: 9781939346780

Volume 2: Switch
ISBN: 9781939346803

Volume 3: And So...
ISBN: 9781939346865

Volume 4: Q2 - The Return
ISBN: 9781682151099

RAI

Volume 1: Welcome to New Japan
ISBN: 9781939346414

Volume 2: Battle for New Japan
ISBN: 9781939346612

Volume 3: The Orphan
ISBN: 9781939346841

SHADOWMAN

Volume 1: Birth Rites
ISBN: 9781939346001

Volume 2: Darque Reckoning
ISBN: 9781939346056

Volume 3: Deadside Blues
ISBN: 9781939346162

Volume 4: Fear, Blood, And Shadows
ISBN: 9781939346278

Volume 5: End Times
ISBN: 9781939346377

SHADOWMAN BY ENNIS & WOOD

ISBN: 9781682151358

IVAR, TIMEWALKER

Volume 1: Making History
ISBN: 9781939346636

Volume 2: Breaking History
ISBN: 9781939346834

Volume 3: Ending History
ISBN: 9781939346995

UNITY

Volume 1: To Kill a King
ISBN: 9781939346261

Volume 2: Trapped by Webnet
ISBN: 9781939346346

Volume 3: Armor Hunters
ISBN: 9781939346445

Volume 4: The United
ISBN: 9781939346544

Volume 5: Homefront
ISBN: 9781939346797

Volume 6: The War-Monger
ISBN: 9781939346902

Volume 7: Revenge of the Armor Hunters
ISBN: 9781682151136

THE VALIANT

ISBN: 9781939346605

VALIANT ZEROES AND ORIGINS

ISBN: 9781939346582

X-O MANOWAR

Volume 1: By the Sword
ISBN: 9780979640940

Volume 2: Enter Ninjak
ISBN: 9780979640995

Volume 3: Planet Death
ISBN: 9781939346087

Volume 4: Homecoming
ISBN: 9781939346179

Volume 5: At War With Unity
ISBN: 9781939346247

Volume 6: Prelude to Armor Hunters
ISBN: 9781939346407

Volume 7: Armor Hunters
ISBN: 9781939346476

Volume 8: Enter: Armorines
ISBN: 9781939346551

Volume 9: Dead Hand
ISBN: 9781939346650

Volume 10: Exodus
ISBN: 9781939346933

Volume 11: The Kill List
ISBN: 9781682151273

VALIANT
HARBINGER
DELUXE EDITION 2

VALIANT
ROBERT VENDITTI MATT KINDT JOSHUA DYSART JOE HARRIS ROBERT GILL
DOUG BRAITHWAITE DIEGO BERNARD TREVOR HAIRSINE STEPHEN SEGOVIA
ARMOR HUNTERS
DELUXE EDITION

VALIANT
JIM SHOOTER | DAVID LAPHAM
CHILDREN OF THE EIGHTH DAY
HARBINGER
VALIANT MASTERS
L8-AGIN

Omnibuses

Archer & Armstrong: The Complete Classic Omnibus
ISBN: 9781939346872
Collecting ARCHER & ARMSTRONG (1992) #0-26, ETERNAL WARRIOR (1992) #25 along with ARCHER & ARMSTRONG: THE FORMATION OF THE SECT.

Quantum and Woody: The Complete Classic Omnibus
ISBN: 9781939346360
Collecting QUANTUM AND WOODY (1997) #0, 1-21 and #32, THE GOAT: H.A.E.D.U.S. #1, and X-O MANOWAR (1996) #16

X-O Manowar Classic Omnibus Vol. 1
ISBN: 9781939346308
Collecting X-O MANOWAR (1992) #0-30, ARMORINES #0, X-O DATABASE #1, as well as material from SECRETS OF THE VALIANT UNIVERSE #1

Deluxe Editions

Archer & Armstrong Deluxe Edition Book 1
ISBN: 9781939346223
Collecting ARCHER & ARMSTRONG #0-13

Archer & Armstrong Deluxe Edition Book 2
ISBN: 9781939346957
Collecting ARCHER & ARMSTRONG #14-25, ARCHER & ARMSTRONG: ARCHER #0 and BLOODSHOT AND H.A.R.D. CORPS #20-21.

Armor Hunters Deluxe Edition
ISBN: 9781939346728
Collecting Armor Hunters #1-4, Armor Hunters: Aftermath #1, Armor Hunters: Bloodshot #1-3, Armor Hunters: Harbinger #1-3, Unity #8-11, and X-O MANOWAR #23-29

Bloodshot Deluxe Edition Book 1
ISBN: 9781939346216
Collecting BLOODSHOT #1-13

Bloodshot Deluxe Edition Book 2
ISBN: 9781939346810
Collecting BLOODSHOT AND H.A.R.D. CORPS #14-23, BLOODSHOT #24-25, BLOODSHOT #0, BLOODSHOT AND H.A.R.D. CORPS: H.A.R.D. CORPS #0, along with ARCHER & ARMSTRONG #18-19

Book of Death Deluxe Edition
ISBN: 9781682151150
Collecting BOOK OF DEATH #1-4, BOOK OF DEATH: THE FALL OF BLOODSHOT #1, BOOK OF DEATH: THE FALL OF NINJAK #1, BOOK OF DEATH: THE FALL OF HARBINGER #1, and BOOK OF DEATH: THE FALL OF X-O MANOWAR #1.

Divinity Deluxe Edition
ISBN: 97819393460993
Collecting DIVNITY #1-4

Harbinger Deluxe Edition Book 1
ISBN: 9781939346131
Collecting HARBINGER #0-14

Harbinger Deluxe Edition Book 2
ISBN: 9781939346773
Collecting HARBINGER #15-25, HARBINGER: OMEGAS #1-3, and HARBINGER: BLEEDING MONK #0

Harbinger Wars Deluxe Edition
ISBN: 9781939346322
Collecting HARBINGER WARS #1-4, HARBINGER #11-14, and BLOODSHOT #10-13

Ivar, Timewalker Deluxe Edition Book 1
ISBN: 9781682151198
Collecting IVAR, TIMEWALKER #1-12

Quantum and Woody Deluxe Edition Book 1
ISBN: 9781939346681
Collecting QUANTUM AND WOODY #1-12 and QUANTUM AND WOODY: THE GOAT #0

Q2: The Return of Quantum and Woody Deluxe Edition
ISBN: 9781939346568
Collecting Q2: THE RETURN OF QUANTUM AND WOODY #1-5

Rai Deluxe Edition Book 1
ISBN: 9781682151174
Collecting RAI #1-12, along with material from RAI #1 PLUS EDITION and RAI #5 PLUS EDITION

Shadowman Deluxe Edition Book 1
ISBN: 9781939346438
Collecting SHADOWMAN #0-10

Shadowman Deluxe Edition Book 2
ISBN: 9781682151075
Collecting SHADOWMAN #11-16, SHADOWMAN #13X, SHADOWMAN: END TIMES #1-3 and PUNK MAMBO #0

Unity Deluxe Edition Book 1
ISBN: 9781939346575
Collecting UNITY #0-14

The Valiant Deluxe Edition
ISBN: 97819393460986
Collecting THE VALIANT #1-4

X-O Manowar Deluxe Edition Book 1
ISBN: 9781939346100
Collecting X-O MANOWAR #1-14

X-O Manowar Deluxe Edition Book 2
ISBN: 9781939346520
Collecting X-O MANOWAR #15-22, and UNITY #1-4

X-O Manowar Deluxe Edition Book 3
ISBN: 9781682151310
Collecting X-O MANOWAR #23-29 and ARMOR HUNTERS #1-4.

Valiant Masters

Bloodshot Vol. 1 - Blood of the Machine
ISBN: 9780979640933

H.A.R.D. Corps Vol. 1 - Search and Destroy
ISBN: 9781939346285

Harbinger Vol. 1 - Children of the Eighth Day
ISBN: 9781939346483

Ninjak Vol. 1 - Black Water
ISBN: 9780979640971

Rai Vol. 1 - From Honor to Strength
ISBN: 9781939346070

Shadowman Vol. 1 - Spirits Within
ISBN: 9781939346018

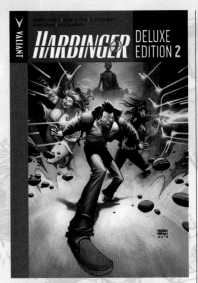

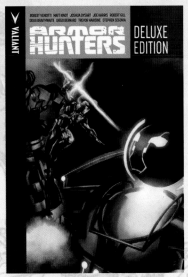

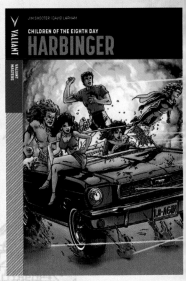

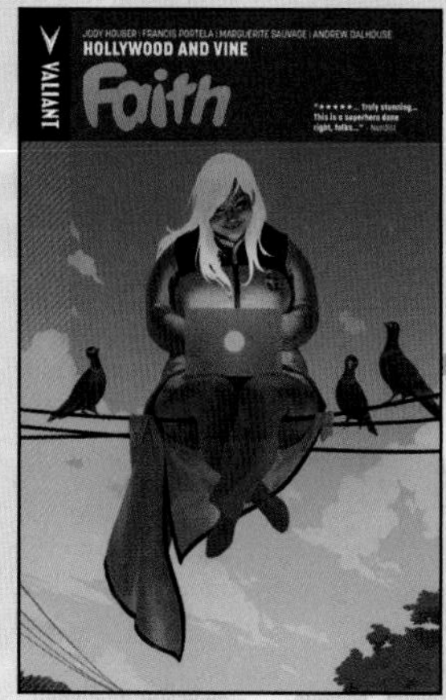
VALIANT
HOLLYWOOD AND VINE
Faith

Faith Vol. 1:
Hollywood and Vine

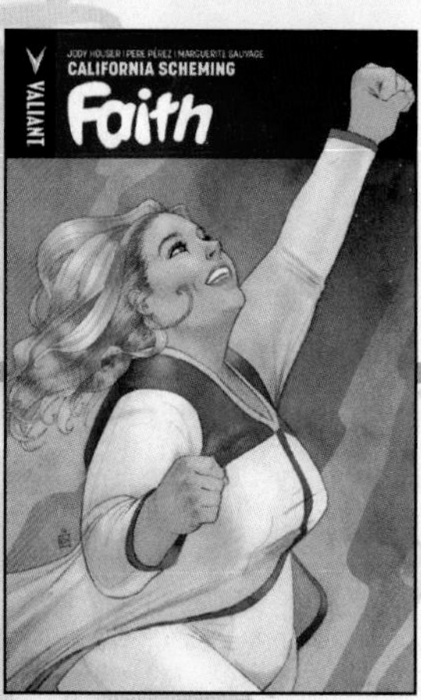
VALIANT
CALIFORNIA SCHEMING
Faith

Faith Vol. 2:
California Scheming

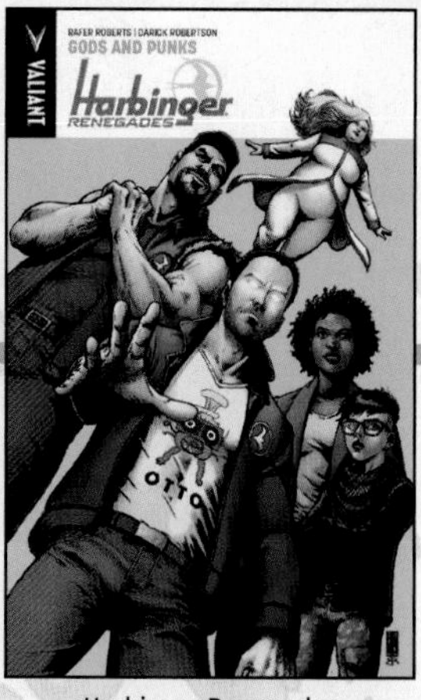
VALIANT
GODS AND PUNKS
Harbinger
RENEGADES

Harbinger Renegades
Vol. 1: Gods and Punks
(OPTIONAL)

Collect the first appearances and cameos of Valiant's high-flying breakout sensation!

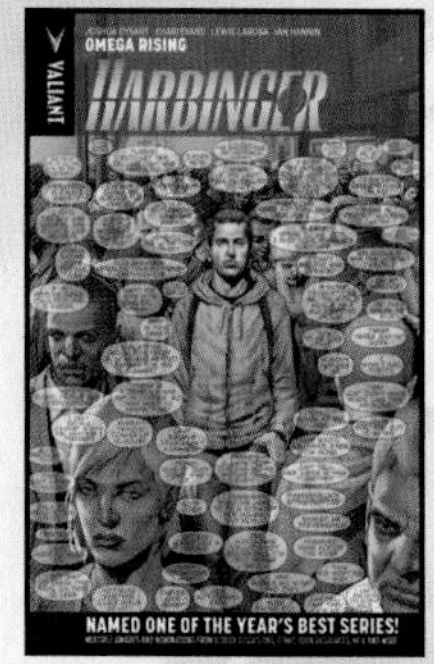
VALIANT
OMEGA RISING
HARBINGER
NAMED ONE OF THE YEAR'S BEST SERIES!

Harbinger Vol. 1:
Omega Rising

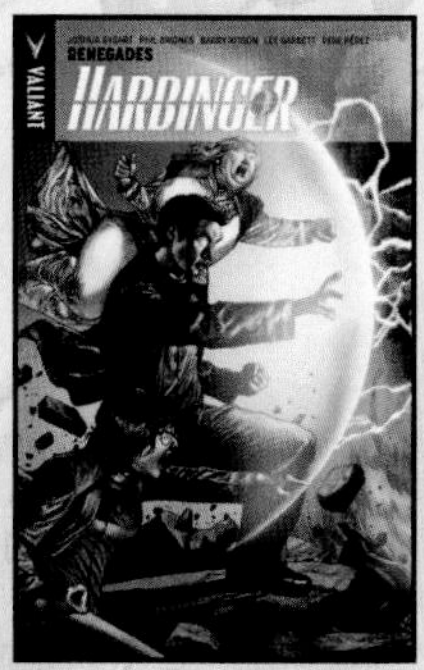
VALIANT
RENEGADES
HARBINGER

Harbinger Vol. 2:
Renegades

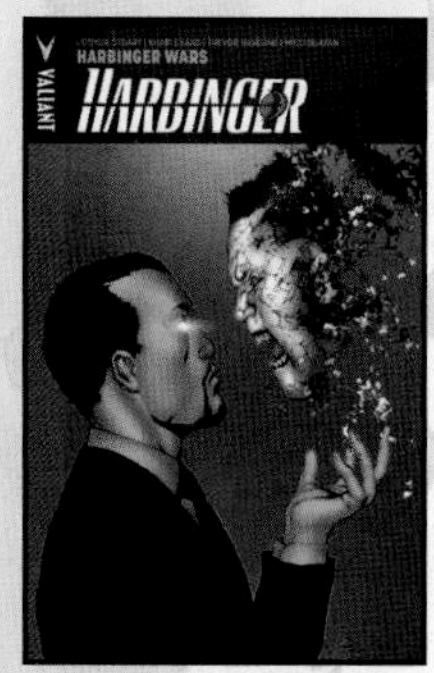
VALIANT
HARBINGER WARS
HARBINGER

Harbinger Vol. 3:
Harbinger Wars

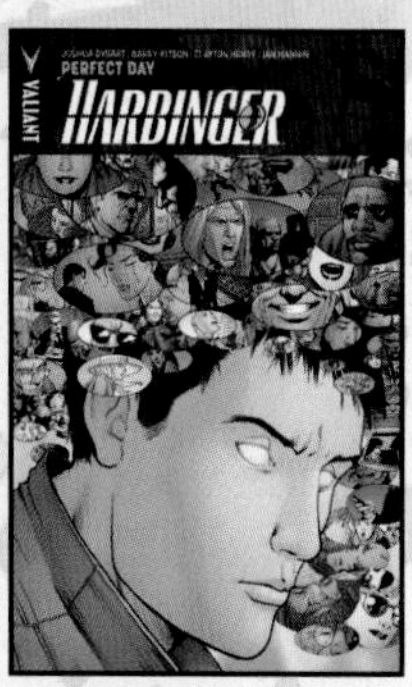
VALIANT
PERFECT DAY
HARBINGER

Harbinger Vol. 4:
Perfect Day

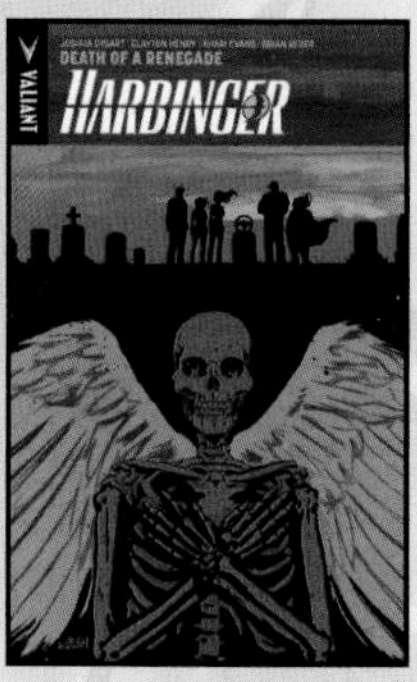
VALIANT
DEATH OF A RENEGADE
HARBINGER

Harbinger Vol. 5:
Death of a Renegade

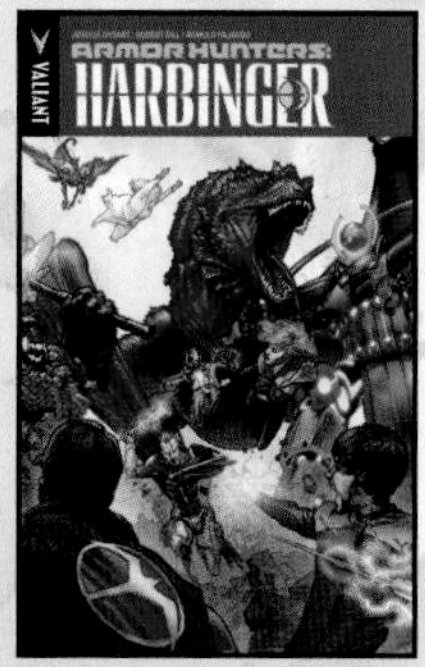
VALIANT
ARMOR HUNTERS:
HARBINGER

Armor Hunters:
Harbinger

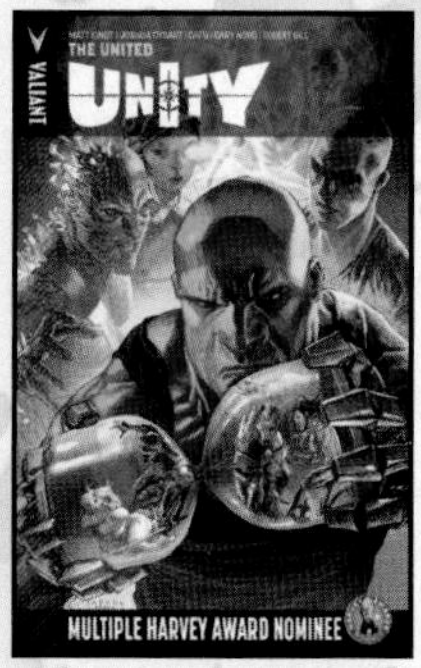
VALIANT
THE UNITED
UNITY
MULTIPLE HARVEY AWARD NOMINEE

Unity Vol. 4:
The United

VALIANT®

Faith™

VOLUME TWO: CALIFORNIA SCHEMING

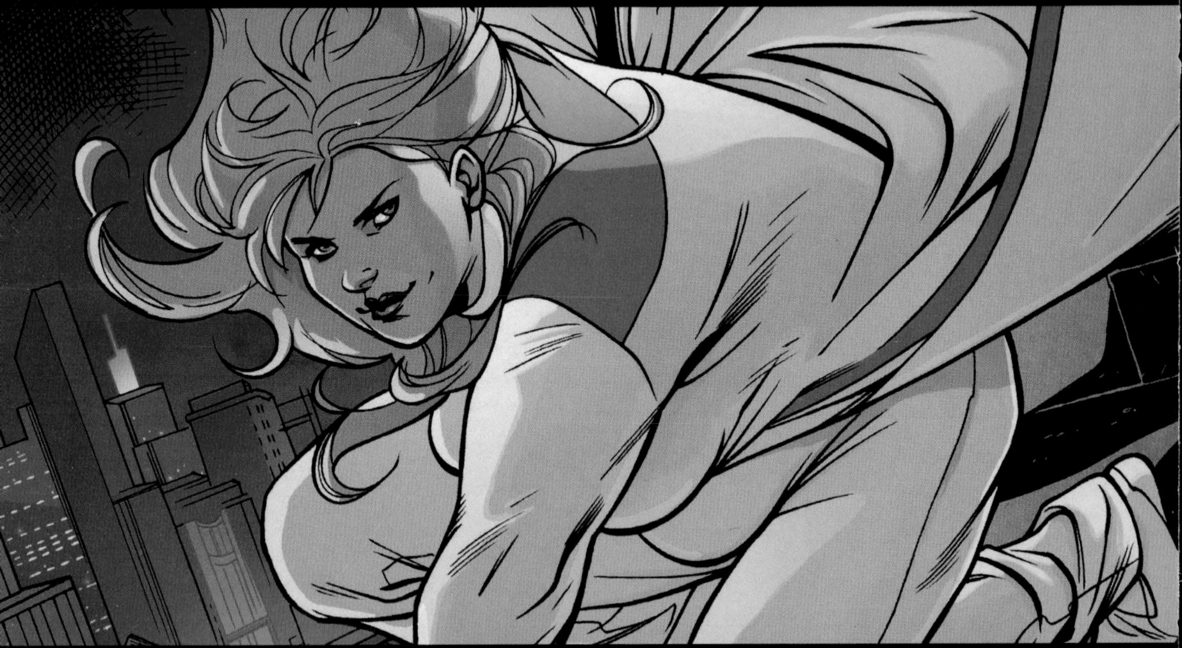

BECAUSE YOU DEMANDED IT...THE HIGH-FLYING HERO THAT CAPTURED THE IMAGINATION OF THE WORLD IS BACK WITH A COLOSSAL NEW COMICS MILESTONE!

In a city under siege by robots, aliens, monsters, and even worse... celebrities, there is only one woman the people of Los Angeles can count on: the stratospheric superhero called Faith! Aspiring reporter by day and dedicated crime-fighter by night, Faith has tackled every obstacle in her path with confidence – like those crushing deadlines at work, the long-distance boyfriend half a world away, and the missing back issues that plague her comics collection! But, unbeknownst to her, Faith is about to collide with the one force she never saw coming: an up-and-coming super-villain bent on snuffing her out once and for all! But who is lurking behind the mask of her new foe...and could they just be the one person capable of rendering Faith powerless?

Faith's headline-grabbing adventures continue here as breakout writer Jody Houser (*Orphan Black*) and sensational artists Pere Pérez (ARCHER & ARMSTRONG) and Marguerite Sauvage (*DC Comics Bombshells*) deliver the next high-flying chapter to the all-new ongoing series read 'round the world!

Collecting FAITH (ONGOING SERIES) #1-4.

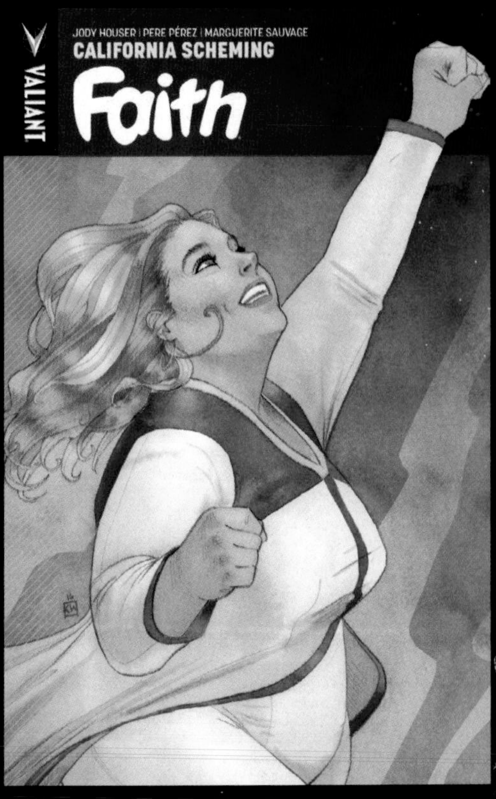

VALIANT
JODY HOUSER | PERE PÉREZ | MARGUERITE SAUVAGE
CALIFORNIA SCHEMING
Faith

TRADE PAPERBACK
ISBN: 978-1-68215-163-1

Y Hou
Houser, Jody,
Faith. Hollywood and Vine